TRAVELS, EXPLORATIONS AND EMPIRES

Volume 7

TRAVELS, EXPLORATIONS AND EMPIRES

WRITINGS FROM THE ERA OF IMPERIAL EXPANSION
1770–1835

Volume 7
LATIN AMERICA
AND THE CARRIBEAN

Edited by Nigel Leask

LONDON
PICKERING & CHATTO
2001

Published by Pickering & Chatto (Publishers) Limited
21 Bloomsbury Way, London, WC1A 2TH

Old Post Road, Brookfield, Vermont 05036, USA

www.pickeringchatto.com

BRITISH LIBRARY CATALOGUING IN PUBLICATION DATA
Travels, explorations and empires : writings from the era of imperial expansion,
1770–1835

Part 2 general editors, Tim Fulford and Peter J. Kitson
advisory editor, Tim Youngs

1. Travelers' writings, European 2. Voyages and travels 3. Europe – Colonies
– Description and travel 4. Europe – Colonies – Social life and customs –18th
century

I. Fulford, Tim II. Kitson, Peter III. Youngs, Tim IV. Lee, Debbie. Africa V.
Ghose, Indira. India VI. Leask, Nigel. South America and Caribbean VII. South
Seas and Australasia

910.9'1712'4'09033

ISBN 1851967214

LIBRARY OF CONGRESS CATALOGING-IN-PUBLICATION DATA
Travels, explorations, and empires : writings from the era of imperial expansion,
1770–1835.

v. <1–4> : facsims. ; 24 cm.
Includes bibliographical references and index.
Contents: v. 1. North America / edited by Tim Fulford with Carol Bolton –
v. 2. Far East / edited by Tim Fulford and Peter J. Kitson – v. 3. North and South
Poles / edited by Peter J. Kitson – v. 4. Middle East / edited by Tilar J. Mazzeo.
ISBN 1-85196-720-6 (set : alk. paper)
1. Voyages and travels – History – Early works to 1800. 2. Voyages and travels
– History – 19th century. 3. Travelers' writings. I. Fulford, Tim, 1962–

G465 .T74 2001
910.4'09'033–dc21   00-051033

This publication is printed on acid-free paper that conforms to the American
National Standard for the Permanence of Paper for Printed Library Materials

New material typeset by
P&C

Printed and bound in Great Britain by
Bookcraft (Bath), Midsomer Norton

CONTENTS

INTRODUCTION

HISTORY AND GEOPOLITICS

> What sympathy does the traveller excite, while he imprints the first step, that
> leads to civilization and all its boundless blessings, along the trackless desert,
> and struggling with the savageness of the untamed wilderness, obtains a victory
> that belongs to mankind.[1]

Helen Maria Williams's euphoric praise for Humboldt's celebrated expedition to tropical Spanish America in the years 1799–1804 set the tone for many
of the Northern European travel accounts about the region which prolifer-
ated over the following decades, and which are the subject of this volume.
Williams represents Latin America as virgin territory, 'nature' unmediated by
civilisation, awaiting the transformative magic of European reason, progress,
and capital to stir it from the long slumber of Spanish and Portuguese colonial misrule. Humboldt himself personifies the restless Romantic spirit of
exploration, turning his back on the bloody battlefields of Europe to win a
victory for all humanity, exploring and evoking the unknown forests, cordilleras, and *llanos* (plains) of the new continent. From being a closed book,
America is now represented as an opportunity for Northern European
explorers, naturalists, merchants and miners. While (as I will demonstrate
below) this was a deeply tendentious description of colonial Latin America on
the eve of its bloody struggle for independence, Williams's praise of Humboldt's 'first step' in civilising the trackless desert aptly illustrates the depths
of foreign ignorance about the present condition, and idealism about the
future prospects, of the region.

Those parts of continental America and the insular Caribbean with which
this volume is concerned were 'discovered' for Europeans in 1492 by Christopher Columbus and claimed for the Spanish crown. The rapid overthrow
of the advanced indigenous civilisations of the New World by conquistadores
like Hernàn Cortés, Francisco Pizarro, Vasco Nunez de Balboa, Diego de
Almagro, Pedro de Valdivia and de Sousa, assisted by the lethal microbes
against which native Americans had no resistance, is one of the most dramatic
and bloody chapters of world history. Spanish and Portuguese rule was con-
solidated by the 1530s, an extraordinary short space of time considering the

---

1 Translator's preface, Alexander von Humboldt and Aimé Bonpland, *Personal Narrative of
Travels to the Equinoctial Regions of the New Continent*, trans. Helen Maria Williams (London,
1814), vol. I, p. v.

geographical scale of the conquest. Despite the rhetoric of civilization and conversion to Christianity, the conquerors were largely motivated by unbridled lust for gold and silver. While the legend of El Dorado long haunted the colonial imagination in the form of an elusive desire for fabled wealth, the mines of Mexico, Colombia and Peru did provide the bullion upon which the Spanish and Portuguese global empires flourished, until their supersession by the new empires of France, Holland and Britain. If the historical pattern of European settlement was initially determined by the quest for gold and silver in highland Mexico and the western cordilleras of the South American Andes, the political geography of Latin America subsequently developed in accordance with Spanish and Portuguese administrative and judiciary divisions. The huge sixteenth-century Spanish viceroyalties of New Spain and Peru (to which New Granada and Río de la Plata were added in the eighteenth century) were divided into captaincy-generals and *audiencias*, partly administrative, partly judicial units. These colonial divisions would largely determine the shape of the Spanish-speaking republics: Mexico in North America, the Central American republics, Venezuela, Columbia, Ecuador, Peru, Chile, Argentina, Uruguay, Paraguay and Portuguese-speaking Brazil. In the case of Brazil, where a more sporadic conquest had created a less centralised authority and a smaller administrative system than in the Spanish colonies, the biggest state in Latin America was divided up into twenty captaincies granted to nobles for tropical plantations worked by imported African slaves.

The massive exploitation of indigenous Indian and later imported African labour in the plantations and mines of America, the notorious *encomienda* and *mita* systems, gave rise in Britain to the so-called 'black legend' of Iberian cruelty and rapacity, not of course without justification. On the other hand, few Britons seemed aware that universities and printing presses had been established in Mexico City and Lima since the middle of the sixteenth century, and that the colonies had developed a rich syncretic culture on the back of conquest and enslavement. Although the systematic brutalisation and legal enslavement of Indians by the *encomenderos* had been successfully challenged by the Dominican friar Bartolomé de las Casas and others, even the church cleaved to the doctrine of 'spiritual conquest' and was only able or willing to mitigate the Indians' harsh yoke to a small degree. The impact of the Catholic missions (Franciscan, Dominican, Augustinian and later Jesuit) in colonising traditional Indian societies is the subject of several excerpts in this volume, notably those by Ulloa, Humboldt and Martin Dobrizhoffer.

The racial amalgamation resulting from these unprecedented programmes of social engineering produced large hybrid populations in all the colonies, and the Spanish obsession with *pureza de sangre* created a proliferation of racial and ethnic categories (the *castas*) ranging from *indios* and *negros* (both free and enslaved Africans) through *mestizos* (product of Indian and European amalgamation), *mulatos* (African and European amalgamation), *zambos* (Indian and African amalgamation), and a bewildering range of sub-categories such as *tercerones* and *cuarterones*, outlined here in the first excerpt from Ulloa's *Voyage to South America*. By about 1800 almost 45 per cent of the Spanish Empire's population of 14.1 million was non-Indian and over 20 per cent was mestizo or otherwise mixed: Europeans were in a clear minority. The poverty and oppression suffered by the *castas*, *indígenas* and *negros* are a recurrent theme in all the travelogues represented here, and they were barely alleviated (sometimes even exacerbated) by republican independence. At the top of the social pyramid sat the European colonisers themselves; pride of place went to those born in Spain (*penisulares*), followed, in a markedly subordinate position, by the American-born Europeans or *criollos*. It was this subordination which, more than any other single factor, would fuel the flames of the Creole independence movements after 1808.

The jealous exclusion of foreigners from the Spanish and Portuguese colonies and their cultural and economic isolation from the rest of the world perhaps helps to explain Williams's Promethean image of Humboldt, although in fact the Prussian explorer never stepped beyond the boundaries and infrastructure of Spanish imperial power, and travelled as its representative. With the default of colonial power from 1808, Latin America was suddenly opened to the outside world, and British, French and North American publics craved information about the newly independent republics, fed by a proliferation of new travel accounts. Although travel books about Latin America had circulated in print during the eighteenth century, most were either plagiarised from sixteenth-century Spanish chroniclers or were the narratives of pirates or freebooters such as Sir Walter Raleigh and William Dampier, whose knowledge was confined to the coastal margins of the continent. William Bullock, in his *Six Months' Residence in Mexico* (1824), claimed that his was the first British travel account of Mexico to be published since Thomas Gage's record of his visit to New Spain during the reign of Charles I. Gage had only been permitted entry because he was an English Dominican priest destined for the Manila missions, but he later absconded and travelled extensively in New Spain. The same closure prevailed in the Portuguese colonies: as one reviewer of John Mawe's *Travels* wrote in 1812, on the eve of independence, 'the extreme jealousy of the Portuguese would not, until very recently, allow a foreigner, touching at any of the ports of Brazil, to sleep on shore, nor even to walk about in the day time, without a soldier at his heels: the interior of the country was *terra incognito*, completely sealed up by a succession of guard houses, which the colonists themselves were not permitted to pass without leave from the highest authority'.[1]

1 *Quarterly Review* (June 1812), p. 346.

Colonial Latin America may have been isolated, but it was not as backward as many European travellers believed. Following Alexis de Tocqueville's paradox, revolution and independence followed in the wake of liberalisation rather than increased oppression, in this case the Bourbon reform programme of the later eighteenth century. In 1737 Phillip V of Spain permitted Charles-Marie de la Condamine's expedition to visit Ecuador and other Spanish colonies in America as part of a belated programme of Spanish Enlightenment. Antonio de Ulloa's *Voyage to South America* (see below, pp. 1–18), the official account of the expedition by its leading Spanish member, portrayed imperial rule in the American colonies in a generally positive light. Unbeknown to his contemporaries, however, Ulloa (and his co-author Jorge Juan) had been commissioned by the Spanish crown to draw up a confidential report on its colonies entitled *Noticias secretas de América*, which contained a devastating condemnation of colonial inertia, corruption and misrule. This work only became public after it fell into British hands in the early nineteenth century, when it caused something of a sensation. Acting on the advice of experts like Ulloa, Charles III of Spain (1759–88) dismantled many of the economic restrictions on his American colonists, introducing *comercio libre* and abolishing the trade monopoly of Cadiz and Seville. Such relaxations were however accompanied by a rigorous new imperialist ideology which sought to subject the colonies to a greater bureaucratic control, increasing dependence upon the metropolis and stirring up creole resentment. The expulsion of the Jesuit order from Spanish territory in 1767 was part of this process of imperial consolidation, and caused widespread unrest throughout Catholic America as well as establishing a diaspora of exiled Jesuits in Europe. Polemical attacks on Spanish imperialism and apologias for American Creole culture by exiled Jesuits like the Mexican Francisco Xavier Clavigero, the Chilean Juan Ignacio Molina and the Austrian Martin Dobrizhoffer contributed to the creation of a new Creole identity which would come into its own in the coming decades. These writers participated in the so-called 'dispute of the New World', parrying the attacks on American culture and nature by Enlightenment savants such as the comte de Buffon, Guillaume-Thomas Raynal and Cornelius de Pauw.[1]

Humboldt does not look quite so Promethean when we realise that his travels were only made possible by a commission from Charles IV of Spain to report on the state of his colonies, especially the mines (Humboldt was a Freiburg-trained mining engineer and mineralogist). In the words of David Brading, 'when he explored the upper reaches of the Orinoco [Humboldt] received every possible assistance from local missionaries and officials and in return he communicated the results of his observations on longitude and latitude (which showed that Portugal had advanced well beyond the agreed

1 See Antonello Gerbi, *The Dispute of the New World*, trans. Jeremy Moyle, (Pittsburgh, 1973).

frontiers) to the government in Caracas for dispatch to Madrid'.[1] For all his subsequent importance in promoting 'creole self-fashioning',[2] Humboldt travelled as 'the spokesperson for the Bourbon enlightenment',[3] transmitting to his European readers a summary of the geographical researches of a generation of Spanish and Creole savants in the supposedly 'backward' colonies of Latin America. Although the Portuguese Enlightenment had not kept pace with that of its more powerful Spanish neighbour, the Derby mineralogist John Mawe was privileged (in a fashion similar to Humboldt) to be one of the first foreigners permitted by the Portuguese crown to enter the Brazilian interior in 1809–10, with the commission of assessing the economic potential of the gold and diamond mines in Minas Gerais province.[4]

By the 1770s, the enfeebled Iberian powers no longer held the monopoly on the whole geographical area covered by this volume, and Spain's territorial losses to its colonial rivals were most evident in the valuable sugar colonies of the Caribbean. Although Santa Domingo, Cuba and Puerto Rico remained under Spanish rule (the latter two were Spain's first and last American colonies), France, Britain, Holland and later Denmark had wrested valuable plantation islands from Spain in the seventeenth century through war and piracy.[5] Both the French sugar colony of Saint-Domingue (renamed Haiti after the revolution against colonial rule initiated by Toussaint L'Ouverture) and British-owned Jamaica had been wrested from Spain, the latter in 1660. Nor was British, French and Dutch power limited to the Caribbean islands: French and Dutch Guyana, (to which British Guyana was formally added after 1815) were relatively small territories on the north-east corner of the South American landmass, and Britain also possessed logging camps in Belize (British Honduras) on the Caribbean coast of Central America. The confusing colonial proprietorship of Guyana is evident in Waterton's *Travels*, which refers to British possessions in 'ci-devant' Dutch Guyana. An earlier travelogue, John Stedman's *Narrative of a Five-Years Expedition against the Revolted Negroes of Surinam* (1796) described the Scottish author's experience as a mercenary soldier in the Dutch service suppressing slave rebellion in Surinam (Dutch Guyana).[6] In common with Matthew Gregory Lewis's celebrated

1 David Brading, *The First America: The Spanish Monarchy, Creole Patriots, and the Liberal State, 1492–1867* (Cambridge, 1991), p. 517.

2 Mary Louise Pratt, *Imperial Eyes: Studies in Travel Writing and Transculturation* (London and New York, 1992), pp. 172–200.

3 Brading, *The First America*, p. 517.

4 Hugh Torrens, 'Under Royal Patronage: The Early Work of John Mawe in Geology and the Background to his Travels in Brazil in 1807–10', in M. Lopes and S. Figueiroa, eds, *O conhecimento geologico na America Latina: questoes de historia e teoria* (Campinas, Brazil, 1990), pp. 103–13. Thanks to Anne Secord for this reference.

5 J. H. Parry and P. M. Sherlock, *A Short History of the West Indies* (London and New York, 1965), pp. 27–62.

6 Despite its importance, Stedman's *Narrative* is not included here because there is a recent annotated edition of the 1796 text by R. A. J. van Lier (Barre, 1971) as well as an edition of Stedman's original manuscript edited by Richard and Sally Price (Baltimore, 1988).

Journal of a West Indian Proprietor, Kept During a Residence in Jamaica (1834),[1] most early nineteenth-century travel accounts of the British Caribbean (such as those of John Stewart and Henry Nelson Coleridge in the present volume) were preoccupied with the reform of the plantation system in the light of the imminent emancipation of the slaves. Britain had pioneered the abolition of the Atlantic slave trade in 1806–7, but slavery was still legal in its colonies until 1834, and there was an overriding fear on the part of white planters of rebellion along the lines of the genocidal Saint-Domingue uprising of 1791, as well as anxiety concerning the economic future of the sugar islands following emancipation.

THE REVOLUTIONARY DECADES

The romantic Spanish America evoked by Helen Maria Williams as a silent and 'trackless' scene of nature could not be further from the turbulent reality of the two decades which followed Humboldt's expedition. The historical background to the travel narratives of Hall, Graham, Head, Proctor and Bullock included in this volume is the protracted and violent struggle for independence of the Spanish and Portuguese colonies.[2] Although rebellion had been endemic in all the colonies before 1800, especially amongst the oppressed Indians, Blacks and *castas*, the Latin American independence struggle was precipitated by Napoleon's invasion of Spain and Portugal in 1808, and the collapse of Bourbon rule. The fact that the Portuguese monarchy fled to exile in Brazil dictated the very different progress of Brazilian independence, surveyed below. In 1812 the new Spanish Cortes (parliament) produced a liberal constitution which claimed for the first time to represent the colonists. The Creole élites were unconvinced, equally distrustful of Napoleon, the Bourbons, and Spanish liberalism, with its strongly imperialist leanings. To support their interests and assert their independence in the face of conflicting messages from the metropolis, the Creoles needed to mobilise entire populations; but at the same time they feared the consequences of racial insurrection on the pattern of Saint-Domingue or the Peruvian Tupac Amaru revolt in 1780–2.

Faced by a crisis of legitimation, local Creole élites began to take power into their own hands, and the flames of independence quickly swept over the whole continent. The first outbreak kindled in Buenos Aires in the wake of the disastrous British invasion attempt of 1806–7. It led, in May 1810, to a declaration of independence in the sparsely settled viceroyalty of Rio de la Plata, and spread across the Pampas and the Andes to Chile and Upper Peru

1 See the new edition by Judith Terry in Oxford World Classics.
2 My brief account here is indebted to John Lynch, *The Spanish American Revolutions, 1808–26*, second edition (New York and London, 1986), and Mark Burkholder and Lyman Johnson, *Colonial Latin America*, third edition (New York and London, 1998).

(Bolivia) in the years that followed. The second (on the heels of the first) was sparked by Venezuela's declaration of independence in December 1811 and spread, with terrible violence and inter-ethnic strife, to New Granada, Ecuador and finally Peru. However the initial, frustrated social revolution of the years 1810–14 quickly suffered a severe setback as the authoritarian Ferdinand VII of Spain, finally rid of the Napoleonic incubus, began to strike back against his rebellious Creole subjects. An enormous Spanish force sailed to Venezuela under the command of General Pablo Morillo ('the Pacifier') in 1815, but despite initial victories in crushing rebellion, the counter-revolution achieved only temporary success.

Although Spanish American independence was finally achieved by a host of *caudillos*, mercenaries, opportunists and idealists, two men emerged to prominence as supreme 'liberators' in South America. From the Río de la Plata came José de San Martín, a Creole soldier and veteran of the peninsular campaign in Spain with strong monarchist leanings, who carried the revolutionary torch from Argentina across the Andes to Chile and Peru. From the north emerged the brilliant Simón Bolívar, scion of a Venezuelan aristocratic family who had travelled widely in Europe (he had met Humboldt in Paris in 1804), educated himself in Enlightenment philosophy and now struggled to accommodate his egalitarian political ideals to the inhospitable conditions of post-colonial Latin America. In 1817 San Martín crossed the Andes from Mendoza into the valleys of central Chile, where he defeated the royalists at the battle of Chacabuco in February 1817, and again at Maipo in April 1818, the latter a decisive victory which, in his own words, 'decided the fate of South America'. Under the directorship of Bernardo O'Higgins, Chile became the power base of the revolution on the Pacific coast of America, from which San Martín launched his expedition to liberate the royalist stronghold of Peru in August 1820. The Chilean navy was led by the brilliant mercenary Admiral Thomas Cochrane, future Earl of Dundonald, who in November 1820 attacked the Spanish navy in the Peruvian port of Calloa and captured its flagship, the 44-gun *Esmeralda*, thereby disabling the fleet from further action against the insurgents. O'Higgins, San Martín and Cochrane all figure prominently in the travel narratives of Basil Hall, Francis Head, Maria Graham and William Proctor. In her *Journal of a Residence in Chile*, Graham, an intimate friend of Cochrane, offers a detailed, if biased, account of Cochrane's increasing frustration with San Martín's softly-softly approach to Peruvian liberation, leading to his eventual resignation and transfer to the Brazilian service in 1823. Proctor's *Journey across the Cordilleras* paints a grim portrait of Peru during the critical years of 1823–4, when civil war divided the country in the wake of San Martín's resignation, and permitted the Spanish to regroup, before their final defeat by Bolívar and his trusted lieutenant Antonio José de Sucre at the battles of Junín and Ayacucho in August and December 1824.

Bolívar had been called to liberate Peru from the north, where he had finally triumphed against massive odds. The Spanish reconquest of Venezuela in 1815 had driven him into exile in Jamaica, where in September 1815 he composed his celebrated 'Jamaica Letter', analysing the failure of the first wave of the revolution and seeking to define the conditions for the success of the second. In December 1816, backed by Alexandre Pétion, ruler of free Haiti and rival of King Henri Christophe, Bolívar launched a new invasion of the mainland and declared the third Venezuelan republic. Attentive to the racial tensions which divided Venezuelan society, and successfully enlisting the support of the *llanero* caudillo José Antonio Páez from the plains of Apure (visited by Humboldt only a decade and a half before), this time Bolívar was successful. At the Congress of Angostura in February 1819, deep in the Guyanan jungle, he sketched his plan for a balanced constitution on the British model, and was declared president of the republic. Reinforced by a legion of British mercenaries, Bolívar joined General Francisco de Paula Santander in May 1819 and crossed the Andes to liberate New Granada (Colombia), defeating the royalists at the battle of Boyaca before returning to Venezuela, where he crushed the Spaniards at the battle of Carabobo in 1821. The fruit of these victories was Bolívar's declaration of the united republic of Gran Colombia, uniting Venezuela, New Granada and Ecuador. Although Bolívar was still to triumph (albeit temporarily) in Peru's reluctant revolution, his idealistic plan for Gran Colombia was doomed to failure. The problem of administering power over huge distances and the regionalism long fostered by Spanish colonial rule led to the breakdown of the republic in 1829–30, and the frustration of Bolívar's ambitious political projects. 'America is ungovernable', he wrote whilst travelling into exile after a failed assassination attempt; 'those who serve the revolution plough the sea. The only thing to do is to emigrate.' He died a month later, a broken man.

Meanwhile, in the enormous viceroyalty of New Spain, which stretched from the shores of Panama to California, a very different kind of revolution had broken out in 1810. With more than 60 million inhabitants, New Spain was home to over 40 per cent of the entire Spanish American population. Its capital, Mexico City, was one of the largest cities in the western hemisphere, with 150,000 inhabitants, and was graced by a university, a college of mining, museums, art galleries and a botanical garden. In 1804, Humboldt had spent a year in Mexico travelling and gathering statistical information from local savants; when his *Political Essay on New Spain* was published in Britain in 1811, it alerted eager investors and entrepreneurs to the wealth of the silver-rich colony. By the time the entrepreneurs arrived in the 1820s, however, the mines had been devastated by a decade of war and bloodshed. Mexico had provided Spain with a staggering two-thirds of her entire imperial revenue in 1800, but her seemingly insatiable appetite for Mexican silver alienated the Creole élite and the church alike.

The Mexican revolution actually began as a pre-emptive Spanish strike against liberal proposals following the imprisonment of the Bourbon monarchy in 1808. This had the effect of stirring up Creole anger, leading to a fierce popular uprising in 1810 instigated by a visionary priest named Miguel Hidalgo y Costilla in the small parish of Dolores near Guanajuato north of Mexico City. The massacre of wealthy Spanish refugees in the Alhóndiga (granary) at Guanajuato by a ragged army of mestizo *campesinos*, miners and Indians revealed the racial antagonism which animated the rebellion, quickly alienating the sympathies of the Creole élite, which had been in the forefront of the South American revolutions. After Hidalgo's defeat by royalist armies at Calderón in 1811, the torch of revolution was taken up by a number of guerrilla leaders, such as Guadalupe Victoria, Vincente Guerrero, and perhaps the most celebrated *insurgente* of them all, José María Morelos, like Hidalgo a rural priest. It was Morelos who formally declared independence in November 1813, but the popular uprising of the *insurgentes* were defeated by the Spanish counter-revolution (like the first wave of the South American revolution) by the end of 1815.

The second Mexican revolution of 1820, led by the conservative counter-insurgent General Agustín de Iturbide, was of a very different stamp. The liberal Spanish Cortes of 1820 had quickly alienated the most powerful interest in Mexico by abolishing forced labour and confiscating church lands. In February 1821 Iturbide took a break from harrying Guerrero's guerrilla bands in the south to publish the Plan de Iguala, which proclaimed Mexican independence from Spain whilst guaranteeing constitutional monarchy, the preservation of the church and property rights. This was a disappointment to the republican revolutionaries, but the church exerted its powers over the masses and the Plan was accepted. Iturbide was a military dictator with an appetite for pomp and circumstance, and when he crowned himself Emperor Agustín I he alienated the republican sympathies of many of his compatriots. Pressurised by a republican party led by Generals Antonio López de Santa Anna and Guadalupe Victoria, and having lost the support of the royalists, he was forced to abdicate on 19 March 1823 (just before William Bullock's arrival in Mexico) and fled into exile in England. A republican constitution was drawn up in October 1824 which sought to balance the conservative centralism of Lucas Alamán's party with the interests of the liberal federalists represented by Victoria, elected as Mexico's first president, and which managed to sustain a precarious stability until 1827.

Independence in Brazil, the background to the excerpt from Maria Graham's *Journal of a Voyage*, followed a different trajectory from the revolutions of Spanish America, on account of the presence of the exiled Portuguese royal family on Brazilian soil. The arrival in 1808 of the court of the Prince Regent John (crowned John VI in 1816) brought with it numerous privileges, including economic liberalisation, increased immigration from

Europe, and social prestige for the Creole élite. In 1815 John declared Brazil to be a co-kingdom equal with Portugal itself. Brazil was virtually untouched by the revolutionary fires that raged across the rest of the continent, with the exception of a short-lived republican uprising in Pernambuco in 1817. Yet as elsewhere in Latin America, events in the metropolis destabilised Brazil, and King John was forced to follow events in Portugal by accepting a liberal constitution in 1821. When he returned to Portugal in July of the same year, he left behind his 22-year-old son Dom Pedro as regent. It would not be so easy to set back the clock, however, as Brazilians were reluctant to revert to colonial status after their king's return to Lisbon. During his father's absence, Dom Pedro became a champion of independence and, aided by his conservative cabinet leader José Bonifácio, assumed leadership of the Brazilian government in 1822. On 7 September he declared himself Pedro I, constitutional emperor of an independent Brazil. Through her friend Admiral Cochrane, Maria Graham was well connected at Dom Pedro's court, and she became close to the Empress Leopoldina when she served as tutor to the Infanta María de Gloria in 1824. Her remarks on independence in the *Journal* present a unique 'insider' view of the rapidly changing course of events.

BRITAIN, LATIN AMERICAN INDEPENDENCE AND THE BOOM OF TRAVEL ACCOUNTS

Part of the enormous appeal of Humboldt's *Personal Narrative* was its contribution to dispelling Northern European ignorance about Spanish America, an ignorance which had only been partly mitigated by the publication of Ulloa and Juan's *Voyage to South America* and other eighteenth-century narratives of the La Condamine expedition. In the wake of Humboldt, and following the outbreak of the wars of independence, the number of travel books about Latin America published in Britain reached a peak between 1815 and 1830 not equalled until after 1850.[1] This clearly reflected both a massive increase in the number of foreigners visiting the region and the involvement of British merchants, diplomats, military men, mercenaries and mining engineers in the revolutions of Spanish and Portuguese America. Britain has unsuccessfully invaded the Río de la Plata in 1806–7 (an eyewitness account is contained in John Mawe's *Travels*) but soon realised that its economic interests would be better served by trade and investment than by foolhardy attempts at colonisation. Although official British sympathy for the independence movement was hampered by the fact that monarchist Spain was Britain's ally against Napoleon after 1808, British merchants were prime beneficiaries of the opening of Spanish American ports in the wake of inde-

---

1 R. A. MacNeil and M. D. Dean, *Europeans in Latin America: Humboldt to Hudson* (Oxford, 1980), p. 23.

pendence, a fact that the government could not ignore. As in the case of Greece fighting free of the Ottoman empire in the same decade, popular opinion was strongly on the side of the *independistas*, despite government recalcitrance. Latin American independence was hotly debated in the British public journals throughout the Romantic period; the Whig *Edinburgh Review* led the way by espousing independence, followed by the *Morning Chronicle* and *The Times*, but the Tory *Quarterly Review* (founded in 1809, it should be remembered, in sympathy with the Spanish monarchist cause belittled by the *Edinburgh Review*) regarded Latin American republicanism as a dangerous extension of French Jacobin principles.[1]

In response to Napoleon's invasion of Spain, the British government established the South American naval squadron with a view to defending British political and mercantile interests in the region against the French threat. Over the next twenty years naval captains like Thomas Graham (Maria Graham's husband) and Basil Hall were sympathetic observers of the independence movement in Brazil, Río de la Plata, Chile, Peru, Venezuela and Mexico. The Admiralty's project of charting South America's coasts and exploring the naval, military and commercial opportunities of the newly independent South Atlantic littoral from Bàhia in Brazil to Bahía Blanco in Argentina (and further south to Patagonia and Tierra del Fuego) was also productive of the most famous South American travel narrative of the nineteenth century, Charles Darwin's *Journal of Researches*. In 1831 Darwin sailed from England with Captain Fitzroy on board HMS *Beagle* in the role of ship's naturalist, although his famous account of the voyage was not published until 1839, just beyond the chronological limits of the present volume.[2] Darwin was one of the many British travellers who credited Humboldt's *Personal Narrative* with having inspired him to visit Latin America; his vivid remarks on Pampas life and on post-independence Chile compliment the accounts of Francis Bond Head and Basil Hall (both of whose books he read on board the *Beagle*) excerpted here.

From the start, the Creole revolutionaries were desperate for British support. In 1810 a delegation from Venezuela consisting of Simón Bolívar, Luis López Méndez and Andrés Bello arrived in London to seek British protection and material assistance for the Junta. Bello, a poet, philosopher and educationalist, remained in Britain for nineteen years as propagandist for the cause of independence. Food, blankets, guns and ammunition were soon on their way to the Caribbean coast of Venezuela. In 1817 and 1818 Bolívar's emissaries recruited five regiments of British mercenaries in London under the nose

1 See José Alberich, 'English Attitudes towards the Hispanic World in the Time of Bello as Reflected by the *Edinburgh* and *Quarterly* Reviews', in John Lynch, ed., *Andrés Bello: The London Years* (London, 1982), pp. 67–81. This article contains a useful list of reviews of Spanish American travelogues in the *Edinburgh* and *Quarterly* reviews between 1803 and 1828.
2 For an excellent recent abridgement of the original 1839 text, see *Charles Darwin's Voyage of the Beagle*, edited and annotated by Janet Browne and Michael Neve (Harmondsworth, 1989).

of the infuriated Spanish ambassador. The following year, under pressure from Spain and the Holy Alliance, an embarrassed Tory government was forced to pass the Foreign Enlistment Act to curtail this practice, but it nonetheless continued in covert fashion. Enlistment in the revolutionary cause, however romantic, was not without its risks: a quarter of Bolívar's British Legion died during the march across the Andes to liberate New Granada in May–July 1819. William Miller, William Brown, Daniel O'Leary, Belford Hinton Wilson and Thomas Cochrane were amongst the most celebrated British generals and admirals in the *independista* service. In 1859, Cochrane published his memoirs, *Narrative of Services in the Liberation of Chili, Peru, and Brazil*. Accounts of the ordeals faced by common soldiers, such as Gustavus Hippisley's *Narrative of the Expedition to the River Orinoco and Apure in South America* (1819) or James Hackitt's *Narrative of the Expedition which Sailed from England in 1817, to Join the South American Patriots* (1818), although unrepresented here, deserve to form a sub-genre in their own right.

In 1826 Bolívar wrote hyperbolically that 'politically, alliance with Great Britain would be a greater victory than Ayacucho, and if we procure it you may be certain that our future happiness is assured. The advantages that will result for Columbia, if we ally ourselves with the mistress of the universe, are incalculable.'[1] Although hindsight might have forced the Liberator to eat his words, given the subsequent history of Latin American economic dependence, at least in the mid-1820s his aspirations were (for once) in the process of being fulfilled. By 1824 up to 100 British commercial houses had been established in Spanish America, and in Buenos Aires, where the British community numbered 3,000, half of the public debt was in British hands.[2] In Mexico, Lucas Alamán, leader of the interim government established after the fall of Iturbide in 1823, showered privileges on the semi-official commercial traveller William Bullock, permitting him to ransack museums and libraries, and to copy rare Aztec sculptures, in return for the reassurance of British capital investment in the country's waterlogged mines.

Britain's most substantial contribution to the independence struggle (apart from men, arms and provisions) was in loans to finance the insurgent armies and support the fragile economies of the new republics. The nominal value of these loans was a staggering 21 million pounds, but the amounts realised were far less, and the sums received by Latin American governments were even smaller still. Speculation in the loans was risky business; interest payments on the Colombian loan of 2 million pounds were suspended in 1826 and many a speculator was bankrupted when the bubbles burst.[3] Robert

---

1 Letter to Sucre, 22 January 1826, cited in John Lynch, 'Great Britain and Spanish American Independence 1810–30', in Lynch, ed., *Andrés Bello*, p. 22.
  2 ibid. p. 9.
  3 ibid. p. 14.

Proctor travelled as an agent for the contractors of the Peruvian loan in 1823–4, and his *Narrative of a Journey* vividly portrays the eagerness with which the loans were awaited and the political complications which rapidly ensnared all parties involved in negotiations. In the 1820s, the newly independent republics were also inundated by a wave of British travellers representing various commercial interests, notably the mining associations which sought to tap the legendary wealth of the Spanish American silver, gold and diamond mines, of which Humboldt had written in glowing terms quarter of a century before. In 1824–5, as many as twenty-six different mining companies were floated in London with a paid-up capital of over 3.5 million pounds.[1] In her pioneering work on Spanish American travel writing, Mary Louise Pratt has aptly described these travellers as the 'capitalist vanguard', indicating the degree to which, in their narratives, the 'contemplative, estheticizing rhetoric of discovery' associated with the Humboldtian traveller is 'often replaced by a goal-orientated rhetoric of conquest and achievement'.[2] Although a cut above the rest in literary terms, Francis Bond Head's *Rough Notes* (excerpted here) is characteristic of this South American sub-genre. John Miers's *Travels in Chile and La Plata* (1826), Joseph Andrews's *Journey from Buenos Aires through the Province of Cordova, Tucuman, and Salta to Potosi* (1827), and Captain Charles Brand's *Journal of a Voyage to Peru* (1828) are other examples not included here.[3]

Another unifying feature of these travel accounts is their shared itinerary. Pratt writes that 'one itinerary in particular became a canonical heroic paradigm for the Englishman's South American journey: landing in the port of Buenos Aires, he made his way overland across the Argentinean pampas, up over the Andean Cordillera and down the other side to the capitals of Chile or Peru, from which he eventually embarked by sea for home'.[4] The equivalent 'beaten track' for Mexico is described in William Bullock's narrative, as well as in works not included here like Henry Ward's *Mexico in 1827* (1828) and (with variations) George Lyons's *Journal of a Residence and Tour in the Republic of Mexico in 1826* (1828). The traveller arrived in the fever-ridden Caribbean port of Veracruz, ascended by the mountainous route via Jalapa and Puebla to Mexico City, and then proceeded to the mining districts of Taxco, Temascaltepec or Guanajuato. Although space has not permitted their inclusion here, narratives such as Charles Cochrane's *Journal of a Residence and Travels in Colombia during the Years 1823–4* (1825) and John Hamilton's *Travels*

---

1 John Ford, 'Rudolph Ackermann: Culture and Commerce in Latin America, 1822–8' in Lynch, ed., *Andrés Bello*, p. 148.

2 Pratt, *Imperial Eyes*, p. 148.

3 See Ricardo Cicerchia, *Journey, Rediscovery and Narrative: British Travel Accounts of Argentina 1800–1850* (London, 1998). Thanks to Angel Gurría Quintana for this and other sources of information.

4 ibid. p. 148.

through the Interior Provinces of Colombia (1827) represent the 'capitalist vanguard' at large in highland Columbia, following the routes of pre-Hispanic
and colonial trade networks and exploiting the labour of indigenous porters,
mule drivers, and the bizarre *silleros* who, like human donkeys, carried afflu-
ent travellers over the cordilleras on upright chairs.[1] Characteristic of all the
narratives of the 'capitalist vanguard' is their obsession with the ruinous state
of the new republics, the dire legacy of colonial misrule and the violence of
recent war: 'neglect becomes the touchstone of a negative esthetic that legiti-
mated European interventionism'.[2]

A deflationary tone thus dominates many of the narratives of the late
1820s, in the wake of the collapse of the mining boom, and Humboldt is
often blamed for having created false hopes and overestimated the economic
potential of the mines. This is exemplified by Francis Head's discovery that
the Uspallata mines promised to his company by the Argentinian government had already been sold off to a rival. Robert Southey wrote of the bubble
in 1827, in a maliciously amusing review of the travel accounts of Miers and
Head, that

> there was scarcely an old lady in the country who did not continue to save
> something from her income to lay out in shares; nor a young and inexperienced
> adventurer in London who was not found dabbling in some mining scheme ...
> Most of the bubbles have long since blown up, and we see the few remaining
> ones bursting daily ... We have been woefully mistaken in all that relates
> to South America – the population, her resources, the activity, industry, and
> integrity of the revolutionists have been intentionally and most grievously
> exaggerated.[3]

To Southey, the nineteenth-century search for El Dorado now seemed just
as quixotic as its sixteenth-century prototype.

Whilst the narratives of the 'capitalist vanguard' are arguably most representative of the travel writing of the capitalist and imperialist nineteenth
century, the present volume seeks to situate these 'goal-orientated' texts
within a broader and more varied context. My selection aims to reflect the
stylistic variety of the whole field of contemporary travel writing, as manifest
in other volumes of this edition. Whilst the objectifying 'statistical' reports
of writers like Ulloa or Stewart exemplify travel writing as a form of degree
zero 'geographical narrative', other texts display a more engaging and imagi-
native literary style. The quirky, pre-scientific 'missionary ethnography' of
Dobrizhoffer, the aestheticising naturalism of Humboldt, or the eccentric
anti-Linnaean natural history of Waterton all represent a distinctively romantic idiom of travel writing, whilst the social commentary of Basil Hall and

---

1 See Michael Taussig, *Shamanism, Colonialism and the Wild Man* (Chicago and London,
1987), pp. 287–335.
2 Pratt, *Imperial Eyes*, p. 149.
3 *Quarterly Review* (January 1827), p. 115.

Maria Graham typify another, more urbane variety. Bullock's Pickwickian narrative persona reveals that even the capitalist vanguard had its more 'literary' moments.

I have aimed at some degree of historical coverage by providing passages pre-dating the wars of independence (the first four), in order to set up a contrast between accounts of colonial and post-colonial Latin America. Space has prevented comprehensive geographical coverage of this enormous continental region: Patagonia, Bolivia, highland Colombia and Central America are unrepresented here, and the far-flung insular Caribbean is only represented by the islands of Cuba, Haiti, Jamaica and Montserrat. The fact that all the texts anthologised here, with the exception of one, are by men reflects the small number of female-authored travel accounts of Latin America in the period; it can only be hoped that quality will substitute for quantity, given that Graham's journal is one of the most accomplished in literary terms. This volume can only aspire to offer a sample of the many travel accounts written about Latin America and the Caribbean in a climacteric period of their history, but it is hoped that the selections are representative to the extent that they map out the terrain and encourage readers to explore further for themselves.

Ulloa and Juan:
Voyage to South America

Antonio de Ulloa and Jorge Juan, *A Voyage to South America. Describing at Large, the Spanish Cities, Towns, Provinces, &c. on that Extensive Continent. Undertaken by Command of the King of Spain. 3rd edition, trans. from the Original Spanish, to which are Added, by Mr John Adams … Occasional Notes and Observations, an Account of Some Parts of Brazil … [and] a Map of S. America Corrected*, 2 vols (London, 1772), vol. I, pp. 29–35; vol. II, pp. 175–84.

In 1737 a joint European expedition, led by the French mathematician Louis Godin and the geographer Charles-Marie de la Condamine, arrived in Ecuador to measure the precise limits of the degrees of latitude at the arc of the Earth's meridian. This was to ascertain whether the Earth bulged at the poles or the equator, and thereby to settle a dispute between Cartesian and Newtonian mathematicians about the shape of the globe. They confirmed Newton's theory that the Earth bulged around its midriff. This was Europe's first modern scientific expedition, equipped with precise instruments never before seen in Spanish America, long closed by its jealous rulers to the outside world. Ecuador was chosen on the grounds that other sites 'under the equinoctial line both in Asia and in Africa, were either inhabited by savages, or not of an extent sufficient for these operations' (vol. I, p. 5).

The expedition was beset by difficulties. Professional and national rivalries between Frenchmen and Spaniards, constant friction with the colonial authorities, technical problems of surveying and damage to equipment in the inhospitable climate all took a heavy toll. The savants complained that 'in the torrid zone … where it was natural to suppose we had most to fear from the heat, our greatest pain was caused by the excessiveness of the cold' (vol. I, p. 211). Between August 1737 and July 1739 Antonio de Ulloa's party suffered the severe conditions of Pichincha, to the bafflement of local inhabitants; 'our hands were covered in chilblains; our lips swelled and chopped; so that every motion, in speaking or the like drew blood' (vol. I, p. 5). Suspected of spying out mineral resources by the authorities, the expedition's surgeon Jean Seniergues was murdered in 1739; La Condamine himself narrowly avoided the same fate. In the end the French delegation fell apart and several more members were murdered, went missing or insane, as they made their separate ways home. The whole grim story was told in La Condamine's *Brief Narrative of Travels through the Interior of South America* (1745).

The expedition's existence depended on the good will of the Spanish King Philip V, who was determined to end Spain's long intellectual isolation. Spain's backwardness dictated that two naval officers (rather than natural philosophers) were sent as official representatives. Jorge Juan y Santacilla (1713–73) and Antonio de Ulloa (1716–95) were graduates of the new Cadiz naval academy, and were encouraged to write a full-length account of the expedition, partly with a view to countering La Condamine's critical perspective. Ulloa's *Relación histórica del viaje a la America meridional* (Juan took a secondary role in its production) was published in 1748, and its English translation by John Adams went through five editions. Its success was due as much to the sheer scarcity of information about Spanish America in the Anglophone world as to any intrinsic literary interest, for the narrative itself is a rather dry compendium, a 'statistical' account in the eighteenth-century meaning of that word, 'an inquiry into the state of a country'. The *Relación* signals the new importance of interior expedition rather than coastal surveying. As the book's translator wrote, 'What idea can we form of a Turkey carpet if we look only at the border, or it may be, at the selvage?' (quoted in Mary Louise Pratt, *Imperial Eyes: Studies in Travel Writing and Transculturation* (New York and London, 1992), p. iii).

Just as important was the credibility of the witnesses themselves. In this respect Ulloa and Juan could not be faulted: on their return journey, their ship was captured by the British and they were brought to Boston and London, where they were welcomed as distinguished members of the La Condamine expedition and elected members of the Royal Society of London. The *Relación*'s English translator made much of this fact in promoting the work to an English readership. In 1763 Ulloa became governor of Louisiana, and in 1772 he published *Noticias americanas*, an account of the natural history of the New World.

The passages excerpted here exemplify the sober, descriptive style which Adams calls 'civil history' (vol. I, p. x). The first describes the complex racial hierarchy of Spanish colonial society and the rigid distinction between *criollos* and *peninsulares*, which would eventually goad the former into revolution. Ulloa propagandised the wealth and economic potential of Spanish America, although precise statistical figures were carefully omitted. It is ironic that the Jesuits praised in the second passage were expelled in 1767 by Charles III. Unbeknown to their contemporaries, Ulloa and Juan had been commissioned to write a secret report on colonial America. *Noticias secretas de América*, a devastating portrait of colonial misrule and corruption, was only published in the early nineteenth century after it had fallen into British hands. But as David Brading has indicated, Ulloa's two narratives reveal him as a zealous servant of the Spanish crown, willing to propagandise in public and criticise in secret, 'the most talented exponent of the recrudescence of the Spanish imperial tradition of commentary on the New World' (Brading, *The First America*, p. 428).

CHAP. IV.

Of the Inhabitants of Carthagena.

THE inhabitants may be divided into different casts or tribes, who derive their origin from a coalition of Whites, Negroes, and Indians. Of each of these we shall treat particularly.

The Whites may be divided into two classes, the Europeans, and Creoles, or Whites born in the country. The former are commonly called Chapetones, but are not numerous; most of them either return into Spain after acquiring a competent fortune, or remove up into inland provinces in order to increase it. Those who are settled at Carthagena, carry on the whole trade of that place, and live in opulence; whilst the other inhabitants are indigent, and reduced to have recourse to mean and hard labour for subsistence. The families of the White Creoles compose the landed interest; some of them have large estates, and are highly respected, because their ancestors came into the country invested with honourable posts, bringing their families with them when they settled here. Some of these families, in order to keep up their original dignity, have either married their children to their equals in the country, or sent them as officers on board the galleons; but others have greatly declined. Besides these, there are other Whites, in mean circumstances, who either owe their origin to Indian families, or at least to an intermarriage with them, so that there is some mixture in their blood; but when this is not discoverable by their colour, the conceit of being Whites alleviates the pressure of every other calamity.

Among the other tribes which are derived from an intermarriage of the Whites with the Negroes, the first are the Mulattos. Next to these the Tercerones, produced from a White and a Mulatto, with some approximation to the former, but not so near as to obliterate

their origin.   After thefe follow the Quarterones, proceeding from a White and a Terceron. The laft are
the Quinterones, who owe their origin to a White and
Quarteron. This is the laft gradation, there being no
vifible difference between them and the Whites, either
in colour or features ; nay, they are often fairer than
the Spaniards.   The children of a White and Quinteron are alfo called Spaniards, and confider themfelves
as free from all taint of the Negro race.   Every perfon
is fo jealous of the order of their tribe or caft, that if,
through inadvertence, you call them by a degree lower
than what they actually are, they are highly offended,
never fuffering themfelves to be deprived of fo valuable
a gift of fortune.

BEFORE they attain the clafs of the Quinterones,
there are feveral intervening circumftances which
throw them back ; for between the Mulatto and the
Negro there is an intermediate race, which they
call Sambos, owing their origin to a mixture between
one of thefe with an Indian, or among themfelves.
They are alfo diftinguifhed according to the cafts their
fathers were of. Betwixt the Tercerones and the
Mulattos, the Quarterones and the Tercerones, &c.
are thofe called Tente en el Ayre, fufpended in the
air, becaufe they neither advance nor recede. Children, thofe parents are a Quarteron or Quinteron,
and a Mulatto or Terceron, are Salto atras, retrogrades,
becaufe, inftead of advancing towards being Whites,
they have gone backwards towards the Negro race.
The children between a Negro and Quinteron are
called Sambos de Negro, de Mulatto, de Terceron, &c.

THESE are the moft known and common tribes or
Caftas ; there are indeed feveral others proceeding
from their intermarriages ; but, being fo various, even
they themfelves cannot eafily diftinguifh them ; and
thefe are the only people one fees in the city, the
eftancias *, and the villages ; for if any Whites, efpe-

* Eftancia properly fignifies a manfion, or place where one ftops
to reft ; but at Carthagena it implies a country-houfe, which, by rea-

cially women, are met with, it is only accidental; thefe generally refiding in their houfes; at leaft, if they are of any rank or charaƈter.

THESE cafts, from the Mulattos, all affeƈt the Spaniſh drefs, but wear very ſlight ſtuffs on account of the heat of the climate. Thefe are the mechanics of the city; the Whites, whether Creoles or Chapitones, difdaining fuch a mean occupation, follow nothing below merchandife. But it being impoſſible for all to fucceed, great numbers not being able to procure fufficient credit, they become poor and miferable from their averfion to thofe trades they follow in Europe; and, inftead of the riches which they flattered themfelves with poſſeſſing in the Indies, they experience the moſt complicated wretchednefs.

THE clafs of Negroes is not the leaft numerous, and is divided into two parts; the free and the flaves. Thefe are again fubdivided into Creoles and Bozares, part of which are employed in the cultivation of the haziandes *, or eftancias. Thofe in the city are obliged to perform the moſt laborious fervices, and pay out of their wages a certain quota to their mafters, fubfifting themfelves on the fmall remainder. The violence of the heat not permitting them to wear any clothes, their only covering is a fmall piece of cotton ſtuff about their waift; the female flaves go in the fame manner. Some of thefe live at the eftancias, being married to the flaves who work there; while thofe in the city fell in the markets all kind of eatables, and dry fruits, fweetmeats, cakes made of the maize, and caffava, and feveral other things about the ftreets. Thofe who have children fucking at their breaft, which is the cafe of the generality, carry them on their fhoulders, in order to have their arms at liberty; and when the infants are hungry,

fon of the great number of flaves belonging to it, often equals a confiderable village.

* Hazianda in this place fignifies a country-houfe, with the lands belonging to it.

they give them the breaft either under the arm or over
the fhoulder, without taking them from their backs.
This will perhaps appear incredible ; but their breafts,
being left to grow without any preffure on them, often
hang down to their very waift, and are not therefore
difficult to turn over their fhoulders for the convenience
of the infant.

THE drefs of the Whites, both men and women, dif-
fers very little from that worn in Spain.   The perfons
in grand employments wear the fame habits as in Europe ; but with this difference, that all their clothes are
very light, the waiftcoats and breeches being of fine
Bretagne linen, and the coat of fome other thin ftuff.
Wigs are not much worn here ; and during our ftay,
the governor and two or three of the chief officers only
appeared in them.   Neckcloths are alfo uncommon,
the neck of the fhirt being adorned with large gold but-
tons, and thefe generally fuffered to hang loofe.   On
their heads they wear a cap of very fine and white linen.
Others go entirely bareheaded, having their hair cut
from the nape of the neck *. Fans are very commonly
worn by men, and made of a very thin kind of palm in
the form of a crefcent, having a ftick of the fame wood
in the middle.   Thofe who are not of the White clafs,
or of any eminent family, wear a cloak and a hat flap-
ped ; though fome Mulattos and Negroes drefs like
the Spaniards and great men of the country.

THE Spanifh women wear a kind of petticoat, which
they call pollera, made of a thin filk, without any lining;
and on their body, a very thin white waiftcoat; but even
this is only worn in what they call winter, it being infup-
portable in fummer.   They however always lace in
fuch a manner as to conceal their breafts. When they
go abroad, they wear a mantelet; and on the days of

* Here, and in moft parts of South America, they have their
hair cut fo fhort, that a ftranger would think every man had a wig,
but did not wear it on account of the heat.—A.

precept, they go to mafs at three in the morning, in order to difcharge that duty, and return before the violent heat of the day, which begins with the dawn *.

WOMEN wear over their pollera a taffety petticoat, of any colour they pleafe, except black ; this is pinked all over, to fhew the other they wear under it. On the head is a cap of fine white linen, covered with lace, in the fhape of a mitre, and, being well ftarched, terminates forward in a point. This they call panito, and never appear abroad without it, and a mantelet on their fhoulders. The ladies, and other native Whites, ufe this as their undrefs, and it greatly becomes them ; for having been ufed to it from their infancy, they wear it with a better air. Inftead of fhoes, they only wear, both within and without doors, a kind of flippers, large enough only to contain the tip of their feet. In the houfe, their whole exercife confifts in fitting in their hammocks †, and fwinging themfelves for air. This is fo general a cuftom, that there is not a houfe without two or three, according to the number of the family. In thefe they pafs the greater part of the day; and often men, as well as women, fleep in them, without minding the inconveniency of not ftretching the body at full length.

BOTH fexes are poffeffed of a great deal of wit and penetration, and alfo of a genius proper to excel in all kinds of mechanic arts. This is particularly confpicuous in thofe who apply themfelves to literature, and who, at a tender age, fhew a judgment and perfpicacity, which, in other climates, is attained only by a long feries of years and the greateft application. This happy difpofition and perfpicacity continues till they are between twenty and thirty years of age, after

---

* The heat is inconfiderable, compared with that of the afternoon, till half an hour after funrife. A.

† Thefe hammocks are made of twifted cotton, and commonly knit in the manner of a net, and make no fmall part of the traffick of the Indians, by whom they are chiefly made. A.

which they generally decline as faft as they rofe; and frequently, before they arrive at that age, when they fhould begin to reap the advantage of their ftudies, a natural indolence checks their farther progrefs, and they forfake the fciences, leaving the furprifing effects of their capacity imperfect.

THE principal caufe of the fhort duration of fuch promifing beginnings, and of the indolent turn fo often feen in thefe bright geniufes, is doubtlefs the want of proper objects for exercifing their faculties, and the fmall hopes of being preferred to any poft anfwerable to the pains they have taken. For as there is in this country neither army nor navy, and the civil employ- ments very few, it is not at all furprifing that the de- fpair of making their fortunes, by this method, fhould damp their ardour for excelling in the fciences, and plunge them into idlenefs, the fure forerunner of vice; where they lofe the ufe of their reafon, and ftifle thofe good principles which fired them when young and under proper fubjection. The fame is evident in the mechanic arts, in which they demonftrate a furprifing fkill in a very little time; but foon leave thefe alfo imperfect, without attempting to improve on the me- thods of their mafters. Nothing indeed is more fur- prifing than the early advances of the mind in this country, children of two or three years of age con- verfing with a regularity and ferioufnefs that is rarely feen in Europe at fix or feven; and at an age when they can fcarce fee the light, are acquainted with all the depths of wickednefs.

THE genius of the Americans being more forward than that of the Europeans, many have been willing to believe that it alfo fooner decays; and that at fixty years, or before, they have outlived that folid judg- ment and penetration, fo general among us at that time of life; and it has been faid that their genius de- cays, while that of the Europeans is haftening to its maturity and perfection. But this is a vulgar prejudice, confuted by numberlefs inftances, and particularly by the celebrated father Fr. Benito Feyjoo, Têatro Critico, vol. iv. effay 6. All who have travelled with any attention through thefe countries, have obferved in the natives of every age a permanent capacity, and uniform brightnefs of intellect; if they were not of that wretched number, who diforder both their minds and bodies by their vices. And indeed one often fees here perfons of eminent prudence and extenfive talents, both in the fpeculative and practical fciences, and who retain them, in all their vigour, to a very advanced age.

★   ★   ★   ★   ★

EVERY town of the miffions of Paraguay, like the cities and great towns of the Spaniards, are under a governor, regidores, and alcaldes. That the important office of governor may be always filled by a person duly qualified, he is chosen by the Indians, with the approbation of the priests. The alcaldes are annually appointed by the regidores, and jointly with them, the governor attends to the maintenance of good order and tranquillity among the inhabitants; and that these officers, who are seldom persons of the most shining parts, may not abuse their authority, and either through interest, or passion, carry their revenge too far against other Indians, they are not to proceed to punishment without previously acquainting the priest with the affair, that he may compare the offence with the sentence. The priest, on finding the person really guilty, delivers him up to be punished, which generally consists in imprisonment for a certain number of days, and sometimes fasting is added to it; but if the fault be very great, the delinquent is whipt, which is the most severe punishment used among them; these people being never known to commit any crime that merits a greater degree of chastisement; for immediately on being registered as converts, the greatest care has been taken in these missions, to imprint on the minds of these new Christians, a detestation of murder, robbery, and such atrocious crimes. The execution of the sentence is preceded by a discourse, made by the priest before the delinquent, in which he represents to the offender, with the greatest softness and sympathy, the nature of his crime, and its turpitude; so that he is brought to acknowledge the justness of the sentence, and to receive it rather as a brotherly correction, than a punishment; so that though nature must feel, yet he receives the correction with the greatest humility and resignation, being conscious that he has brought it upon himself. Thus the priests are in no danger of any malice being harboured against them; indeed the love and veneration the Indians pay them is so great, that could they be guilty of enjoining an unjust punishment, the suffering party would impute it to his own demerits, being firmly persuaded that the priests never do any thing without a sufficient reason.

EVERY town has a particular armory, in which are kept all the fire-arms, swords, and weapons used by the militia, when they take the field, whether to repel the insults of the Portuguese, or any heathen Indians inhabiting on their frontiers. And that they may be dexterous in the management of them, they are exercised on the evening of every holiday in the market-places of the towns. All persons capable of bearing arms in every town, are divided into companies, and have their proper officers, who owe this distinction to their military qualifications: their uniform is richly laced with gold and silver, according to their rank, and embroidered with the device of their towns. In these they always appear on holidays, and at the times of exercise. The governor, alcaldes, and regidores, have also very magnificent habits of ceremony, which they wear on solemn occasions.

No town is without a school for teaching reading, writing, dancing, and music : and in whatever they undertake they generally excel, the inclination and genius of every one being carefully consulted before they are forwarded in any branch of science. Thus many attain a very good knowledge of the Latin tongue. In one of the courts of the house belonging to the priest of every town, are shops or workhouses for painters, sculptors, gilders, silversmiths, locksmiths, carpenters, weavers, watchmakers, and all other mechanic arts and trades. Here every one works for the benefit of the whole town, under the inspection of the priests coadjutors ; and boys are there also instructed in those trades and arts, to which they have the greatest inclination.

THE churches are large, and well built : and, with regard to decorations, not inferior to the richest in Peru. Even the houses of the Indians are built with that symmetry and convenience, and so completely and elegantly furnished, as to excel those of the Spaniards in many towns in this part of America. Most of them however are only of mud walls, some of unburnt bricks, and others of stone ; but all, in general, covered with tiles. Every thing in these towns is on such good footing, that all private houses make

gunpowder, that a sufficient quantity of it may not be
wanting, either on any exigency, or for fireworks on
holidays, and other anniversary rejoicings which are
punctually kept.   But the most splendid ceremony is
on the accession of the new monarch to the Spanish
throne, when the governor, alcaldes, regidores, together with all the civil and military officers, appear
in new uniforms, and other ornaments, to express the
ardent affection they bear their new sovereign.

EVERY church has its band of music, consisting
of a great number both of vocal and instrumental performers. Divine service is celebrated in them with all
the pomp and solemnity of cathedrals.   The like is
observed in public processions, especially that on
Corpus Christi day, at which the governor, alcaldes,
and regidores, in their habits of ceremony, and the
militia in their uniforms, assist : the rest of the people carry flambeaux : so that the whole is conducted
with an order and reverence suitable to the occasion.
These processions are accompanied with fine dancing,
but very different from that in the province of Quito,
described in the first volume; and the performers
wear particular dresses, extremely rich, and well adapted to the characters represented. In short, a missionary town omits no circumstance either of festivity
or devotion, practised in opulent cities.

EVERY town has a kind of beaterio, where women
of ill fame are placed, it also serves for the retreat of
married women who have no families, during the
absence of their husbands.   For the support of this
house, and also of orphans and others, who by age
or any other circumstance are disabled from earning
a livelihood, two days in the week are set apart ;
when the inhabitants of every village are obliged to
sow and cultivate a certain piece of ground, called
Labor de la Comunidad, the labour of the community; and the surplus of the produce is applied to
procure furniture and decorations for the church, and

to clothe the orphans, the aged, and the disabled persons.   By this benevolent plan all distress is precluded, and the inhabitants provided with every necessary of life.   The royal revenues are punctually paid; and by the union of the inhabitants, the uninterrupted peace they enjoy, and the wisdom of their policy, which is preserved inviolable, these places, if there are any such on earth, are the habitations of true religion and felicity.

THE jesuits, who are the priests of these missions, take upon them the sole care of disposing of the manufactures and products of the Guaranies Indians, designed for commerce; these people being naturally careless and indolent, and doubtless without the diligent inspection and pathetic exhortations of the fathers, would be buried in sloth and indigence.   The case is very different in the missions of the Chiquitos, who are industrious, careful, and frugal; and their genius so happily adapted to commerce, as not to stand in need of any factors.   The priests in the villages of this nation are of no expence to the crown, the Indians themselves rejoicing in maintaining them; and join in cultivating a plantation filled with all kinds of grain and fruits for the priest; the remainder, after this decent support, being applied to purchase ornaments for the churches.

THAT the Indians may never be in any want of necessaries, it is one part of the minister's care to have always in readiness a stock of different kinds of tools, stuffs, and other goods; so that all who are in want repair to him, bringing by way of exchange wax, of which there are here great quantities, and other products.   And this barter is made with the strictest integrity, that the Indians may have no reason to complain of oppression; and that the high character of the priests for justice and sanctity may be studiously preserved.   The goods received in exchange are by the priests sent to the superior of the missions, who is a different person from the superior of the Guaranies: and with the produce, a fresh stock of goods is laid in. The principal intention of this is, that the Indians may have no occasion to leave their own country, in order to be furnished with necessaries ; and by this means are kept from the contagion of those vices, which they would naturally contract in their intercourse with the inhabitants of other countries, where the depravity of human nature is not corrected by such good examples and laws.

If the civil government of these towns be so admirably calculated for happiness, the ecclesiastical government is still more so. Every town and village has its particular priest, who in proportion to its largeness, has an assistant or two of the same order. These priests, together with six boys who wait on them, and also sing in the churches, form in every village a kind of small college, where the hours are under the same regulation, and the exercises succeed each other with the same formalities as in the great colleges of cities. The most laborious part of the duty belonging to the priest, is to visit personally the chacaras or plantations of the Indians; and in this they are remarkably sedulous, in order to prevent the ill consequences of that slothful disposition so natural to the Guaranies ; who, were they not frequently roused and stimulated by the presence of the priest, would abandon their work, or, at least, perform it in a very superficial manner. He also attends at the public slaughter-house, where every day are killed some of the cattle; large herds of which are kept for the public use by the Indians. The flesh of these beasts are dealt out by the priest, in lots proportionable to the number of persons each family consists of; so that every one has a sufficiency to supply the calls of nature, but nothing for waste. He also visits the sick, to see that they want for nothing, and are attended with that care and tenderness their state requires. These charitable employments take up so great a part of the day, as often to leave him no time for assisting the father coadjutor in the services of the church. One useful part of the duty of the latter is to catechize, and explain some portion of scripture in the church every day in the week, Thursdays and Saturdays excepted, for the instruction of the young of both sexes; and these in every town are not less than two thousand. On Sundays all the inhabitants never fail to attend divine service. The priest also visits the sick to confess them; and if the case requires it, to give them the viaticum; and to all these must be added the other indispensable duties of a priest.

By the strictness of the law these priests should be nominated by the governor, as vice-patron, and be qualified for their function by the consecration of the bishop; but as among the three persons recommended on such occasions to the governor, there will of consequence be one, whose virtues and talents render him most fit for the office; and as no better judges of this can be supposed than the provincials of the order, the governor and bishop have receded from their undoubted rights, and the provincials always collate and prefer those whose merits are most conspicuous.

The missions of the Guaranies are also under one superior, who nominates the assistant priests of the other towns. His residence is at Candelaria, which lies in the centre of all the missions; but he frequently visits the other towns, in order to superintend their governments; and at the same time, concerts measures that some of the fathers may be sent among the heathen Indians, to conciliate their affections, and by degrees work their conversion. In this important office he is assisted by two vice-superiors, one of whom resides at Parana, and the other on the river Uruguay.

All these missions, though so numerous and dispersed, are formed as it were into one college, of which the superior may be considered as the master or head; and every town is like a family governed by a wise and affectionate parent, in the person of the priest.

In the missions of the Guaranies, the king pays the stipends of the priests, which, including that of the assistant, is three hundred dollars per annum. This sum is lodged in the hands of the superior, who every month supplies them with necessary food and apparel, and on any extraordinary demand, they apply to him, from whom they are sure of meeting with a gracious reception.

The missions of the Chiquito Indians have a distinct superior; but with the same functions as he who presides over the Guaranies; and the priests also are on the same footing, but have less anxiety and labour; the industry and activity of these Indians, saving them the trouble of coming among them to exhort them to follow their employments, or of being the storekeepers and agents in disposing of the fruits of their labours; they themselves vending them for their own advantage.

All these Indians are very subject to several contagious distempers; as the small-pox, malignant fevers, and others, to which, on account of the dreadful havock attending them, they give the name of pestilence. And to such diseases it is owing, that these settlements have not increased in a manner proportional to their numbers, the time since their establishment, and the quietness and plenty in which these people live.

The missionary fathers will not allow any of the inhabitants of Peru, whether Spaniards, or others, Mestizos, or even Indians, to come within their missions in Paraguay. Not with a view of concealing their transactions from the world; or that they are afraid lest others should supplant them of part of the products and manufactures; nor for any of those causes, which even with less foundation, envy has dared to suggest; but for this reason, and a very prudent one it is, that their Indians, who being as it were new born from savageness and brutality, and initiated into morality and religion, may be kept steady in this state of innocence and simplicity. These Indians are strangers to sedition, pride, malice, envy, and other passions, which are so fatal to society. But were strangers admitted to come among them, their bad examples would teach them what at present they are happily ignorant of; but should modesty, and the attention they pay to the instructions of their teachers, be once laid aside, the shining advantages of these settlements would soon come to nothing; and such a number of souls, who now worship the true God in the beauty of holiness, and live in tranquillity and love (of which such slender traces are seen among civilized nations), would be again seduced into the paths of disorder and perdition.

THESE Indians live at present in an entire assurance, that whatever their priests advise them to is good, and whatever they reprehend is bad. But their minds would soon take a different turn, by seeing other people, on whom the doctrine of the gospel is so far from having any effect, that their actions are absolutely repugnant to its precepts. At present they are firmly persuaded, that in all bargains and other transactions, the greatest candour and probity must be used, without any prevarication or deceit. But it is too evident, that were others admitted among them, whose leading maxim is to sell as dear, and buy as cheap as they are able, these innocent people would soon imbibe the same practice together with a variety of others which seem naturally to flow from it. The contamination would soon spread through every part of their behaviour, so as never more to be reclaimed. I do not here mean to lessen the characters of those Spaniards or inhabitants of other nations, whose countries are situated conveniently for trading with Paraguay, by insinuating that they are universally fraudulent and dissolute: but, on the other hand, among such numbers, it would be very strange if there was not some; and one single person of such a character would be sufficient to infect a whole country. And who could pretend to say, that, if free admisson were allowed to foreigners, there might not come in, among a multitude of virtuous, one of such pestilent dispositions? Who can say that he might not be even the very first? Hence it is that the Jesuits have inflexibly adhered to their maxim of not admitting any foreigners among them: and in this they are certainly justified by the melancholy example of the other missions of Peru, whose decline from their former happiness and piety is the effect of an open intercourse.

THOUGH in the several parts of Paraguay, where the missions have been always settled, there are no mines of gold and silver; several are to be found in some adjacent countries under the dominion of the king of Spain; but the Portuguese reap the whole benefit of them: for having encroached as far as the lake Xarayes, near which, about twenty years ago, a rich mine of gold was discovered; they without any other right than possession, turned it to their own use: the ministry in Spain, in consideration of the harmony subsisting between the two nations, and their joint interest, forbearing to make use of any forcible methods.

Dobrizhoffer:
Account of the Abipones

Martin Dobrizhoffer, *An Account of the Abipones, an Equestrian People of Paraguay, from the Latin of Martin Dobrizhoffer, 18 years a Missionary in that Country*, trans. Sara Coleridge, 3 vols (London: John Murray, 1822), vol. II, pp. 110–26, 233–7; vol. III, pp. 394–402.

Father Martin Dobrizhoffer (1717–91), an Austrian Jesuit missionary, was born in Gratz in Styria in 1717 and entered the Jesuit order in 1736. In 1749 he arrived in South America to work in the Jesuit missions of Paraguay, isolated areas of the interior where the native Guarani Indians were concentrated into planned villages, each dominated by a parish church, where they were trained to work as artisans and subjected to a strict disciplinary regime. The fact that Spanish settlers were excluded from the missions, each of which was defended by a Jesuit-led indigenous militia, caused bitter rivalry between Spanish *encomenderos* and the Jesuit order. In Europe the missions were alternately idealised as utopian settlements and castigated as collective prisons, most famously in Voltaire's 1758 novel *Candide*. Dobrizhoffer worked first in the Guarani 'reductions' (as these settlements were called), subsequently in the more difficult and dangerous circumstances of the mission to the warlike equestrian Abipones, who for many years actively resisted Spanish colonial expansion in their native land.

Upon the expulsion of his order from Spanish America in 1767, Dobrizhoffer returned to Austria, residing in Vienna until his death in 1791. His skill in narrating his experiences during his long sojourn on Europe's colonial frontier earned him the patronage of the Empress Maria Theresa, who frequently called upon him to relieve the tedium of court life. In 1784 he published an account of the Abipones, combined with a spirited defence of the much maligned Jesuit missions, entitled *Historia de Abiponibus, equestri, bellicosaque paraquariae natione*; allegedly he preferred to write in Latin as his long residence in Paraguay had caused him almost to forget his native German. The work was quickly recognised as not only a masterpiece of modern Latin composition (Robert Southey commented on the 'lively singularity of the old man's Latin'), but also a unique record of the culture of the Abipones and other nomadic indigenous societies in Paraguay, who were rapidly being decimated by contact with Europeans. In the German-language version published in the same year, the translator estimated that 'there is no other work which contains so full, so faithful, and so lively an account of the South American tribes'. Dobrizhoffer prided himself on his style, although he wrote apologetically in the book's introduction 'who can expect the graces of Livy, Sallust, Caesar, Strada, or Maffeus, from one who, for so many years, has had no commerce with the muses, no access to classical literature? Yet in writing of savages, I have taken especial care that no barbarisms should creep into my language' (vol. I, p. vi).

While researching his *History of Brazil*, the poet Robert Southey first encountered Dobrizhoffer's narrative via John Pinkerton's *Modern Geography*. In 1818 he recommended that his charge, Derwent Coleridge (the poet's son), should translate it into English to pay his university fees. Derwent reluctantly began to translate the first volume, delegating work on the third volume to his teenage sister Sara Coleridge, later to achieve renown as a writer and editor of her father's works, and wife of H. N. Coleridge. When Derwent abandoned the project, Sara single-handedly took it over, and *An Account of the Abipones, an Equestrian People of Paraguay, from the Latin of Martin Dobrizhoffer* was published in January 1822, in three volumes, shortly after Sara's nineteenth birthday. In the same year the poet S. T. Coleridge read through the work, later opining that 'I hardly know anything more amusing than the honest German Jesuitry of Dobrizhoffer', adding proudly 'My dear daughter's translation of this book is, in my judgement, unsurpassed for pure mother English by anything I have read for a long time' (Coleridge, *Table Talk*, p. 191). An incident related in Dobrizhoffer's book inspired one of Southey's least-read poems, *A Tale of Paraguay*, published in three cantos in 1825. A family of Guarani Indians, survivors of the smallpox epidemic that ravaged native Americans after contact with Europeans, are rescued from a 'state of nature' in the wilderness by Martin Dobrizhoffer and resettled in the Jesuit mission of St Joachin. Mother, daughter and son all quickly succumb to the disease once they have been 'civilised', but their death is amply compensated (in Southey's view) by the fact that their souls are saved. Dobrizhoffer is cast as the Jesuit hero who feels no need to justify his action in 'reducing' this Guarani family with such fatal consequences. *A Tale of Paraguay* is based on an anecdote in the first volume of Dobrizhoffer's book; the passages excerpted here are from the second and third volumes, which describe the harsh life and 'savage' customs of the Abipones, who unlike the Guarani refused to relinquish easily their nomadic life and the rigorous freedom of the Pampas.

CHAPTER XIII.

OF THE FOOD, JOURNEYS, AND OTHER PARTICULARS OF THE ECONOMY OF THE ABIPONES.

THE wild Abipones live like wild beasts. They neither sow nor reap, nor take any heed of agriculture. Taught by natural instinct, the instructions of their ancestors, and their own experience, they are acquainted with all the productions of the earth and the trees, at what part of the year they spontaneously grow, what animals are to be found in what places, and what arts are to be employed in taking them. All things are in common with them. They have no proprietors, as with us, of lands, rivers, and groves, who possess the exclusive right of hunting, fishing, and gathering wood there. Whatever flies in the air, swims in the water, and grows wild in the woods, may become the property of the first person that chooses to take it. The Abipones are unacquainted with spades, ploughs, and axes; the arrow, the spear, the club, and horses, are the only instruments they make use of in procuring food, clothing, and habitation. As all lands do not bear all things, and as various productions grow at various times of the year, they cannot continue long in one situation. They remove from place to place, wherever they can most readily satisfy the demands of hunger and thirst. The plains abound in emus, and their numerous eggs, in deer, tigers, lions, various kinds of rabbits, and other small animals peculiar to America, and also in flocks of partridges. Numbers of stags, exactly like those of our country, frequent the banks of the larger rivers. Innumerable herds of wild boars are almost constantly to be seen in marshy places, which they delight in, in the neighbourhood of a wood. The groves, besides antas, and tamanduas, contain swarms of monkeys and parrots. The lakes and rivers, which abound in fish, produce water-wolves, water-dogs, capibaris, innumerable otters, and flocks of geese and ducks. I do not mention the great multitude of tortoises, as neither the Abipones nor Spaniards eat them in Paraguay. At stated times of the year, they collect quantities of young cormorants, on the banks of rivers, and reckon them amongst the delicacies of the table. Were none of these things to be procured, tree fruits and hives of excellent honey would never be wanting. The various species of palms alone will supply meat, drink, medicine, habitation, clothes, arms, and what not, to those that are in need. Under the earth, and even under the water, grow esculent roots. Two species of the alfaroba, commonly called St. John's bread, throughout great part of the year, produce extremely wholesome, and by no means unsavoury food, both meat and drink. See the munificence of God even towards those by whom he is not worshipped! Behold a rude image of the golden age! The Abipones have it in their power to procure all the appurtenances of daily life, with little or no labour, and though unacquainted with money of every kind, are commodiously supplied with all necessaries; for if a long drought have exhausted the rivers, they will find water even in the most desert plains, under the leaves of the caraquatà, or they can suck little apples, which are full of a watery liquor like melons, and grow under the earth, or dig a well in the channel of a dried-up river, and see water sufficient for themselves and their horses spring up from thence. A Spaniard, in the wilds of America, will pine with thirst, either from being ignorant of these things, or impatient of the labour of obtaining them.

As the supports of life are not all found collected together in one place, nor will suffice for a long time, or a great number of hordesmen, the Abipones are obliged to change their residence, and travel about continually. Neither rugged roads, nor distances of places, prevent them from a journey; for both men and women travel on horses which are swift and numerous there, and if they are in haste, traverse vast tracts of land every day. I shall now describe the equipment of the horse, and the method of riding. The bit which they use is composed of a cow's horn fastened on each side to four little pieces of wood placed transversely, and to a double thong which supplies the place of a bridle. Some use iron bits, of which they are very proud. The major part have saddles like English ones, of a raw bull's hide stuffed with reeds. Stirrups are not in general use. The men leap on to their horse on the right side. With the right hand they grasp the bridle, with the left a very long spear, leaning upon which they jump up with the impulse of both feet, and then fall right upon the horse's back. The same expedition in dismounting, which would excite the admiration of a European, is very useful to them in skirmishes. They use no spurs even at this day. For a whip, they make use of four strips of a bull's hide twisted together, with which they stimulate new or refractory horses to the course, not by the sense of pain, but by the fear excited by the cracking of the whip. The

saddles used by the women are the same as
those of the men, except that the former, more
studious of external elegance, have theirs
made of the skin of a white cow. When
an Abiponian woman wants to mount her horse,
she throws herself up to the middle upon its
neck, like men in Europe, and then separating
her feet on both sides, places herself in the
saddle, which has no cushion; nor does the
hardness of it offend her in journeys of many
days; from which you may perceive that the
skin of the Abipones is harder than leather,
being rendered callous by their constantly
riding without a cushion. Indians who ride
much and long without saddles, frequently hurt
and wound the horse's back, without receiving
any injury themselves. I will now describe
their manner of travelling when they remove
from one place to another. The wife, besides
her husband's bow and quiver, carries all the
domestic furniture, all the pots, gourds, jugs,
shells, balls of woollen and linen thread, wea-
ving instruments, &c. These things are contained in boar-skin bags, suspended here and
there from the saddle; where she also places
the whelps, and her young infant if she have
one. Besides these things, she suspends from
the sides of the saddle a large mat, with two
poles, to fix a tent wherever they like, and a
bull's hide to serve for a boat in crossing rivers.

No woman will set out on a journey without a stake like a palm branch, broad at each side and slender in the middle, made of very hard wood, and about two ells long, which serves admirably for digging eatable roots, knocking down fruits from trees, and dry boughs for lighting a fire, and even for breaking the heads and arms of enemies, if they meet any by the way. With this luggage, which you would think a camel could hardly carry, are the women's horses loaded in every journey. But this is not all. You often see two or three women or girls seated on one horse : not from any scarcity of beasts, all having plenty, but because they are sworn enemies to solitude and silence. As few horses will bear more than one rider, unless accustomed to it, they immediately throw the female trio, but generally without doing them any injury, except that these Amazons, when seen sprawling like snails upon the ground, excite the mirth of the spectators, and amidst mutual laughter, try to scramble again on to the rustic steed, as often as they are thrown off.

The company of women is attended by a vast number of dogs. As soon as they are mounted, they all look round, and if one be missing out of the many which they keep, begin to call him with their usual *nè nè nè*, repeated as loud as possible a hundred

times, till at last they see them all assembled.
I often wondered how, without being able to
count, they could so instantly tell if one were
missing out of so large a pack. Nor should
they be censured for their anxiety about their
dogs; for these animals, in travelling, serve as
purveyors, being employed, like hounds, to hunt
deer, otters, and emus. It is chiefly on this
account that every family keeps a great number
of dogs, which are supported without any
trouble; plenty of provender being always supplied by the heads, hearts, livers, and entrails
of the slaughtered cattle; which, though made
use of by Europeans, are rejected by the savages. The fecundity of these animals in Paraguay corresponds to the abundance of victuals.
They scarce ever bring forth fewer than twelve
puppies at a birth. When the period of par-
turition draws nigh, they dig a very deep
burrow, furnished with a narrow opening, and
therein securely deposit their young. The
descent is so artfully contrived with turnings
and windings, that, however rainy the weather
may be, no water can penetrate to this subterranean cave. The mother comes out every
day to get food and drink, when she moans and
wags her tail as if to excuse her absence to her
master; at length, at the end of many days,
she shows her whelps abroad, though she cer-

tainly cannot boast of their beauty: for the
Indian dogs have no elegance of form, they are
generally middle-sized, and of various colours,
as with us.   They are neither so small as the
dogs of Malta and Bologna, nor so large as
mastiffs.   You never see any of those shaggy
curly dogs, which are so fond of the water, and
so docile, except amongst the Spaniards, who
have them sent over in European ships.   But
though the Indian dogs do not excel in beauty,
they are by no means inferior to those of Europe in quickness of scent, in activity, vigilance, and sincere affection for their masters.
In every Abiponian colony, some hundred dogs
keep continual watch, and by the terrible howling and barking which they nightly utter in
chorus, at the slightest motion, perpetually
disturbed our sleep, but never secured us from
being surprized by the enemy; a troop of whom
would often steal into the colony, whilst the
whole of the dogs maintained a profound silence.
Yet none of the Abipones ever blamed them,
foolishly imagining them bewitched by the magic
arts of the enemy's jugglers.   It may be reckoned amongst the blessings of Paraguay, that
it is unacquainted with madness in dogs, or any
kind of cattle, and that hydrophobia is unknown
here.   This must be accounted a singular benefit
of Providence, and one of the wonders of nature

in a country where beasts are frequently distress-
ed both with the burning heat of heaven, and
with long thirst, for want of water, which is not
to be got for many leagues. But let us now take
leave of the female riders, and of the dogs that
accompany them, and direct our attention to
the Abipones, their husbands.

The luggage being all committed to the
women, the Abipones travel armed with a
spear alone, that they may be disengaged to
fight or hunt, if occasion require. If they spy
any emus, deer, stags, boars, or other wild
animals, they pursue them with swift horses, and
kill them with a spear. If they can meet with
nothing fit to kill and eat, they set fire to the
plain which is covered with tall dry grass, and
force the animals, concealed underneath, to
leap out by crowds, and in flying from the fire
to fall into the cruel hands of the Indians, who
kill them with wood, iron, or a string, and
afterwards roast them. Should every thing
else be wanting, the plains abound in rabbits,
to afford a breakfast, dinner, or supper. To
strike fire, they have no occasion for either
flint or steel, the place of which is supplied by
pieces of wood, about a span long, one of which
is soft, the other hard. The first, which is a
little pierced in the middle, is placed underneath; the harder wood, which has a point

like an acorn, is applied to the bole of the softer, and whirled quickly round with both hands. By this mutual and quick attrition of both woods, a little dust is rubbed off which at the same moment catches fire and emits smoke; to this the Indians apply straw, cow-dung, dry leaves, &c. for fuel. The soft wood used for this purpose is taken either from the tree ambaỹ, from the shrub caraquatà, or from the cedar; but the harder, which they whirl round with the hand, comes from the tree tataỹi, which affords a saffron-coloured wood, as hard as box, and fit for dying clothes yellow, together with mulberries very like those of our own country.

Whenever they think fit to sleep at noon, or pass the night by the way, they anxiously look out for some place affording an opportunity of water, wood, and pasture. If there arise any suspicion of a hostile ambuscade, they hide themselves in lurking holes, rendered inaccessible by the nature of the place. You would say that they and their families are at home, wherever they go, for they carry about mats to serve for a house, as a snail does its shell. Two poles are fixed into the ground, and to them is tied a mat, twice or thrice folded to exclude the wind and rain. That the ground upon which they lie may not be wetted by a heavy shower, they providently dig a little channel at the side of their tent, that the waters may flow off, and be carried elsewhere. They generally send a tame mare with a bell about her neck to a drove of horses, when they are sent to pasture; for they will never go out of sight of her, and if dispersed up and down the plain, through fear of a tiger, return to her as to their mother; on which account the Spaniards call this mare *la madrina*, and the Abipones, *latè*, which means a mother. For the same reason, on a few of the horses they place shackles of soft leather, that they may crop the grass without wandering far from the tent, and be at hand, if it be found necessary to travel in the night. Not only the men, but even very young women cross rivers without ford, bridge, or boat, by swimming. The children, the saddles, and other luggage are sent over on a bull's hide, called by the Abipones, *ñatac*, and by the Spaniards, *la pelota*, and generally made use of in crossing the smaller rivers. I will describe the rude structure of it. A hairy, raw, and entirely un-dressed hide is made almost square, by having the extremities of the feet and neck cut off. The four sides are raised like a hat, to the height of about two spans, and each is tied with a thong, that they may remain erect, and pre-serve their squareness of form. At the bottom of the pelota, the saddles and other luggage are

thrown by way of ballast, in the midst of which
the person that is to cross the river, sits, taking
care to preserve his balance.   Into a hole in
the side of the pelota, they insert a thong instead of a rope, which a person, swimming, lays
hold of with his teeth and with one hand,
whilst he uses the other for an oar, and thus
gently draws the pelota along the river, without shaking or endangering the person within
in the least, though a high wind may have
greatly agitated the waves.   If the coldness of
the water cramps the man that drags the pelota,
so that he is disenabled from swimming, and
would otherwise be drowned, he will be carried
safely along with the pelota to the opposite
bank, by the force of the waves.   If rivers of a
wider channel and a more rapid stream are to
be crossed, the swimmer holds the tail of the
horse, which swims before, with one hand, to
support himself, and drags the pelota with the
other.   In so many and such long journies, I
practised this sort of navigation almost daily,
and not unfrequently repeated it often on the
same day.   At first it appeared very formidable and dangerous to me.   But instructed by
frequent practice, I have often laughed at myself and my imaginary danger, and always preferred a hide in crossing a river, to a tottering
skiff or boat, which is constantly liable to be

overturned.   If many days' rain has wetted the hide, and made it as soft as linen, boughs of trees are placed under the four sides, and the bottom of the pelota, which supports the hide, and strengthens it to cross the river in safety. American captains of Spanish soldiers will not swim, although they know how, that they may not be obliged to strip before their men.   To reach, therefore, the opposite shore, they sit upon a pelota, which, scorning the assistance of another person, they impel forwards by two forked boughs for oars.

The Abipones enter even the larger rivers on horseback: but when the ford begins to fail, they leap from their horse into the water.   With their right hand they hold the reins of the horse, and row with the same; in their left they grasp a very wide spear, at the end of which they suspend their clothes in the air, that they may not be wetted.   Every now and then they give the horse a blow, if he suffers himself to be carried down with the stream, to bring him back to the right course, and make him strain to the appointed part of the opposite shore, which should be neither marshy nor weedy, nor of a very high bank, so that it may afford an easy ascent.   It was laughable to see the crowds of savages swimming at my side, with nothing but their heads above water, yet conversing as plea-

santly as others would on the green turf. How
often have I crossed those tremendous rivers
sitting on a hide in the midst of them! You
would have called them so many Neptunes, so
familiar were they with the water.   Their bold-
ness exceeds the belief of Europeans.   Whenever they had a mind to go from St. Ferdinand
to Corrientes, they swam across that vast sea,
which is composed of the united streams of the
great Paraguay and the great Parana, with
their horses swimming beside them, to the great
astonishment of the Spaniards : for in this part
the river is formidable to ships even, from
its width, depth, and incredible rapidity, and
often filled myself and my companions with
terror when we sailed upon it, whilst I resided
in that colony.   Formerly those savage plun-
derers, whenever they hastened home with a
great number of beasts taken from the Spaniards, prudently crossed this immense river
towards the South, going from island to island;
by which means they had time to recruit themselves and their beasts, after the fatigue of
swimming, in each of the islands.   It will be
worth while to describe the manner in which
many thousands of horses, mules, and oxen, are
sent across great rivers to the opposite shore.
The herd of beasts is not all driven by one
person, but divided into companies, each of

which is inclosed behind and on both sides, by
men on horseback, to keep them from running
away : to prevent which, some erect two
hedges, wider at the beginning, and narrower
at the shore itself, through which the beasts are
driven, so that more than two or three cannot
enter the river at a time. The tame oxen and
horses are sent first into the water, and the
wild ones follow without delay. Great care
must be taken, that they be not deprived of the
power of swimming, by being too much
crowded. Behind and on both sides the beasts
are watched by Indians, either swimming, or
conveyed in a little bark, that they may make
straight for the opposite shore : for when left
alone, they suffer themselves to be carried
down by the stream, and float to those places
which forbid all access, on account of the high
banks, marshes, or trees, by which they are
impeded. If an ox or a horse be whirled round
in swimming, it will be sucked up by the water,
unable to exert itself any longer. To prevent
this, the Abipones, even in the midst of the
river, mount those oxen, that are either sluggish
or refractory, and taking hold of their horns
with both hands, sit upon their backs, striking
their sides with both feet, till, in spite of themselves, they are guided to the opposite shore.
When arrived at land, fear gives way to rage,

and they attack every thing that comes in their way, with their threatening horns. You will hardly believe that I always found fierce bulls less dexterous in crossing rivers, than cows, which, on account of the greater timidity of their nature, are more obedient to the driver, and strain more eagerly to the shore. Oxen tied by the horns to a tolerably large boat often swim across in perfect security : for as the heads of the animals are suspended on each side the boat, their bodies scarcely find any difficulty in swimming. In this manner I sent twenty oxen at a time from the estate, to the colony of the Rosary, across the river Paraguay. More or fewer oxen may be tied to the bark, according to the size of it. Sometimes the herd of beasts is surrounded by long barks or skiffs on every side, lest, when weary of swimming, they should float down with the stream, and wander from that part of the shore that had been fixed on for their ascent. But the Abipones, not needing these precautions of the Spaniards, could successfully transport crowds of swimming oxen across any rivers, themselves swimming beside them. This expertness of the Abipones in swimming across rivers, I have long desired to see in European armies, which are often prevented from attacking the enemy, by the intervention of some large river, though every thing conspired to yield them an easy victory, if the soldiers could cross the river by swimming, without the noise of bridges or boats. But, alas! out of a numerous army, how few are able to swim! Much service has indeed been rendered the Austrian camp, by the Croatian forces, who, not waiting for boats or bridges, have so often surprized the enemy on the opposite shore, apprehending no hostilities.

★ ★ ★ ★ ★

CHAPTER XXII.

OF A CERTAIN DISEASE PECULIAR TO THE ABIPONES.

During an eighteen years' acquaintance with Paraguay and its inhabitants, I discovered a disease amongst the Abipones Nakaiketergehes, entirely unknown elsewhere. This disease affects the mind more than the body, though I should think it occasioned by the bad temperature of the former. They sometimes begin to rave and storm like madmen. The credulous and superstitious crowd think them reduced to this state by the magic arts of jugglers, and call them *Loaparaika*. These persons, agitated, as I think, by the intemperature of black bile, and filled with gloomy ideas, betray their madness chiefly at sun-set. The distracted persons suddenly leap out of their tents, run into the country on foot, and direct their course straight to the burying-place of their family. In speed they equal ostriches, and those who pursue them on the swiftest horses can hardly overtake and bring them home. Seized with fury in the night, they burn with the desire of committing slaughter somewhere; and for this purpose snatch up any arms they can lay hold of. Hence, as soon as a report is spread through a town of any one's being seized with this kind of madness, every body takes up a spear. The hordesmen, as they can neither calm the furious man, nor keep him at home, suffer him to go out into the street, armed with a stick, and accompanied with as many people as possible. A crowd of boys assembling to behold the spectacle, they make a circuit about all the streets. The insane person strikes the roof and mats of every tent again and again with the stick, none of the inmates daring to utter a word. If through the negligence of his guards, or his own cunning, he gets possession of arms, Heavens! what a universal terror is excited! a terror not confined to women and unwarlike boys, but felt by men who account themselves heroes; for they say it is wrong and irrational to use arms against those who are not in possession of their senses. The women, therefore, with their children used to crowd to the court-yard of our house which was fortified with stakes against the assaults of savages, and through fear of the insane person, pass hours, nay whole nights there.

Persons seized with this madness take scarcely any food or sleep, and walk up and down pale with fasting and melancholy: you would imagine that they were contemplating some new system of the figure of the earth, or studying how to square the circle. By day, however, they betray no signs of alienation of mind, nor are they to be feared before evening. A person of this description, who was very turbulent at night, visited me in the middle of the day. In familiar conversation I asked him who it was that disturbed the rest by his furiousness every night. He replied with a calm countenance, that he did not know. The Spaniard, my companion, seeing him take his leave, said, " This is the man you have long wished to know. This is he that raves at night." Yet I could discover nothing indicative of derangement either in his countenance or manners. Another insane person of the kind, whom I knew, met me as we were both riding in the plain, and joined company with me. But, pretending business, I put spur to my horse and hastened home. Twice when I was shutting the door of my hut, and once when I was tying a horse to a stake to feed, I should have been destroyed by a madman, had not persons come to my succour and averted the danger. Sometimes many persons of both sexes began to rave at once; sometimes one, and often no one was in this deplorable state. This madness lasted eight, fourteen, or more days, before tranquillity and intellect were restored. All the Abipones subject to this malady, whom I have known, were uniformly of a melancholy turn of mind, always in a state of perturbation from their hypochondriac or choleric temper, and of a fierce, threatening countenance. When this bile was excited by bad air, or immoderate drinking, it is neither strange nor surprising, that derangement and raving madness ensued. The stupid or ignorant alone attribute that to magic art, which is solely to be ascribed to the fault or strength of nature.

We have found the fear of death a powerful antidote to the licence of raving amongst the Abipones. Within a few days the number of mad persons increased unusually: one of them in the dead of the night got through the fence, and was stealing into our house, but was carried away by people who came to our assistance. Alaykin, the chief Cacique, being informed of our danger, called all the people into the market-place next day, and declared, that if any one henceforward took to raving, he should immediately put to death all the female jugglers, as well as the insane themselves. From that time I never heard of any more tumults occasioned by these furious persons. Might not some of them have feigned madness in the first instance, because they

loved to be objects of terror to their hordesmen, and to be pointed at with the finger?
I never can believe with the savages, that a
magical charm was the cause of their insanity.

★   ★   ★   ★   ★

It certainly ought to be reckoned amongst
the noble victories of our age, that the Abipones who, from the time of Charles the Fifth,
had continued to defy the arms of the Spaniards,
when so many other nations of Paraguay were
put under the yoke, have at last been induced
to enter colonies. The fruitlessness of innumerable expeditions undertaken against them at
length convinced the Spanish soldiers that the
Abipones were an overmatch for all the force
and cunning of the Europeans, by their craft,
their swiftness, and above all by the situation

of the places they óccupied, thè nature of which itself defended, and rendered them invincible. Their stations served for strong-holds, thick woods for walls, rivers and pools for fosses, lofty trees for watch-towers, and the Abipones themselves for guards and spies. To prevent the possibility of their ever being utterly extermi- nated, they were separated into various hordes, and dwelt in different places, both that they might mutually warn and assist one another, and that, if any danger were apprehended, that they might with more certainty avoid the enemy. Indeed the old complaint of the Spaniards was, that they had more difficulty in finding the Abi- pones, than in conquering them when found. Though to-day you learn from your spies that they are settled in a neighbouring plain, you will hear to-morrow that they are removed to a great distance from their yesterday's residence, and are buried amidst woods and marshes. Whenever the savages have any suspicion of danger, they mount swift horses, hasten to places of greater security, and, sending scouts in all directions, generally disconcert the plans of the enemy by unremitting vigilance. I do not think the Abipones are much to be cen- sured for having delayed to enter our colonies so long : for whilst they live in towns, banished from their lurking-places, and exposed to attacks of every kind, they think they have sold their liberty and security, incapable of any firm reliance on the faith and friendship of the Spaniards, which the cruelty and deceit formerly practised towards their ancestors have taught them to suspect.

I can truly say, that my most earnest endeavour was to inspire the Abipones with love and confidence towards the Spaniards. " Had they not come to Paraguay," said I, " you would still be unacquainted with horses, oxen, and dogs, all which you take such delight in. You would have been obliged to creep along like tortoises. You could never have tasted the flesh of oxen, but must have subsisted entirely on that of wild animals. How laborious would you think it to hunt otters without hounds, which likewise by their barking prevent you from being surprized by the enemy in your sleep! Horses, your delight, your deities, if I may be allowed to make use of the expression, your chief instruments of war, hunting, travelling, and sportive contests, have been bestowed on you by the Spaniards. But all this is nothing in comparison with the light of divine religion kindled for you by that people, whose anxiety for your happiness has led them to offer you teachers of Christianity brought from Europe in their ships, and at their expense. From all this, it is evident what love and fidelity you ought to show to the Spaniards, who have conferred such benefits on you, and are so studious of your welfare. I do not mean to deny that they once turned their arms against yourselves and your ancestors, but you, not they, were the aggressors. The Spaniards will henceforward return love for love, if, ceasing to cherish hatred and suspicion towards them, you will cultivate their friendship by all the means in your power." These ideas I constantly strove to inculcate into the minds of my disciples, but though none of them ventured openly to contradict me, they gave more credit to their eyes than their ears, to the deeds of the Spaniards than to the words of the Missionaries, and sometimes in familiar conversation during our absence whispered their sentiments with regard to the Spaniards, who, they said, attend solely to their own interests, and care little for the convenience of the Indians; preserve peace only so long as they fear war; and are most to be dreaded when they speak the fairest; whose deeds correspond not with their words, and whose conduct is inconsistent with the law they profess to observe. When reproved for stealing horses from the estates of the Spaniards, they denied it to be a theft, affirming that their country was usurped by the Spaniards, and that whatever

was produced there belonged of right to them.
Your whole stock of rhetoric was exhausted before you could eradicate these erroneous notions
from the minds of the Indians, which, however,
by excessive toil was at length effected; for all
of them knew that, unless they promised peace
and sincere friendship to the Spaniards, they
would never be received into our colonies, and
have the benefit of our instructions. All the
Indians in America intrusted to our care were
soldiers and tributaries of the Spanish Monarch,
not slaves of private individuals. This is to be
understood not only of the Guaranies and Chiquitos, but also of the Christian Mocobios,
Abipones, and all the other nations which we
civilized in Paraguay.

But let us suppose the Abipones to have
been prevailed upon to enter a colony, and
accept the friendship of the Spaniards; ye
saints, what numerous and almost insurmount-
able obstacles remain to be overcome in effecting their civilization! From boyhood they had
spent their whole time in rapine and slaughter,
and had acquired riches, honours, and high-
sounding names in the pursuit. How hard
then must it have been for them to refrain their
hands from the Spaniards, to sit down in a
colony indigent and inglorious, to cut wood
instead of enemies' heads, to exchange the spear

for the axe and the plough; with bended knees
to learn the rudiments of religion amongst
children; and in some sort to become children
themselves! These were arduous trials to veteran warriors, who remembered the time when
they were formidable, not to one little town
only, but to the whole province; and though
many of the more advanced in age gradually
laid aside their ferocity, and conformed to the
discipline of our colonies, we often had to experience the truth of the apophthegm,

Naturam expelles furcâ, tamen usque recurret.

The greatest difficulties were to be encountered
in taming the old women and the young men:
the former, blindly attached to their ancient
superstitions, the source of their profits, and stay
of their authority, thought it a crime to yield up
a tittle of the savage rites; the latter, burning
with the love of liberty, and disgusted with
any sort of labour, strove by plundering horses
to acquire renown, that they might not seem to
have degenerated from the valour of their
ancestors.

They had never even heard of a benevolent
Deity, the creator of all things, and were
accustomed to fear and reverence the evil
spirit, as I have shown more fully in a former
chapter. Instructed by us they learnt to know

worship frequently; evince considerable industry in tilling the fields and building houses;
yet after all this, it was scarcely possible to
prevent them from assembling together, and
intoxicating themselves with drink made of
honey or the alfaroba.

The pernicious examples of the Christians,
which often meet the eyes of the Abipones,
frequently prevent them from amending their
conduct. Paraguay is inhabited by Spaniards,
Portugueze, native Indians and Negroes, and
those born from their promiscuous marriages,
Mulatos, Mestizos, &c. Amid such a various
rabble of men, it cannot be wondered at that
many are to be found who *say that they know
God, yet deny him with their deeds,—who, though
they believe like Catholics, live like Gentiles,
enemies of the cross of Christ, whose God is their
belly.* Such licence in plundering, such shame-
less profligacy of manners, such impunity in
slaughters and other atrocities, prevailed for a
long time in the cities and estates, that, compared with them, the hordes of the most savage
Indians might be called theatres of virtue,
humanity, and chastity. These reprobates,
either strangers or natives, infect the savages
with the contagion of their manners, teach
them crimes of which they were formerly
ignorant, and prevent them from lending an

and adore the one, and to despise the other. All those pitiful, superstitious, absurd opinions which had been sucked in with their mothers' milk, and, heard from the mouths of old women, as from a Delphic tripod, had received the ready assent of their infancy, they were com- manded to look upon as ridiculous falsehoods, and at the same time to yield their belief to mysteries of religion, which surpass the com- prehension of the wisest. It was somewhat hard immediately to forego notions which had been sanctioned by the approbation of their grandfathers, and great-grandfathers, and to embrace laws brought from a strange land, and every way contrary to their habits of life. Formerly they had been permitted to marry as many wives as they pleased, and to repudiate them in like manner whenever it suited their fancy. To repress such unbounded liberty by the perpetual marriage tie, this was the diffi- culty, this was the great obstacle to their embracing religion, and their frequent incite- ment to desert it.

The custom of drinking had taken such firm root amongst the Abipones, that it required more time and labour to eradicate drunkenness than any other vice. They would abstain from slaughter and rapine, and superstitious rites; confine themselves to one wife; attend divine ear to the instructions of the priests, when they daily hear and see words and actions so discordant to them in the old Christians. Indians returned from captivity amongst the Spaniards, Spaniards in captivity amongst the Indians, stranger from the cities, soldiers sent for the defence of the colonies, and Spanish guards appointed to take care of the cattle, were all certain plagues of the Abiponian colonies. I should never make an end were I to relate all I know on this subject. That the bad examples of the Christians greatly retarded the progress of religion amongst the Abipones, cannot be controverted. Let the old Christians of America become Christians in their conduct, and the Abipones, Mocobios, Tobas, Mataguayos, Chiriguanos, in a word, all the Indians of Paraguay will cease to be savages, and will embrace the law of Christ. This subject was treated of in the pulpit before the Royal Governor, Joseph Andonaegui, and a noble congregation, by the Jesuit P. Domingo Muriel, a Spaniard eminent for sanctity and learning, afterwards master of theology in the academy at Cordoba, and author of a most useful work intituled *Fasti Novi Orbis*, printed at Venice in the year 1776.

Humboldt and Bonpland:
Personal Narrative

Alexander von Humboldt and Aimé Bonpland, *Personal Narrative of Travels to the Equinoctial Regions of the New Continent, During the Years 1799–1804*, trans. Helen Maria Williams, 7 vols in 6 (London, 1814–29), vol. II, pp. 19–22, 239–41; vol. III, pp. 46–9, 119–31; vol. IV, pp. 342–50, 357–8, 419–22, 436–8, 531–4; vol. V, pp. 81–5, 137–40, 233–8, 289–92, 617–23; vol. VI, pp. 116–18; vol. VII, pp. 7–10.

'When I began to read the numerous relations of voyages, which compose so interesting a part of modern literature, I regretted that travellers, the most enlightened in the insulated branches of natural history, were seldom possessed of a sufficient variety of knowledge, to avail themselves of every advantage arising from their position' (vol. I, p. iv). Returning to Europe in 1804 after his five-year expedition to Spanish America with the French botanist Aimé Bonpland, Alexander von Humboldt set about harnessing his polymathic energies in justifying the project of scientific travel. He spent the next three decades publishing the thirty-volume *Voyage aux regions equinoxiales du Nouveau Continent*, containing the records of their travels and researches. The *Voyage* has assumed legendary proportions in European travel writing and established Humboldt as the paramount traveller of the period.

Humboldt was uniquely qualified to revolutionise travel writing. Scion of an aristocratic Prussian family, he was brought up amongst the leading lights of Romanticism and *naturphilosophie*. His training as a mining engineer at Freiburg and his liberal politics encouraged him to attempt a synthesis between the idealism of the German Romantics and the empirical programme of late Enlightenment French physics. His expedition was an attempt to transport his early experiments in mineralogy, galvanism and botany 'into the field' of tropical nature. Humboldt's 'global physics' sought, by rigorously empirical means, to establish the physical laws underlying phenomena and their relationship with the unified system of the world. As Mary Louise Pratt has reminded us in *Imperial Eyes*, Humboldt more than any other writer created the dominant image of South American nature for nineteenth-century Europeans, as well as offering Creole élites an important resource for cultural self-fashioning on the eve of their wars of independence.

More problematic was Humboldt's splendid but uncompleted *Personal Narrative*, which he began to write reluctantly in the years following his return to Paris, but which terminated abruptly as he and Bonpland set off down the Magdalena river in March 1801, headed for Ecuador and Peru, leaving the second half of the expedition un-narrated. The three volumes of the *Relation historique* were published in 1814–25. It is the longest of Humboldt's publications, and indeed one of the longest travel books ever written.

Humboldt confessed that originally he had intended to 'arrange the facts, not in the order in which they successively presented themselves, but according to the relation they bore to each other. Amidst the overwhelming majesty of Nature, and the stupendous objects she presents at every step, the traveller is little disposed to record in his journal what relates only to himself, and the ordinary details of life' (vol. I, p. xxxviii). Eventually, however, public demand overcame his scruples and he set out to convert his field notebooks into a 'personal narrative', combining meticulous scientific detail with his personal responses to the rich stimuli of tropical America. The method he adopted was to begin by narrating the itinerary in temporal sequence, with some acknowledgement of his own reactions, and then to consider objects of interest in their general, scientific relations. He suppressed personal incidents that were not susceptible to this sort of generalisation. Scientific generalisation is here often forestalled by description of the 'picturesque beauties' of tropical America, but Humboldt rejects the egotistical focus conventionally communicated by a rhetoric of emotional intensity. The Humboldtian picturesque urges a 'phenomalist' interpretation of nature quite distinct from the associative intensity of more conventional formulations.

Several of these passages describe transactions with the inhabitants of the Venezuelan coastal town of Cumana, with white *campesinos* in the hinterland and, perhaps most compellingly, with isolated Spanish missionaries and their Indian proselytes deep in the Orinoco interior. Humboldt vividly portrays the forests and *llanos* of Venezuela and Colombia. Although he never left European-ruled territory, and depended on the infrastructure of colonial Spain, he wrote as if he were discovering South America for the first time.

Generalised description gradually overtook 'personal narrative' as the work progressed. The English volumes 1–5 are largely a conventional travel narrative, albeit one which includes lengthy scientific dissertations. A dramatic shift is noticeable, however, in volumes 6–7. The *Personal Narrative* was gradually transforming itself into a 'geographical narrative', a digest of scientific, statistical and anthropological information. Despite its tortuous genesis and truncated form, the book is one of the major achievements of nineteenth-century travel writing; Charles Darwin admitted that his whole course of life had been determined by his enthusiastic reading of it. Robert Southey commented that Humboldt 'is among travellers what Wordsworth is among poets. The extent of his knowledge and the perfect command which he has of it are truly surprising; and with this he unites a painter's eye and a poet's feelings' (*New Letters of Southey*, ed. Kenneth Curry, vol. II, p. 231).

The lower regions of the air were loaded with vapors for some days. We saw distinctly for the first time the Cross of the south only in the night of the 4th and 5th of July, in the sixteenth degree of latitude; it was strongly inclined, and appeared from time to time between the clouds, the centre of which, furrowed by uncondensed lightnings, reflected a silver light. If a traveller may be permitted to speak of his personal emotions, I shall add, that in this night I saw one of the reveries of my earliest youth accomplished.

When we begin to fix our eyes on geographical maps, and read the narratives of navigators, we feel for certain countries and climates a sort of predilection, for which we know not how to account at a more advanced period of life. These impressions, however, exercise a considerable influence over our determinations; and from a sort of instinct we endeavour to connect ourselves with objects, on which the mind has long been fixed as by a secret charm. At a period when I studied the heavens, not with the intention of devoting myself to astronomy, but only to acquire a knowledge of the stars, I was agitated by a fear unknown to those who love a sedentary life. It seemed painful to me to renounce the hope of beholding those beautiful constellations, which border the southern pole. Impatient to rove in the equinoctial regions, I could not raise my eyes

towards the starry vault without thinking of the
Cross of the South, and without recalling the sublime passage of Dante, which the most celebrated
commentators have applied to this constellation;

> Io mi volsi a man destra e posi mente
> All' altro polo e vidi quattro stelle
> Non viste mai fuor ch' alla prima gente.

> Goder parca lo ciel di lor fiammelle ;
> O settentrional vedovo sito
> Poi che privato se' di mirar quelle !

The pleasure we felt on discovering the southern
Cross was warmly shared by such of the crew as
had lived in the colonies. In the solitude of the
seas, we hail a star as a friend, from whom we have
long been separated. Among the Portuguese and
the Spaniards peculiar motives seem to increase
this feeling ; a religious sentiment attaches them to
a constellation, the form of which recalls the sign of
the faith planted by their ancestors in the deserts
of the new world.

The two great stars which mark the summit and
the foot of the Cross having nearly the same
right ascension, it follows hence, that the constellation is almost perpendicular at the moment
when it passes the meridian. This circumstance
is known to every nation, that lives beyond the
tropics, or in the southern hemisphere. It has
been observed at what hour of the night, in different seasons, the Cross of the south is erect, or

inclined. It is a time-piece that advances very regularly near four minutes a day, and no other group of stars exhibits, to the naked eye, an observation of time so easily made. How often have we heard our guides exclaim in the savannas of Venezuela, or in the desert extending from Lima to Truxillo, " Midnight is past, the Cross begins to bend!" How often those words reminded us of that affecting scene, where Paul and Virginia, seated near the source of the river of Lataniers, conversed together for the last time, and where the old man, at the sight of the southern Cross, warns them that it is time to separate.

★ ★ ★ ★ ★

CHAPTER V.

*Peninsula of Araya.—Salt-marshes.—Ruins of
the Castle of San Giacomo.*

THE first weeks of our abode at Cumana were employed in verifying our instruments, in herbalizing
in the neighbouring fields, and in examining the
traces of the earthquake of the 14th of December,
1797.   Overpowered at once by a great number of
objects, we were somewhat embarrassed to lay
down a regular plan of study and observation.   If
every thing around us was fitted to inspire us with
the most lively interest, our physical and astronomical instruments in their turns excited strongly
the curiosity of the inhabitants.   We were distracted by frequent visits ; and in order not to dis-
satisfy persons, who appeared so happy to see the
spots of the Moon through Dollond's telescope,
the absorption of two gazes in a eudiometrical tube,
or the effects of galvanism on the motions of a
frog, we were obliged to answer questions often
obscure, and repeat for whole hours the same
experiments.

These scenes were renewed for the space of five
years, every time that we took up our abode in a

place where it was understood, that we were in possession of microscopes, telescopes, and electrical apparatus. They were in general so much the more fatiguing, as the persons who visited us had confused notions of astronomy and physicks; two sciences, which in the Spanish colonies are designated under the singular name of the new philosophy, *nueva filosophia*. The half-scientific looked on us with a sort of disdain, when they learnt that we had not brought in our collection of books the *Spectacle de la Nature* by Abbé Pluche, the *Cours de Physique* of Sigaud la Fond, or the Dictionary of Valmont de Bomare. These three works, and the *Traité d'Economie politique* of Baron Bielfeld, are the foreign work smost known and esteemed in Spanish America, from Caracas and Chili to Guatimala and the north of Mexico. No one is thought learned, who cannot quote their translations; and it is only in the great capitals, at Lima, at Santa Fe de Bogota, and at Mexico, that the names of Haller, Cavendish, and Lavoisier, begin to take the place of those, that have enjoyed popular celebrity for these fifty years past.

The curiosity excited respecting the phænomena of the heavens, and various objects of the natural sciences, takes a very different character among anciently civilized nations, and among those who have made but little progress in the unfolding of their intellectual faculties. Each of them exhibits in the highest classes of society frequent examples of persons unacquainted with science; but in the colonies, and among new people, curiosity, far from being idle or transient, arises from an ardent desire of instruction, and discovers itself with an ingenuousness and simplicity, which in Europe are the characteristics only of youth.

I could not begin a regular course of astronomical observations before the 28th of July, though it was highly important for me to know the longitude given by Berthoud's time-keeper; but it happened, that in a country, where the sky is constantly clear and serene, no stars appeared for several nights. Every day, two hours after the Sun had passed the meridian, a storm gathered; and I had great difficulty in obtaining correspondent altitudes of the Sun, though I took three or four sets at different intervals. The chronometrical longitude of Cumana differed only four seconds in time from that which I deduced from the celestial phænomena; yet our voyage had lasted more than forty days, and during the excursion to the top of the Peak of Teneriffe, the watch had been exposed to great variations of temperature *.

★   ★   ★   ★   ★

In this village lives a labourer, Francisco Lozano, who presented a physiological phenomenon, highly calculated to strike the imagination, though it is very conformable to the known laws of organized nature. This man has suckled a child with his own milk. The mother having fallen sick, the father, to quiet the infant, took it into his bed, and pressed it to his bosom. Lozano, then thirty-two years of age, had never remarked till that day that he had milk : but the irritation of the nipple, sucked by the child, caused the accumulation of that liquid. The milk was thick and very sweet. The father, astonished at the increased size of his breast, suckled his child two or three times a day during five months. He drew on himself the attention of his neighbours, but he never thought, as he probably would have done in Europe, of deriving any advantage from the curiosity he excited. We saw the certificate, which had been drawn up on the spot, to attest this remarkable fact, eye-witnesses of which are still living. They assured us, that, during this suckling, the child had no other nourishment than the milk of his father. Lozano, who was not at Arenas during our journey in the Missions, came to us at Cumana. He was accompanied by his son, who was then thirteen or fourteen years of age. Mr. Bonpland examined with attention the father's breast, and found it wrinkled like those of women who have given suck. He observed, that the left breast in particular was much enlarged; which Lozano explained to us from the circumstance, that the two breasts did not furnish milk in the same abundance. Don Vicente Empa-

ran, Governor of the province, sent a circum-
stantial account of this phenomenon to Cadiz.

It is not a very uncommon circumstance, to
find, both among humankind and animals *,
males whose breasts contain milk; and the climate does not appear to exert any marked influence on the more or less abundance of this
secretion. The ancients cite the milk of the he
goats of Lemnos and Corsica. In our own time,
we have seen in the country of Hanover, a he
goat, which for a great number of years was
milked every other day, and yielded more milk
than a female goat †. Among the signs of the
pretended weakness of the Americans, travellers
have mentioned the milk contained in the
breasts of men ‡. It is however improbable,
that it has ever been observed in a whole tribe,
in some part of America unknown to modern
travellers; and I can affirm, that at present it
is not more common in the new continent, than
in the old. The labourer of Arenas, whose his
tory we have just related, is not of the copper-

* Athanas. Joannides de Mammarum Struct., 1801, p. 0.
Haller, Elem. Physiol., T. 7, P. II. page 18.

† Blumenbach, Vergleich. Anat., 1805, p. 504. Hanœ-
vrisches Magaz., 1787, page 753. Reil, Arch. der Physiol.,
T. 3, p. 449. Montegre, Gazette de Santé, 1812, p. 110.

‡ It has even been seriously related, that in a part of
Brazil it is the men, and not the women, that suckle children. Clavigero, Storia di Messico. T. 4. 169.

coloured race of Chayma Indians: he is a white man, descended from Europeans. Moreover, the anatomists of Petersburg * have observed, that among the lower orders of the people in Russia, milk in the breasts of men is much more frequent, than among the more southern nations; and the Russians have never been deemed weak and effeminate.

* Comment. Petrop., Tom. 3, p. 278.

★　　★　　★　　★　　★

What gives most celebrity to the valley of Caripe, beside the extraordinary coolness of the climate, is the great *Cueva*, or Cavern of the *Guacharo* *. In a country where the people love what is marvellous, a cavern that gives

* The province of Guacharucu, which Delgado visited in 1534, in the expedition of Hieronimo de Ortal, appears to have been situate South, or South-east from Macarapana. Has it's name any connexion with those of the cavern and the bird? or is this last of Spanish origin? (Laet, Nov. Orb., p. 676). Guacharo means in Castilian " one who cries and laments himself"; now the bird of the cavern of Caripe, and the guacharaca (phasianus parraka), are very noisy birds.

birth to a river, and is inhabited by thousands
of nocturnal birds, the fat of which is employed
in the Missions to dress food, is an everlasting
object of conversation and discussion. Scarcely has a stranger arrived at Cumana, when he
is told of the stone of Araya for the eyes; of
the labourer of Arenas, who suckled his child;
and of the cavern of Guacharo, which is said
to be several leagues in length; till he is tired
of hearing of them. A lively interest in the
phenomena of nature is preserved wherever
society may be said to be without life; where,
in dull monotony, it presents only simple relations little fitted to excite the ardour of curiosity.

The cavern, which the natives call *a mine
of fat,* is not in the valley of Caripe itself,
but at three short leagues distance from the
convent, toward the West-south-west. It opens
into a lateral valley, which terminates at the
Sierra del Guacharo. We set out toward
the Sierra on the 18th of September, accompanied by the Alcaids, or Indian magistrates,
and the greater part of the monks of the Convent. A narrow path led us at first during
an hour and a half toward the South, across
a fine plain, covered with a beautiful turf. We
then turned toward the West, along a small river, which issues from the mouth of the cavern
We ascended during three quarters of an hour,

walking sometimes in the water, which was shallow, sometimes between the torrent and a wall of rocks, on a soil extremely slippery and miry. The falling down of the earth, the scattered trunks of trees over which the mules could scarcely pass, the creeping plants that covered the ground, rendered this part of the road fatiguing. We were surprised to find here, at scarcely 500 toises of elevation above the level of the sea, a cruciferous plant, raphanus pinnatus. It is well known how scarce the plants of this family are between the tropics; they display in some sort a northern form, and as such we never expected to see it on the plain of Caripe at so little an elevation, Those northern forms seem also to appear in the galium caripense, the valeriana scandens, and a sanicle not unlike the s. marilandica.

At the foot of the lofty mountain of Guacharo, we were only four hundred steps from the cavern, without yet perceiving the entrance. The torrent runs in a crevice, which has been hollowed out by the waters; and we went on under a cornice, the projection of which prevented us from seeing the sky. The path winds like the river: at the last turning we came suddenly before the immense opening of the grotto. The aspect of this spot is majestic even to the eye of a traveller accustomed to the picturesque scenes of the higher Alps. I had before this seen the

caverns of the Peak of Derbyshire, where, extended in a boat, we traversed a subterranean
river, under a vault of two feet high. I had
visited the beautiful grotto of Treshemienshiz,
in the Carpathian mountains, the caverns of the
Hartz, and those of Franconia which are vast
cemeteries * of bones of tigers, hyenas, and
bears, as large as our horses. Nature in every
zone follows immutable laws in the distribution
of rocks, in the exterior form of mountains,
and even in those tumultuous changes, which
the exterior crust of our planet has undergone.
So great a uniformity led me to believe, that
the aspect of the cavern of Caripe would differ
little from what I had observed in my preceding travels. The reality far exceeded my ex-
pectations. If the configuration of the grottoes,
the splendor of the stalactites, and all the phe-

---

* The mould, that has covered for thousands of years the
soil of the caverns of Gaylenreuth and Muggendorf in Franconia, emits even now choke-damps, or gazeous mixtures
of hydrogen and nitrogen, that rise to the roof of their
caves. This fact is known to all those who show these
caverns to travellers ; and when I had the direction of the
mines of the Fichtelberg, I observed it frequently in the
summer time. Mr. Laugier found in the mould of Muggendorf, beside phosphate of lime, 0·10 of animal matter. (Cuvier, Recherches sur les Ossemens fossiles, T. 4. Ours, p.
14.) I was struck, during my stay at Steeben, with the
ammoniacal and fetid smell produced by it, when projected
on a red hot iron.

nomena of inorganic nature, present striking
analogies, the majesty of equinoxial vegetation
gives at the same time an individual character
to the aperture of the cavern.

The Cueva del Guacharo is pierced in the vertical profile of a rock. The entrance is toward
the South, and forms a vault eighty feet broad,
and seventy-two feet high. This elevation is
but a fifth less than that of the colonnade of
the Louvre. The rock, that surmounts the
grotto, is covered with trees of gigantic height.
The mammee-tree, and the genipa * with large
and shining leaves, raise their branches vertical-
ly toward the sky; while those of the courbaril
and the erythrina form, as they extend them=
selves, a thick vault of verdure. Plants of the
family of pothos with succulent stems, oxalises,
and orchideæ of a singular structure †, rise in
the driest clefts of the rocks; while creeping
plants, waving in the winds, are interwoven in
festoons before the opening of the cavern. We
distinguished in these festoons a bignonia of a
violet blue, the purple dolichos, and for the
first time that magnificent solandra ‡, the

---

* Caruto, genipa americana. The flower, at Caripe, has
sometimes five, sometimes six stamens.

† A dendrobium, with a golden flower, spotted with
black, three inches long.

‡ Solandra scandens. It is the gousaticha of the Chayma Indians.

orange flower of which has a fleshy tube more
than four inches long. The entrance of grottoes,
like the view of cascades, derive their principal
charm from the situation, more or less majestic,
in which they are placed, and which in some
sort determines the character of the landscape.
What a contrast between the Cueva of Caripe,
and those caverns of the North crowned with
oaks and gloomy larch-trees !

But this luxury of vegetation embellishes not
only the outside of the vault, it appears even
in the vestibule of the grotto. We saw with
astonishment plantain-leaved heliconias eighteen feet high, the praga palm-tree, and arbor-
escent arums, follow the banks of the river,
even to those subterranean places. The vegetation continues in the cave of Caripe, as in
those deep crevices of the Andes, half excluded
from the light of day ; and does not disappear,
till, advancing in the interior, we reach thirty
or forty paces from the entrance. We measured the way by means of a cord: and we
went on about four hundred and thirty feet,
without being obliged to light our torches.
Daylight penetrates even into this region, because the grotto forms but one single channel,
which keeps the same direction, from South-east
to North-west. Where the light begins to fail,
we heard from afar the hoarse sounds of the
nocturnal birds ; sounds, which the natives

think belong exclusively to those subterrane-ous places.

The guacharo is of the size of our fowls, has the mouth of the goatsuckers and procnias, and the port of those vultures, the crooked beak of which is surrounded with stiff silky hairs. Suppressing, with Mr. Cuvier, the order of picæ, we must refer this extraordinary bird to the passeres, the genera of which are connected with each other by almost imperceptible transitions. I have noted it under the name of steatornis, in a particular monography, contained in the second volume of my Observations on Zoology and Comparative Anatomy. It forms a new genus *, very different from the goat-sucker by the force of it's voice, by the considerable strength of it's beak, containing a double tooth, by it's feet without the mem-branes that unite the anterior phalanxes of the claws. It is the first example of a nocturnal bird among the *passeres dentirostrati*. In it's manners it has analogies both with the goat-suckers and the alpine crow †. The plumage of the guacharo is of a dark bluish gray, mixed with small streaks and specks of black. Large

---

* It's essential characters are : rostrum validum, lateribus compressum, apice aduncum, mandibula superiori subbiden-tata, dente anteriori acutiori. Rictus amplissimus. Pedes breves, digitis fissis, unguibus integerrimis.

† Corvus pyrrhocorax.

white spots, which have the form of a heart,
and which are bordered with black, mark the
head, the wings, and the tail. The eyes of the
bird are hurt by the blaze of day ; they are blue,
and smaller than those of the goat-suckers. The
spread of the wings, which are composed of se-
venteen or eighteen quill feathers, is three feet
and a half. The guacharo quits the cavern at
night-fall, especially when the moon shines.
It is almost the only frugiferous nocturnal bird,
that is yet known ; the conformation of it's
feet sufficiently shows, that it does not hunt
like our owls. It feeds on very hard fruits ;
as the nut-cracker * and the pyrrhocorax. The
latter nestles also in clefts of rocks, and is
known under the name of *night-crow*. The
Indians assured us, that the guacharo does not
pursue either the lamellicornous insects, or
those phalænæ which serve as food to the goat-
suckers. It is sufficient to compare the beaks
of the guacharo and goat-sucker, to conjecture
how much their manners must differ. It is difficult to form an idea of the horrible noise occasioned by thousands of these birds in the
dark part of the cavern, and which can only

---

* Corvus caryocatactes, c. glandarius. Our alpine crow
builds it's nest, toward the top of Mount Libanus, in subterranean caverns, nearly like the guacharo; the horribly
shrill voice of which it also has. (Labillardière, Ann. du
Musée, T. 18, p. 455.)

be compared to the croaking of our crows, which, in the pine forests of the North, live in society, and construct their nests upon trees, the tops of which touch each other. The shrill and piercing cries of the guacharoes strike upon the vaults of the rocks, and are repeated by the echo in the depth of the cavern. The Indians showed us the nests of these birds, by fixing torches to the end of a long pole. These nests were fifty or sixty feet high above our heads, in holes in the shape of funnels, with which the roof of the grotto is pierced like a sieve. The noise increased as we advanced, and the birds were affrighted by the light of the torches of copal. When this noise ceased a few minutes around us, we heard at a distance the plaintive cries of the birds roosting in other ramifications of the cavern. It seemed as if these bands answered each other alternately.

The Indians enter into the Cueva del Guacharo once a year, near midsummer, armed with poles, by means of which they destroy the greater part of the nests. At this season several thousands of birds are killed ; and the old ones, as if to defend their brood, hover over the heads of the Indians, uttering terrible cries. The young *, which fall to the ground, are opened on the spot. Their peritoneum is extremely

* Los pollos del Guacharo.

loaded with fat, and a layer of fat reaches from
the abdomen to the anus, forming a kind of
cushion between the legs of the bird. This
quantity of fat in frugivorous animals, not exposed to the light, and exerting very little muscular motion, reminds us of what has been long
since observed in the fattening of geese and oxen.
It is well known how favourable darkness and
repose are to this process. The nocturnal birds
of Europe are lean, because, instead of feeding
on fruits, like the guacharo, they live on the
scanty produce of their prey. At the period
which is commonly called at Caripe *the oil har-
vest**, the Indians build huts with palm leaves,
near the entrance, and even in the porch of the
cavern. Of these we still saw some remains.
There, with a fire of brush-wood, they melt in
pots of clay the fat of the young birds just
killed. This fat is known by the name of but-
ter or oil *(manteca* or *aceite)* of the guacharo.
It is half liquid, transparent, without smell, and
so pure that it may be kept above a year without becoming rancid. At the convent of Caripe no other oil is used in the kitchen of the
monks but that of the cavern; and we never
observed, that it gave the aliments a disagreeable taste or smell.

The quantity of this oil collected little corres-

---

* La cosecha de la manteca.

ponds with the carnage made, every year in the grotto by the Indians. It appears, that they do not, get above 150 or 160 bottles* of very pure *manteca;* the rest, less transparent, is preserved in large earthen vessels. This branch of industry reminds us of the harvest of pigeons' oil †, of which some thousands of barrels were formerly collected in Carolina. At Caripe, the use of the oil of guacharoes is very ancient, and the missionaries have only regulated the method of extracting it. The members of an Indian family, which bears the name of Morocoymas, pretend, as descendants of the first colonists of the valley, to be the lawful proprietors of the cavern, and arrogate to themselves the monopoly of the fat; but, thanks to the monastic institutions, their rights at present are merely honorary. In conformity to the system of the missionaries, the Indians are obliged to furnish guacharo-oil for the church lamp: the rest, we were assured, is purchased of them. We shall not decide either on the legitimacy of the rights of the Morocoymas, or on the origin of the obligation imposed on the natives by the monks. It would seem natural, that the produce of the chace should belong to those who hunt: but in the forests of the New World, as in the centre of

* Sixty cubic inches each.

† This *pigeon oil* comes from the columba migratoria (Pennant's Arctic Zoology, T. 2, p. 13).

European cultivation, public might is modified according to the relations, which are established between the strong and the weak, the victors and the vanquished.

The race of the guacharoes would have been long ago extinct, had not several circumstances contributed to it's preservation. The natives, restrained by their superstitious ideas, have seldom the courage to penetrate far into the grotto. It appears also, that birds of the same species dwell in neighbouring caverns, which are too narrow to be accessible to man. Perhaps the great cavern is repeopled by colonies, that abandon the small grottoes; for the missionaries assured us, that hitherto no sensible diminution of the birds had been observed. Young guacharoes have been sent to the port of Cumana, and have lived there several days without taking any nourishment; the seeds offered to them not suiting their taste. When the crops and gizzards of the young birds are opened in the cavern, they are found to contain all sorts of hard and dry fruits, which furnish, under the singular name of guacharo seed, *semilla del guacharo*, a very celebrated remedy against intermittent fevers. The old birds carry these seeds to their young. They are carefully collected, and sent to the sick at Cariaco, and other places of the low regions, where fevers are prevalent.

We followed, as we continued our progress through the cavern, the banks of the small river, which issued from it, and is from twenty-eight to thirty feet wide. We walked on the banks, as far as the hills formed of calcareous incrustations permitted us. When the torrent winds among very high masses of stalactites, we were often obliged to descend into it's bed, which is only two feet in depth. We learnt, with surprise, that this subterraneous rivulet is the origin of the river Caripe, which, at a few leagues distance, after having joined the small river of Santa Maria, is navigable for canoes. It enters into the river Areo under the name of *Canno de Terezen*. We found on the banks of the subterraneous rivulet a great quantity of palm-tree wood, the remains of trunks, on which the Indians climb to reach the nests hanging to the roofs of the cavern. The rings, formed by the vestiges of the old footstalks of the leaves, furnish as it were the footsteps of a ladder perpendicularly placed.

★　　★　　★　　★　　★

We found at Calabozo, in the midst of the

Llanos, an electrical machine with large plates, electrophori, batteries, and electrometers; an apparatus nearly as complete as our first scientific men in Europe possess. All these articles had not been purchased in the United States; they were the performance of a man, who had never seen any instrument, who had no person to consult, and who was acquainted with the phenomena of electricity only by reading the treatise of Sigaurd de la Fond, and Franklin's Memoirs. Mr. Carlos del Pozo, the name of this worthy and ingenious man, had begun to make cylindrical electrical machines, by employing large glass jars, after having cut off the necks. It was only within a few years he had been able to procure, by way of Philadelphia, two plates, to construct a plate machine, and to obtain more considerable effects. It is easy to judge what difficulties Mr. Pozo had to encounter, since the first works upon electricity had fallen into his hands; and that he had the courage to resolve to procure himself, by his own industry, all that he had seen described in the books. Till now he had enjoyed only the astonishment and admiration produced by his experiments on persons destitute of all information, and who had never quitted the solitude of the Llanos; our abode at Calabozo gave him a satisfaction altogether new. It may be supposed, that he set some value on the opinions of two travellers, who could compare his apparatus with those constructed in Europe. I had brought with me electrometers, with straws, with pith balls, and with gold leaves; and also a small Leyden vial, which could be charged by friction according to the method of Ingenhousz, and which served for my physiological experiments. Mr. Pozo could not contain his joy, on seeing for the first time instruments which he had not made, and which appeared to be copied from his own. We also showed him the effect of the contact of heterogeneous metals on the nerves of frogs. The name of Galvani and Volta had not yet resounded in those vast solitudes.

After this electrical apparatus, the work of the industrious sagacity of an inhabitant of the Llanos, nothing at Calabozo excited in us so great an interest as the gymnoti, which are animated electrical apparatuses. Occupied daily for a great number of years by the phenomena of galvanic electricity; given up to that enthusiasm, which excites us to research, but prevents us from seeing accurately what we have discovered; having constructed, unconsciously, real *piles*, by placing metallic disks one upon another, and making them alternate with pieces of muscular flesh, or with other humid substances*; I was impatient, from the time of my

---

* See my Experiments on the irritable Fibre, vol. i, p. 74, pl. iii, iv, v, of the German edition.

arrival at Cumana, to procure electrical eels. We had been promised them often, but our hopes had always been disappointed. Money loses it's value as you withdraw from the coast; and how is the imperturbable phlegm of the vulgar to be vanquished, when they are not excited by the desire of gain?

The Spaniards confound all electrical fishes under the name of *tembladores (producers of trembling*, literally *tremblers)*. There are some in the Caribbean sea, on the coast of Cumana. The Guayqueria Indians, who are the most skilful and industrious fishermen in those parts, brought us a fish, which, they said, had benumbed their hands. This fish ascends the little river Manzanares. It is a new species of the ray, the lateral spots of which are scarcely visible, and which much resembles the torpedo of Galvani. The torpedoes, furnished with an electric organ that is externally visible, on account of the transparency of the skin, form a genus or subgenus, different from the rays properly so called *. The torpedo of Cumana was

---

* *Cuvier, Regne Animal*, vol. ii, p. 136. The Mediterranean contains, according to Mr. Risso, four species of electrical torpedoes, all formerly confounded under the name of raia torpedo; these are torpedo narke, t. unimaculata, t. galvanii, and t. marmorata. The torpedo of the Cape of Good Hope, the subject of the recent experiments of Mr. Todd, is no doubt a nondescript species.

very lively, very energetic in it's muscular movements, and yet the electrical shocks it gave us
were extremely feeble. They became stronger
on *galvanizing* the animal by the contact of
zinc and gold. Other *tembladores*, real gymnoti
or electrical eels, inhabit the Rio Colorado, the
Guarapiche, and several little streams, that
cross the missions of the Chayma Indians. They
abound also in the large rivers of America, the
Oroonoko, the Amazon, and the Meta; but the
strength of the current, and the depth of the
water, prevent their being caught by the Indians.
They see these fish less frequently than they
feel electrical shocks from them when swimming or bathing in the river. In the *Llanos*,
particularly in the environs of Calabozo, between the farms of Morichal and the missions
de arriba and *de abaxo*, the basins of stagnant
water, and the confluents of the Oroonoko,
(the Rio Guarico and the *Canos* of Rastro,
Berito, and Paloma) are filled with electrical
eels. We at first wished to make our experiments in the house we inhabited at Calabozo;
but the dread of the electrical shocks of the
gymnoti is so great, and so exaggerated among
the vulgar, that during three days we could not
obtain one, though they are easily caught, and
we had promised the Indians two piastres for
every strong and vigorous fish. This fear of the
Indians is the more extraordinary, as they do

not attempt to employ means in which they profess to have great confidence. When interrogated on the effect of the *tembladores*, they never fail to tell the Whites, that they may be touched with impunity, while you are chewing tobacco. This fable of the influence of tobacco on animal electricity is as general on the continent of South America, as the belief among mariners of the effect of garlick and tallow on the magnetic needle.

Impatient of waiting, and having obtained very uncertain results from an electrical eel that had been brought to us alive, but much enfeebled, we repaired to the Cano de Bera, to make our experiments in the open air, on the borders of the water itself. We set off on the 19th of March, at a very early hour, for the village of *Rastro de abaxo ;* thence we were conducted by the Indians to a stream, which, in the time of drought, forms a basin of muddy water, surrounded by fine trees *, the clusia, the amyris, and the mimosa with fragrant flowers. To catch the gymnoti with nets is very difficult, on account of the extreme agility of the fish, which bury themselzes in the mud like serpents. We would not employ the *barbasco*, that is to say, the roots of the piscidea erithyrna, jacquinia armillaris, and some species of phyllanthus, which, thrown

---

* Amyris *lateriflora*, a. *coriacea*, laurus *pichurin*, myroxylon *secundum*, malpighia *reticulata*.

into the pool, intoxicate or benumb these animals. These means would have enfeebled the gymnoti; the Indians therefore told us, that they would " fish with horses," *embarbascar con cavallos* *. We found it difficult to form an idea of this extraordinary manner of fishing; but we soon saw our guides return from the savannah, which they had been scouring for wild horses and mules. They brought about thirty with them, which they forced to enter the pool.

The extraordinary noise caused by the horses' hoofs makes the fish issue from the mud, and excites them to combat. These yellowish and livid eels, resembling large aquatic serpents, swim on the surface of the water, and crowd under the bellies of the horses and mules. A contest between animals of so different an organization furnishes a very striking spectacle. The Indians, provided with harpoons and long slender reeds, surround the pool closely; and some climb upon the trees, the branches of which extend horizontally over the surface of the water. By their wild cries, and the length of their reeds, they prevent the horses from running away, and reaching the bank of the pool. The eels, stunned by the noise, defend themselves by the repeated discharge of their electric

---

* Properly *to set to sleep*, or *intoxicate* the fish by means of horses.

batteries. During a long time they seem to prove victorious. Several horses sink beneath the violence of the invisible strokes, which they receive from all sides in organs the most essential to life; and stunned by the force and frequency of the shocks, disappear under the water. Others, panting, with mane erect, and haggard eyes, expressing anguish, raise themselves, and endeavour to flee from the storm by which they are overtaken. They are driven back by the Indians into the middle of the water; but a small number succeed in eluding the active vigilance of the fishermen. These regain the shore, stumbling at every step, and stretch themselves on the sand, exhausted with fatigue, and their limbs benumbed by the electric shocks of the gymnoti.

In less than five minutes two horses were drowned. The eel, being five feet long, and pressing itself against the belly of the horses, makes a discharge along the whole extent of it's electric organ. It attacks at once the heart, the intestines, and the *plexus cœliacus* of the abdominal nerves. It is natural, that the effect felt by the horses should be more powerful, than that produced upon man by the touch of the same fish at only one of his extremities. The horses are probably not killed, but only stunned. They are drowned from the impossibility of rising amid the prolonged struggle between the other horses and the eels.

We had little doubt, that the fishing would terminate by killing successively all the animals engaged; but by degrees the impetuosity of this unequal combat diminished, and the wearied gymnoti dispersed. They require a long rest *, and abundant nourishment, to repair what they have lost of galvanic force. The mules and horses appear less frightened; their manes are no longer bristled, and their eyes express less dread. The gymnoti approach timidly the edge of the marsh, where they are taken by means of small harpoons fastened to long cords. When the cords are very dry, the Indians feel no shock in raising the fish into the air. In a few minutes we had five large eels, the greater part of which were but slightly wounded. Some were taken by the same means toward the evening.

★   ★   ★   ★   ★

Gymnoti are neither charged conductors, nor batteries, nor electromotive apparatuses, the shock of which is received every time they are touched with one hand, or when both hands are applied to form a conducting circle between two heterogeneous poles. The electric action of the fish depends entirely on it's will; whether because it do not keep it's electric organs always charged; or by the secretion of some fluid, or by any other means alike mysterious to us, it be capable of directing the action of it's organs to an external object. We often tried, both insulated and uninsulated, to touch the fish, without feeling the least shock. When Mr. Bonpland held it by the head, or by the middle of the body, while I held it by the tail, and, standing on the moist ground, did not take each other's hand, one of us received shocks, which the other did not feel. It depends upon the gymnotus to act toward the point, where it finds itself the most strongly irritated. The discharge is then made at one point only, and not at the neighbouring points. If two persons touch the belly of the fish with their fingers, at an inch distance, and press it simultaneously, sometimes one, sometimes the other will receive the shock. In the same manner, when one insulated person holds the tail of a vigorous gymnotus, and another pinches the gills, or pectoral fin, it is often the first only by whom the shock is received. It did not appear to us, that these differences could be attributed to the dryness or dampness of our hands, or to their unequal conducting power. The gymnotus seemed to direct it's strokes sometimes from the whole surface of it's body, sometimes from one point only. This effect indicates less a partial discharge of the organ composed of an innumerable quantity of leaves; than the faculty which the animal possesses, perhaps by the instantaneous secretion of a fluid spread through the cellular membrane, of establishing the communication between it's organs and the skin only, in a very limited space.

★ ★ ★ ★ ★

Having passed the Diamante, we entered a land inhabited only by tigers, crocodiles, and *chiguires*, a large species of the genus cavia of Linneus. We saw flocks of birds, crowded so close together, as to appear against the sky like a dark cloud, that every instant changed it's form. The river widens by degrees. One of it's banks is generally barren and sandy from the effect of inundations; the other is higher, and covered with lofty trees. Sometimes the river is bordered by forests on each side, and forms a straight canal a hundred and fifty toises broad. The manner in which the trees are disposed is very remarkable. We first find bushes of *sauso* *, forming a kind of hedge four feet high; and appearing as if they had been clipped by the hand of man. A copse of cedars, brazillettoes, and lignum vitæ, rises behind this hedge. Palm-trees are rare; we saw only a few scattered trunks of the thorny piritu and corozo. The large quadrupeds of those regions, the tigers, tapirs, and pecaris, have made openings in the hedge of *sausos* which we have just described. Through these the wild animals pass, when they come to drink at the river. As they fear but little the approach of a boat, we had the pleasure of viewing them pace slowly along the shore, till they disappeared in the forest, which they entered by one of the narrow passes left here and there between the bushes. I confess that these scenes, which were often repeated, had ever for me a peculiar attraction. The pleasure they excite is not owing solely to the interest, which the naturalist takes in the objects of his study; it is connected with a feeling common to all men, who have been brought up in the habits of civilization. You find yourself in a new world, in the midst of untamed and savage nature. Now it is the jaguar, the beautiful panther of America, that appears upon the shore; and now the hocco * with it's black plumage and it's tufted head, that moves slowly along the sausoes. Animals of the most different classes succeed each other. " *Esse como en el Paraiso* †," said our pilot, an old Indian of the missions. Every thing indeed here recalls

---

* Craix alector, the peacock pheasant; c. pàuxi, the cashew bird.

† " It is just as it was in Paradise."

to mind that state of the primitive world, the innocence and felicity of which ancient and venerable traditions have transmitted to all nations : but, in carefully observing the manners of animals between themselves, we see that they mutually avoid and fear each other. The golden age has ceased ; and in this Paradise of the American forests, as well as every where else, sad and long experience has taught all beings, that benignity is seldom found in alliance with strength.

The night was calm and serene, and there was a beautiful moonlight. The crocodiles were stretched along the shore. They placed themselves in such a manner as to be able to see the fire. We thought we observed, that it's splendour attracted them, as it attracts fishes, crayfish, and other inhabitants of the water. The Indians showed us the traces of three tigers in the sand, two of which were very young. A female had no doubt conducted her little ones to drink at the river. Finding no tree on the strand, we stuck our oars in the ground, and to these we fastened our hammocks. Every thing passed tranquilly till eleven at night; and then a noise so terrific arose in the neighbouring forest, that it was almost impossible to close our eyes. Amid the cries of so many wild beasts howling at once, the Indians discriminated such only as were heard separately. These were the little soft cries of the sapajous, the moans of the alouates, the howlings of the tiger, the couguar, or American lion without mane, the pecari, and the sloth, and the voices of the curassoa, the parraka, and some other gallinaceous birds. When the jaguars approached the skirt of the forest, our dog, which till then had never ceased barking, began to howl and seek for shelter beneath our hammocks. Sometimes, after a long silence, the cry of the tiger came from the tops of the trees; and in this case it was followed by the sharp and long whistling of the monkeys, which appeared to flee from the danger that threatened them.

I notice every circumstance of these nocturnal scenes, because, being recently embarked on the Rio Apure, we were not yet accustomed to them. We heard the same noises repeated, during the course of whole months, whenever the forest approached the bed of the rivers. The security displayed by the Indians inspires travellers with confidence. You persuade yourself with them, that the tigers are afraid of fire, and do not attack a man lying in his hammock. These attacks are in fact extremely rare ; and, during a long abode in South America, I remember only one example of a Llanero, who was found torn in his hammock opposite the island of Achaguas.

When the natives are interrogated on the causes of this tremendous noise made by the beasts of the forest at certain hours of the night, they reply gaily, " they are keeping the feast of the full moon."

I believe this agitation is most frequently the effect of some contest, that has arisen in the depths of the forest. The jaguars, for instance, pursue the pecaris and the tapirs, which, having no defence but in their numbers, flee in close troops, and break down the bushes they find in their way. Affrighted at this struggle, the timid and mistrustful monkies answer from the tops of the trees the cries of the large animals. They awaken the birds that live in society, and by degrees the whole assembly is in movement. We shall soon find, that it is not always in a fine moonlight, but more particularly at the time of a storm and violent showers, that this tumult takes place among the wild beasts. " May Heaven grant them a quiet night and repose, and us also!" said the monk who accompanied us to the Rio Negro, when, sinking with fatigue, he assisted in arranging our accommodations for the night. It was indeed a strange situation, to find no silence in the solitude of woods. In the inns of Spain we dread the sharp sounds of guitars from the next apartment; in those of the Oroonoko, which are an open beach, or the shelter of a solitary tree, we are afraid of being disturbed in our sleep by voices issuing from the forest.

★   ★   ★   ★   ★

The missionary of the *Raudales* made the preparations for the voyage with greater activity than we wished. From fear of not having a sufficient number of Maco and Guahibe Indians, who are acquainted with the labyrinth of small channels and cascades, of which the *Raudales* or cataracts are composed, two Indians were put during the night in the *cepo;* that is to say, made to lie with their legs placed between two pieces of wood, notched and fastened together by a chain with a padlock. Early in the morning we were awakened by the cries of a young man, mercilessly beaten with a whip of manatee skin. His name was *Zerepe,* a very intelligent Indian, who was highly useful to us in the sequel, but who now refused to accompany us. Born in the mission of Atures, of a Maco father, and a mother of the nation of the Maypures, he had returned to the woods (*al monte*), and had lived some years with the unsubdued Indians. He had thus acquired the knowledge of several languages, and the missionary employed him as an interpreter. We obtained with difficulty the pardon of this young man. " Without these acts of severity," we were told, " you would want for every thing. The Indians of the *Raudales* and the Upper Oroonoko are a stronger and more laborious race than the inhabitants of the Lower Oroonoko. They know, that they are much sought after at Angostura. If left to their own will, they would all go down the river to sell their productions, and live in full liberty among the Whites. The missions would be deserted."

These reasons are, I confess, more specious than true. Man, in order to enjoy the advantages of a social state, must no doubt sacrifice a part of his natural rights, and his ancient independence. But, if the sacrifice imposed on him be not compensated by the benefits of civilization, the savage, wise in his simplicity, retains the wish of returning to the forests that gave him birth. It is because the Indian of the woods is treated like a person in a state of villanage in the greater part of the missions, because he enjoys not the fruits of his labours, that the Christian establishments on the Oroonoko remain deserts. A government founded on the ruins of the liberty of the natives extinguishes the intellectual faculties, or stops their progress.

When it is said, that the savage, like the child, can be governed only by force, this is to establish false analogies. The Indians of the Oroonoko have something infantine in the expression of their joy, and the quick succession of their emotions; but they are not great children; they are as little so as the poor labourers in the East of Europe, whom the barbarism of our feudal institutions has held in the rudest state. To

consider the employment of force as the first and
sole means of the civilization of the savage, is a
principle as far from being true in the education
of nations, as in the education of youth.   Whatever may be the state of weakness or degradation in our species, no faculty is entirely annihilated.   The human understanding exhibits
only different degrees of strength and development.   The savage, like the child, compares the
present with the past; he directs his actions,
not according to blind instinct, but from motives
of interest.   Reason can every where enlighten
reason; and it's progress will be retarded in
proportion as the men, who think themselves
called upon to bring up youth, or govern nations,
proud of the feeling of their superiority, and
despising those on whom they should act, think
proper to substitute constraint and force for that
moral influence, which can alone unfold the
rising faculties, calm the irritated passions, and
give stability to social order.

★   ★   ★   ★   ★

It was among the cataracts that we began to hear of the hairy man of the woods, called salvaje, that carries off women, constructs huts, and sometimes eats human flesh. The Tamanacks call it *achi**, and the Maypures *vasitri*, or *great devil*. The natives and the missionaries have no doubt of the existence of this anthropomorphous monkey, which they singularly dread. Father Gili✝ gravely relates the history of a lady in the town of San Carlos‡, who much praised the gentle character and attentions of the man of the woods. She lived several years with one in great domestic harmony, and only requested some hunters to take her back, "because she was tired, she and her children (a little hairy also), of living far from the church and the sacraments." The same author, notwithstanding his credulity, confesses, that he had not been able to find an Indian, who asserted positively that he had seen the *salvaje* with his own eyes. This fable, which the missionaries, the European planters, and the negroes of Africa, have no doubt embellished with many features taken from the description of the manners of the

---

* Pronounce *atschi.*

✝ Saggio, vol. i, p. 248, 315.

‡ In the Llanos of Venezuela.

ourang outang*, the gibbon, the jocko or chim-
panzee, and the pongo, pursued us during five
years from the northern to the southern hemisphere; and we were every where blamed, in the
most cultivated class of society, for being the only
persons to doubt the existence of the great anthropomorphous monkey of America.   We shall
first observe, that there are certain regions,
where this belief is particularly prevalent among
the people; such are the banks of the Upper
Oroonoko †, the valley of Upar near the lake of
Maracaybo, the mountains of Santa Martha and
of Merida, the provinces of Quixos, and the
banks of the Amazon near Tomependa.   In all
these places, so distant one from the other, it is
repeated, that the *salvaje* is easily recognized by
the traces of it's feet, the toes of which are

---

* Simia satyrus.   We must not believe, notwithstanding
the assertions of almost all zoological writers, that the word
orang outang is applied exclusively in the Malay language to
the simia satyrus of Borneo.   This expression, on the contrary, means any very large monkey, that resembles man in
figure. (*Marsden, Hist. of Sumatra,* 3d edit., p. 117).   Modern zoologists have arbitrarily appropriated provincial
names to certain species y and by continuing to prefer these
names, strangely disfigured in their orthography, to the latin
systematic names, the confusion of the nomenclature has
been increased.

† Near the Rio Paruasi (see vol. iv, p. 540) a mountain
bears the name of Achi-tipuiri, which means in Tamanack
mountain of the man of the woods.

turned backward. But if there exist a monkey of a large size in the New Continent, how has it happened, that during three centuries no man worthy of belief has been able to procure the skin of one? Several hypotheses present themselves to the mind, in order to explain the source of so ancient an error or belief. Has the famous *capuchin* monkey of Esmeralda*, the canine teeth of which are more than six lines and a half long, the physiognomy much more like man's† than that of the ourang outang, and which, when irritated, rubs it's beard with it's hand, give rise to the fable of the *salvaje*? It is not so large indeed as the coaïta *(simia paniscus)*; but when seen at the top of a tree, and the head only visible, it might easily be taken for a human being. It may be also (and this opinion appears to me the most probable), that the man of the woods was one of those large bears, the footsteps of which resemble those of a man, and which is believed in every country to attack women. The animal killed in my time at the foot of the mountains of Merida, and sent, by the name of *salvaje*, to Colonel Ungaro, the governor of the province Varinas, was in fact a bear with black and smooth fur. Our fellow-traveller, Don

---

* Simia chiropotes. See my *Obs. de Zool.*, vol. i, p. 312.

† The whole of the features, the expression of the physiognomy, not the forehead.

Nicolas Sotto, had examined it closely. Did the strange idea of a plantigrade animal, the toes of which are placed as if it walked backward, take it's origin from the habit of the real savages of the woods, the Indians of the weakest and most timid tribes, of deceiving their enemies, when they enter a forest, or cross a sandy shore, by covering the traces of their feet with sand, or walking backward?

I have just expressed my doubts of the existence of an unknown species of large monkey in a continent, which appears entirely destitute of quadrumanes of the family of the ourangs, cynocephali, mandrils, and pongoes. Let us not forget, that all articles of popular belief, even the most absurd in appearance, repose on real facts, but ill observed. In treating them with disdain, the traces of a discovery may often be lost in natural philosophy, as well as in zoology. We will not then admit, with a Spanish author, that the fable of the man of the woods was invented by the artifice of Indian women, who pretended to have been carried off, when they had been long absent unknown to their husbands; we rather counsel travellers, who shall visit after us the missions of the Oroonoko, to continue our researches on the *salvaje* or *great devil* of the woods; and examine whether it be some unknown species of bear, or some very rare monkey analogous to the simia chiropotes, or simia satanas, that can have given rise to such singular tales.

★   ★   ★   ★   ★

To take in at one view the grand character of these stupendous scenes, the spectator must be stationed on the little mountain of Manimi, a granitic ridge, that rises from the savannah, north of the church of the mission, and is itself only a continuation of the steps, of which the *raudalito* of Manimi is composed. We often visited this mountain, for we were never weary of the view of this astonishing spectacle, concealed in one of the most remote corners of the Earth. Arrived at the summit of the rock, the eye suddenly takes in a sheet of foam, extending a whole mile. Enormous masses of stone, black as iron, issue from it's bosom. Some are paps grouped in pairs, like basaltic hills ; others resemble towers, strong castles, and ruined buildings. Their gloomy tint contrasts with the silvery splendour of the foam. Every rock, every islet is covered with vigorous trees, collected in clusters. At the foot of those paps, far as the eye can reach, a thick vapour is suspended over the river, and through this whitish fog the tops of the lofty palm-trees shoot up. What name shall we give to these majestic plants? I suppose them to be the *vadgiaï*, a new species of the genus oreodoxa, the trunk of which is more than eighty feet high. The leafy plume of this palm-tree had a brilliant lustre, and rises almost straight toward the sky. At every hour of the day the sheet of foam displays different aspects. Sometimes the hilly islands and the palm-trees project their broad shadows, sometimes the rays of the setting sun are refracted in the humid cloud, that shrouds the cataract. Coloured arcs are formed, and vanish and appear again alternately; light sport of the air, their images wave above the plain.

Such is the character of the landscape discovered from the top of the mountain of Manimi, which no traveller has yet described. I do not hesitate to repeat, that neither time, nor the view of the Cordilleras, nor any abode in the temperate vallies of Mexico, have effaced from my mind the powerful impression of the aspect of the cataracts. When I read a description of those places in India, that are embellished by running waters and a vigorous vegetation, my imagination retraces a sea of foam and palm-trees, the tops of which rise above a stratum of vapour. The majestic scenes of nature, like the sublime works of poetry and the arts, leave remembrances that are incessantly awakening, and through the whole of life mingle with all our feelings of what is grand and beautiful.

The calm of the atmosphere, and the tumultuous movement of the waters, produce a contrast peculiar to this zone. Here no breath of wind ever agitates the foliage, no cloud veils the splendour of the azure vault of Heaven; a great mass of light is diffused in the air, or the earth strewn with plants with glossy leaves, and on the bed of the river, which extends far as the eye can reach. This appearance surprises the traveller born in the north of Europe. The idea of wild scenery, of a torrent rushing from rock to rock, is linked in his imagination with that of a climate, where the noise of the tempest is mingled with the sound of the cataracts; and where in a gloomy and misty day, sweeping clouds seem to descend into the valley, and rest upon the tops of the pines. The landscape of the tropics in the low regions of the continents has a peculiar physiognomy, something of greatness and repose, which it preserves even where one of the elements is struggling with invincible obstacles. Near the equator, hurricanes and tempests belong to islands only, to deserts destitute of plants, and to those spots, where parts of the atmosphere repose upon surfaces, from which the radiation of heat is very different.

★   ★   ★   ★   ★

We left the mission at a late hour in the morning, and continued to go up the Atabapo for five miles; then, instead of following that river to it's source in the east, where it bears the name of Atacavi, we entered the Rio Temi. Before we reached it's confluence, a granitic hummock, that rises on the western bank, near the mouth of the Guasacavi, fixed our attention; it is called the *Rock of the Guahiba woman**, or the Rock of the Mother, *Piedra de la Madre.* We inquired the cause of so singular a denomination. Father Zea could not satisfy our curiosity; but some weeks after, another missionary, one of the predecessors of this ecclesiastic, whom we found settled at San Fernando as president of the missions, related to us an event, which I recorded in my journal, and which excited in our minds the most painful feelings. If, in these solitary scenes, man scarcely leaves behind him any trace of his existence, it is doubly humiliating for a European to see perpetuated by the name of a rock, by one of those imperishable monu-

---

* *Piedra de la Guahiba.*

ments of nature, the remembrance of the moral degradation of our species, and the contrast between the virtue of a savage, and the barbarism of civilized man!

In 1797 the missionary of San Fernando had led his Indians to the banks of the Rio Guaviare, on one of those hostile incursions, which are prohibited alike by religion and the Spanish laws. They found in an Indian hut a Guahiba mother with three children, two of whom were still infants. They were occupied in preparing the flour of cassava. Resistance was impossible; the father was gone to fish, and the mother tried in vain to flee with her children. Scarcely had she reached the savannah, when she was seized by the Indians of the mission, who go to *hunt men*, like the Whites and the Negroes in Africa. The mother and her children were bound, and dragged to the bank of the river. The monk, seated in his boat, waited the issue of an expedition, of which he partook not the danger. Had the mother made too violent a resistance, the Indians would have killed her, for every thing is permitted when they go to the conquest of souls (*à la conquista espiritual*), and it is children in particular they seek to capture, in order to treat them in the mission as *poitos*, or slaves of the Christians. The prisoners were carried to San Fernando in the hope, that the mother would be unable to find her way back to her home by land.   Far from those children who had accompanied their father on the day in which she had been carried off, this unhappy woman shewed signs of the deepest despair. She attempted to take back to her family the children, who had been snatched away by the missionary; and fled with them repeatedly from the village of San Fernando, but the Indians never failed to seize her anew; and the missionary, after having caused her to be mercilessly beaten, took the cruel resolution of separating the mother from the two children, who had been carried off with her.   She was conveyed alone toward the missions of the Rio Negro, going up the Atabapo.   Slightly bound, she was seated at the bow of the boat, ignorant of the fate that awaited her; but she judged by the direction of the Sun, that she was removing farther and farther from her hut and her native country.   She succeeded in breaking her bonds, threw herself into the water, and swam to the left bank of the Atabapo.   The current carried her to a shelf of rock, which bears her name to this day.   She landed, and took shelter in the woods, but the president of the missions ordered the Indians to row to the shore, and follow the traces of the Guahiba.   In the evening she was brought back.   Stretched upon the rock *(la Piedra de la Madre)* a cruel punishment was inflicted on her with those straps of manatee leather, which serve for whips in that country, and with which the alcades are always furnished. This unhappy woman, her hands tied behind her back with strong stalks of *mavacure*, was then dragged to the mission of Javita.

She was there thrown into one of the caravanseras that are called *Casa del Rey*. It was the rainy season, and the night was profoundly dark. Forests till then believed to be impenetrable separated the mission of Javita from that of San Fernando, which was twenty-five leagues distant in a straight line. No other path is known than that of the rivers; no man ever attempted to go by land from one village to another, were they only a few leagues apart. But such difficulties do not stop a mother, who is separated from her children. Her children are at San Fernando de Atabapo; she must find them again, she must execute her project of delivering them from the hands of Christians, of bringing them back to their father on the banks of the Guaviare. The Guahiba was carelessly guarded in the caravansera. Her arms being wounded, the Indians of Javita had loosened her bonds, unknown to the missionary and the alcades. She succeeded by the help of her teeth in breaking them entirely; disappeared during the night; and at the fourth rising Sun was seen at the mission of San Fernando, hovering around the hut where her children were confined.   "What that woman performed," added the missionary, who gave us this sad narrative, "the most robust Indian would not have ventured to undertake.   She traversed the woods at a season, when the sky is constantly covered with clouds, and the Sun during whole days appears but for a few minutes.   Did the course of the waters direct her way? The inundations of the rivers forced her to go far from the banks of the main stream, through the midst of woods where the movement of the waters is almost imperceptible.   How often must she have been stopped by the thorny lianas, that form a network around the trunks they entwine! How often must she have swam across the rivulets, that run into the Atabapo! This unfortunate woman was asked how she had sustained herself during four days? She said, that exhausted with fatigue, she could find no other nourishment than those great black ants called *vachacos*, which climb the trees in long bands, to suspend on them their resinous nests."   We pressed the missionary to tell us, whether the Guahiba had peacefully enjoyed the happiness of remaining with her children; and if any repentance had followed this excess of cruelty.   He would not satisfy our curiosity; but at our return from the Rio Negro we learnt, that the Indian mother was not allowed time to cure her wounds, but was again separated from her children, and sent to one of the missions of the Upper Oroonoko. There she died, refusing all kind of nourishment, as the savages do in great calamities.

Such is the remembrance annexed to this fatal rock, to the *Piedra de la Madre*. In the relation of my travels I feel no propensity to pause at a picture of individual calamity, of evils which are every where frequent, where there are masters and slaves, civilized Europeans living with people in a state of barbarism, and priests executing the plenitude of arbitrary power on men ignorant and without defence. Historian of the countries through which I passed, I generally confine myself to pointing out what is imperfect, or fatal to humanity, in their civil or religious institutions. If I have dwelt longer on the *Rock of the Guahiba*, it was to display an affecting instance of maternal tenderness in a race of people so long calumniated ; and because I thought some benefit might accrue from publishing a fact, which I had from the monks of St. Francis, and which proves how much the system of the missions calls for the care of the legislator.

★   ★   ★   ★   ★

The morning was cool and beautiful. We had been confined thirty-six days in a narrow boat, so unstable, that it would have been over-set by any person rising imprudently from his seat, without warning the rowers to preserve her trim, by leaning on the opposite side. We had suffered severely from the sting of insects, but we had withstood the insalubrity of the climate; we had passed without accident the great number of falls of water and bars, that impede the navigation of the rivers, and often render it more dangerous than long voyages by sea. After all we had endured, I may be permitted, perhaps, to speak of the satisfaction we felt in having reached the tributary streams of the Amazon, having passed the isthmus that separates two great systems of rivers, and in being sure of having fulfilled the most important object of our voyage, the determining astronomically the course of that arm of the Oroonoko, which falls into the Rio Negro, and of which the existence has been alternately proved and denied during half a century. In proportion as we draw near to an object we have long had in view, it's interest seems to augment. The uninhabited banks of the Cassiquiare, covered with forests, without memorials of times past, then occupied my imagination, as do now the banks of the Euphrates, or the Oxus, celebrated in the annals of civilized nations. In that interior part of the New Continent we almost accustomed ourselves to regard men as not being essential to the order of nature. The earth is loaded with plants, and nothing impedes their free development. An immense layer of mould manifests the uninterrupted action of organic powers. The crocodiles and the boas are masters of the river; the jaguar, the pecari, the dante, and the monkeys, traverse the forest without fear, and without danger; there they dwell as in an ancient inheritance. This aspect of animated nature, in which man is nothing, has something in it strange and sad.   To this we reconcile ourselves with difficulty on the ocean, and amid the sands of Africa; though in these scenes, where nothing recalls to mind our fields, our woods, and our streams, we are less astonished at the vast solitude through which we pass.   Here, in a fertile country adorned with eternal verdure, we seek in vain the traces of the power of man; we seem to be transported into a world different from that which gave us birth.   These impressions are so much the more powerful, in proportion as they are of longer duration.   A soldier, who had spent his whole life in the missions of the Upper Oroonoko, slept with us on the bank of the river.   He was an intelligent man, who, during a calm and serene night, pressed me with questions on the magnitude of the stars, on the inhabitants of the Moon, on a thousand subjects of which I was as ignorant as himself.   Being unable by my answers to satisfy his curiosity, he said to me in a firm tone; " with respect to men, I believe there are no more above, than you would have found, if you had gone by land from Javita to Cassiquiare.   I think I see in the stars, as here, a plain covered with grass, and a forest (*mucho monte*) traversed by a river." In citing these words, I paint the impression produced by the monotonous aspect of those solitary regions. May this monotony not be found to extend itself to the journal of our navigation, and tire the reader accustomed to the description of the scenes and historical memorials of the ancient continent!

★　　★　　★　　★　　★

The most remote part of the valley is covered by a thick forest. In this shady and solitary spot, on the declivity of a steep mountain, the cavern of Ataruipe opens itself; it is less a cavern than a jutting rock, in which the waters have scooped a vast hollow, when, in the ancient revolutions of our planet, they attained that height *. We soon reckoned in this tomb of a whole extinct tribe near six hundred skeletons well preserved, and so regularly placed, that it would have been difficult to make an error in their number. Every skeleton reposes in a sort of basket, made of the petioles of the palm-tree.

* I saw no vein, no *four* filled with crystal. (See vol. iii, p. 138.) The decomposition of granitic rocks, and their separation into large masses, dispersed in the plains and valleys under the form of *blocks* and of *balls* with concentric layers, appear to favor the enlarging of these natural excavations, which resemble real caverns.

These baskets, which the natives call *mapires*, have the form of a square bag. Their size is proportioned to the age of the dead; there are some for infants cut off at the moment of their birth. We saw them from ten inches to three feet four inches long, the skeletons in them being bent together. They are all ranged near each other, and are so entire, that not a rib, or a phalanx is wanting. The bones have been prepared in three different manners, either whitened in the air and the sun; dyed red with onoto, a colouring matter extracted from the bixa orellana; or, like real mummies, varnished with odoriferous resins, and enveloped in leaves of the heliconia or of the plantain tree. The Indians related to us, that the fresh corpse is placed in damp ground, in order that the flesh may be consumed by degrees; some months after, it is taken out, and the flesh remaining on the bones is scraped off with sharp stones. Several hordes in Guyana still observe this custom. Earthen vases half-baked are found near the *mapires*, or baskets. They appear to contain the bones of the same family. The largest of these vases, or funeral urns, are three feet high, and five feet and a half long. Their colour is greenish gray; and their oval form is sufficiently pleasing to the eye. The handles are made in the shape of crocodiles, or serpents; the edge is bordered with meanders, labyrinths, and real *grecques,* in straight lines variously combined. Such paintings are found in every zone, among nations the most remote from each other, either with respect to the spot which they occupy on the Globe, or to the degree of civilization which they have attained. The inhabitants of the little mission of Maypures still execute them on their commonest pottery*; they decorate the bucklers of the Otaheiteans, the fishing implements of the Eskimoes, the walls of the Mexican palace of Mitla †, and the vases of ancient Greece. Every where a rhythmic repetition of the same forms flatters the eye, as the cadenced repetition of sounds soothes the ear. Analogies founded on the internal nature of our feelings, on the natural dispositions of our intellect, are not calculated to throw light on the filiation and the ancient connections of nations.

We could not acquire any precise idea of the period, to which the origin of the *mapires* and the painted vases, contained in the ossuary cavern of Ataruipe, can be traced. The greater part seemed not to be more than a century old; but it may be supposed, that, sheltered from all humidity, under the influence of a uniform tem-

* See above, chap. xxi, p. 154.

† See my *Views of the Cordilleras, and Monuments of the Ancient Inhabitants of America,* Pl. 50. [Vol. ii, English edition, or xiv of the present work, p. 158, Pl. 19.]

perature, the preservation of these articles would
be no less perfect, if it dated from a period
far more remote.   A tradition circulates among
the Guahiboes, that the warlike Atures, pursued
by the Caribbees, escaped to the rocks that
rise in the middle of the Great Cataracts ; and
there that nation, heretofore so numerous, became gradually extinct, as well as it's language*.
The last families of the Atures still existed in
1767, in the time of the missionary Gili.   At
the period of our voyage an old parrot was
shown at Maypures, of which the inhabitants
related, and the fact is worthy of observation,
that, " they did not understand what it said,
because it spoke the language of the Atures."

We opened, to the great concern of our guides,
several *mapires*, in order to examine attentively
the form of the skulls; they all displayed the
characteristics of the American race, with
the exception of two or three, which approached indubitably to the Caucasian.   We have
observed above†, that in the middle of the Cataracts, in the most inaccessible spots, cases are
found strengthened with iron bands, and filled
with European tools, vestiges of clothes, and glass
trinkets.   These articles, which have given rise
to the most absurd reports of treasures hidden

---

* See above, chap. xx, p. 13 ; and chap. xxi, p. 144.
† See above, chap. xxi, p. 121.

by the Jesuits, probably belonged to Portugueze traders, who had penetrated into these savage countries. Now may we suppose, that the skulls of European race, which we saw mingled with the skeletons of the natives, and preserved with the same care, were the remains of some Portugueze travellers, who had died of sickness, or had been killed in battle? The aversion which the natives affect for whatever is not of their own race renders this hypothesis little probable. Perhaps fugitive mestizoes of the missions of the Meta and Apure may have come and settled near the Cataracts, marrying women of the tribe of the Atures. Such mixed marriages sometimes take place in this zone, though they are more rare than in Canada, and in the whole of North America, where hunters of European origin unite themselves with savages, assume their habits, and sometimes acquire great political influence.

We took several skulls, the skeleton of a child of six or seven years old, and two of full-grown men of the nation of the Atures, from the cavern of Ataruipe. All these bones, partly painted red, partly varnished with odoriferous resins, were placed in the baskets (*mapires* or *canastos*), which we have just described. They made almost the whole load of a mule; and as we knew the superstitious aversion of the Indians for dead bodies, when they have given them sepulture, we had carefully enveloped the *canastos* in mats recently woven. Unfortunately for us, the penetration of the Indians, and the extreme quickness of their senses, rendered all our precautions useless. Wherever we stopped, in the missions of the Caribbees, amid the Llanos, between Angostura and Nueva Barcelona, the natives assembled round our mules to admire the monkeys which we had purchased at the Oroonoko. These good people had scarcely touched our baggage, when they announced the approaching death of the beast of burden, "that carried the dead." In vain we told them, that they were deceived in their conjectures; and that the baskets contained the bones of crocodiles and manatees: they persisted in repeating, that they smelt the resin, that surrounded the skeletons, and "that they were their *old relations*." We were obliged to make the monks interpose their authority, in order to conquer the aversion of the natives, and procure for us a change of mules.

One of the skulls, which we took from the cavern of Ataruipe, has appeared in the fine work published by my old master, Blumenbach, on the varieties of the human species. The skeletons of the Indians were lost on the coast of Africa, together with a considerable part of our collections, in a shipwreck, in which perished our friend and fellow-traveller, Fray Juan Gonzales*, a young monk of the order of Saint Francis.

★ ★ ★ ★ ★

The population of the New Continent yet surpasses but little that of France or Germany. It doubles in the United States in twenty-three or twenty-five years; and at Mexico, even under the government of the mother country, it doubles in forty or forty-five years. Without indulging too flattering hopes of the future, it may be admitted, that in less than a century and a half the population of America will equal that of Europe. This noble rivalship in civilization, and the arts of industry and commerce, far from impoverishing the ancient continent, which has been so often prognosticated, at the expense of the new, will augment the wants of the consumer, the mass of productive labour, and the activity of exchange. No doubt after the great revolutions, which human societies undergo, the public fortune, which is the common patrimony of civilization, is found differently divided among the nations of the two worlds : but by degrees the equilibrium is restored; and it is a fatal, I had

* See vol. iii, chap. 11, p. 350.

almost said an impious prejudice, to consider the growing prosperity of any other part of our planet as a calamity for ancient Europe. The independance of the colonies will not contribute to isolate them from the old civilized nations, but will rather bring them closer. Commerce tends to unite what a jealous policy has long separated. It may be added, that it is the nature of civilization to go forward, without becoming extinct for this reason in the spot that gave it birth. It's progression from east to west, from Asia to Europe, proves nothing against this axiom. A clear light preserves the same splendor, even when it illumines a wider space. Intellectual cultivation, that fertile source of national wealth, communicates itself from step to step, and extends itself without being displaced. It's movement is not a migration : and if it appear such to us in the east, it is because barbarous hordes have seized upon Egypt, Asia Minor, and that Greece, heretofore free, the forsaken cradle of the civilization of our ancestors.

The barbarism of nations is the consequence of the oppression exercised either by interior despotism, or foreign conquest ; and it is always accompanied by a progressive impoverishment, a diminution of the public fortune. Free and powerful institutions, adapted to the interests of all, remove these dangers ; and the growing civilization of the world, the rivalship of labour, and that of trade, are not the ruin of states, the welfare of which flows from a natural source. Productive and commercial Europe will profit from the new order of things in Spanish America, as it would profit by the increase of it's consumption, from events that might put an end to barbarism in Greece, or the northern coast of Africa, and in other countries subjected to the tyranny of the Ottomans. What most menaces the prosperity of the ancient continent is the prolongation of those intestine struggles, which stop production, and diminish at the same time the number and wants of the consumers. This struggle, begun in Spanish America six years after my departure, is drawing gradually to an end. We shall soon see independent nations, ruled by very different forms of government; but united by the remembrance of a common origin, the uniformity of language, and the wants to which civilization gives rise, inhabit the two shores of the Atlantic. It may be said, that the immense progress of the art of navigation has narrowed the basin of the seas. The Atlantic Ocean already appears to us in the form of a narrow channel, which as little removes the New World from the commercial states of Europe, as the basin of the Mediterranean, in the infancy of navigation, removed the Greeks of Peloponnesus from those of Ionia, Sicily, and the Cyrenaic region.

★   ★   ★   ★   ★

The aspect of the Havannah, at the entrance of the port, is one of the gayest and most picturesque on the shore of Equinoxial America, north of the equator.   This spot, celebrated by travellers of all nations, has not the luxury of vegetation that decorates the banks of the river Guayaquil, nor the wild majesty of the rocky coast of Rio Janeiro, two ports of the southern hemisphere; but the graces which in those climates embellish the scenes of cultivated nature, are here mingled with the majesty of vegetable forms, and the organic vigour that characterizes the torrid zone.   Amidst a variety of soothing impressions, the European forgets the dangers that menace him in the populous cities of the Caribbean islands; he seeks to seize the different elements of a vast landscape; to contemplate the fortified castles that crown the rocks on the east of the port; the inland basin, surrounded by villages and farms; those palms that rise to a majestic height; and that city, half concealed by a forests of masts and the sails of vessels.   In entering the port of the Havannah you pass between the fortress of Morro *(Castillo de los Santos Reyes,)* and the fort of *San Salvador de la Punta :* the opening is only from one hundred and seventy to two hundred toises wide. It preserves this breadth during three-fifths of a mile. Having passed this narrow entrance, and left on the north the fine castle of *San Carlos de la Cabana*, and the *Casa Blanca*, we reach a basin in the form of a trefoil, of which the great axis, stretching from S.S.W. to N.N.E., is two miles and one-fifth long. This basin communicates with three creeks, that of Regla, Guanavacoa, and Atares, of which the last has some springs of fresh water. The town of the Havannah, surrounded by walls, forms a promontory bounded on the south by the arsenal, and on the north by the fort of la Punta. Beyond the vestiges of some vessels sunk in the shoals of la Luz, we no longer find eight to ten, but five to six fathoms of water. The castles of *Santo Domingo de Atares* and *San Carlos del Principe*, defend the town towards the west ; they are distant from the interior wall on the land side, the one 660 toises, the other 1240. The intermediate space is filled by the suburbs (*arrabales* or *barrios extra muros*) of the Horcon, Jesus Maria, Guadaloupe, and Senor de la Salad, which from year to year contract the Field of Mars *(Campo de Marte)*. The great edifices of the Havannah, the cathedral, the *Casa del Govierno*, the house of the commandant of the marine, the arsenal, the *Correo* or General Post Office, and the factory of tobacco, are less remarkable for their beauty than the solidity of their construction ; the streets are for the most part narrow, and the greater number are not paved. The stones coming from Vera Cruz, and their transport being very expensive, the idea was conceived a short time before my voyage, of joining great trunks of trees together, as is done in Germany and Russia, when dykes are constructed across marshy places. This project was soon abandoned, and travellers recently arrived saw with surprize the fine trunks of *Cahoba* (mahogany) sunk in the mud of the Havannah. At the time of my stay, few towns of Spanish America presented, from the want of a good police, a more hideous aspect. People walked in mud up to the knee ; and the multitude of caleches or *volantes*, the characteristic equipage of the Havannah, the carts loaded with cases of sugar, the porters who elbow the passengers, rendered walking disagreeable and humiliating. The smell of *tasajo*, or meat ill dried, often poisons the houses, and the winding streets ; but it appears that of late the police has interposed, and that a sensible improvement has taken place in the cleanliness of the streets; that the houses are more airy, and that the *Calle de los Mercadares* presents a fine aspect. Here, as in the oldest towns of Europe, an ill-traced plan of streets can only be slowly amended.

Mawe:
Travels in the Interior of Brazil

John Mawe, *Travels in the Interior of Brazil, Particularly in the Gold and Diamond Districts of that Country, by Authority of the Prince Regent of Portugal. Including a Voyage to the Rio de la Plata, and an Historical Sketch of the Revolution of Buenos Aires* (London: Longman, 1812), pp. 219–26.

The Derbyshire mineralogist John Mawe (1764–1829) spent much of his earlier life at sea, but in the 1790s set himself up as a mineral dealer collecting specimens for the King of Spain's cabinet. In 1802 he publishing a technical treatise entitled *The Mineralogy of Derbyshire*. Two years later he set out for South America, but his journey to Río de la Plata was interrupted by the outbreak of war between Britain and Spain, and he found himself blockaded at Cadiz. In March 1805 he finally arrived in Montevideo, only to find himself locked up as an English spy. He was freed when Montevideo fell into the hands of General Beresford and the invading British expeditionary force; he then accompanied General Whitelock's army in its disastrous bid to capture Buenos Aires. On returning to Montevideo after the humiliating British defeat, he purchased a ship and sailed for Brazil, where, upon presenting a letter of introduction from San Domingo de Souza Coutinho in London, he was well received by the Portuguese regent Dom Pedro, currently in exile with the royal court in Brazil.

In 1809–10 Mawe was granted permission to visit the Brazilian interior and the rich Minas Gerais mines. Along with Henry Koster (author of *Travels in Brazil*), Mawe was the first foreigner to be entrusted with such a commission in a country the interior of which was virtually unknown to the outside world. The Portuguese-language newspaper in London naturally accused him of diamond smuggling and espionage. Mawe's official task was to ascertain the quantity of gold and diamonds which remained to be exploited; his conclusion was that both were well-nigh exhausted and, although the industry might be revitalised, the miners would be better off turning their present energies to cattle farming. In 1811 Mawe returned to England, setting up as a commercial mineralogist and opening a shop in the Strand. The following year he published his *Travels in the Interior of Brazil*, capitalising not only on the public's interest in unknown Brazil but also on his eyewitness account of the Rio de la Plata humiliation in 1806–7. As can be seen from this extract describing the diamond mines on the river Jigitonhonha and the harsh labour regime imposed on the black miners, Mawe wrote in the bald, descriptive style of the professional who travelled on business rather than for pleasure. Mawe typified the sort of artisan mineralogist whose interactions with the polite world of the Geological Society helped lay the foundation of the modern science of geology; he is also remembered as one of the first and last foreign travellers to describe the Brazilian interior on the eve of the colony's independence from Portugal.

CHAP. XIII.

Visit to the Diamond Works on the River Jigitonhonha. — General Description of the Works. — Mode of Washing. — Return to Tejuco. — Visit to the Treasury. — Excursion to Rio Pardo. — Miscellaneous Remarks.

THE continual fatigues, and want of accommodation on the journey, had rendered me very unwell, and I was therefore desirous of resting a week at Tejuco before I proceeded to the diamond mines ; but, learning that I had been expected for the last two or three days, I sent one of my soldiers up to the house of Mr. Fernando de Camara, the governor, to announce my arrival, and to state that I was prevented by indisposition from personally paying my respects to him. He immediately came with a few friends to visit me, gave me a most hearty welcome to Tejuco, and staid with me at least three hours. I delivered to him my public and private letters, passports, and other credentials, which he perused with great satisfaction, observing to the Ouvidor and his friends, that I possessed the same privileges which they did, having permission from the court to see every place I wished, which they were directed to shew me. He then told me that, in expectation of my arrival, he had delayed a journey to the greatest of the diamond works, called Mandanga, situated on the river Jigitonhonha, which employs about a thousand negroes, and on particular occasions double that number. He was desirous that I should see this great work with all the machinery in operation, which would be very speedily removed, the late rains having swoln the river so much as to render working more, impracticable. He therefore kindly invited me to breakfast at his house on the following morning, when he would have all in readiness for a journey of about thirty miles to the place above-mentioned.

At an early hour I arose ; and, though so unwell as to be scarcely more than half alive, I could not resist the favourable opportunity now offered me of gratifying the curiosity which had so long occupied my mind, by visiting the diamond mines, in company with the principal officer in the administration of them, who was therefore qualified to furnish me with the amplest information.   A fine horse was waiting for me at the door, and I rode up to the house of the governor, who introduced me to his amiable lady, daughters, and family, with whom I had the honour to take breakfast.   Several officers of the diamond establishment arrived on horseback to accompany us, their presence being required on this occasion.

At nine o'clock we set out, and crossed the ravine, watered by the small rivulet of St. Francisco, which separates Tejuco from the opposite mountains.   The road was very rough and uneven, continually ascending or descending mountains of considerable extent, the strata of which were grit alternating with micaceous schistus, and presenting an immense quantity of rude masses, composed of grit and rounded quartz, forming a loose and friable kind of pudding-stone.   The country appeared almost destitute of wood, presenting occasionally a few poor shrubs ;   there were no cattle to be seen, yet some of the tracts would certainly maintain sheep in great numbers.   Having halted at a place about half way, we descended a very steep mountain, full a mile in the declivity, and entered a ravine where we crossed a very good wooden bridge over the river Jigitonhonha, which is larger than the Derwent at Derby.   We rode along its margin, where the land appears much richer, presenting a good vegetable soil covered with underwood ; and, proceeding about a league, arrived at the famed place called Mandanga. The habitations, which are about one hundred in number, are built detached, and are generally of a circular form, with very high thatched roofs, like African huts, but much larger.   The walls are formed of upright stakes, interwoven with small branches and coated with clay inside and out.   The houses of the officers are of the

A View of the manner in which the bed of the River Jigitonhonha is laid dry by an Aqueduct, in order to search for Diamonds.

same materials but of much more convenient form, and white-washed within. Near some of the houses we observed inclosures for gardens, which, in some degree, enlivened the prospect, and gave an air of comfort to these rude and simple dwellings.

I remained here five days, during which 1 was occupied in viewing and examining various parts of the works, of which I shall here attempt to give a general description.

This rich river, formed by the junction of a number of streams which will be hereafter noted, is as wide as the Thames at Windsor; and in general from three to nine feet deep. The part now in working is a curve or elbow, from which the current is diverted into a canal cut across the tongue of land round which it winds, the river being stopped just below the head of the canal by an embankment formed of several thousand bags of sand. This is a work of considerable magnitude, and requires the co-operation of all the negroes to complete it; for, the river being wide and not very shallow, and also occasionally subject to overflows, they have to make the embankment so strong as to resist the pressure of the water, admitting it to rise four or five feet.

The deeper parts of the channel of the river are laid dry by means of large caissons, or chain-pumps, worked by a water-wheel. The mud is then carried off, and the cascalhão is dug up and removed to a convenient place for washing. This labour was, until lately, performed by the negroes, who carried the cascalhão in gamellas on their heads, but Mr. Camara has formed two inclined planes about one hundred yards in length, along which carts are drawn by a large water-wheel, divided into two parts, the ladles or buckets of which are so constructed that the rotatory motion may be altered by changing the current of water from one side to the other; this wheel, by means of a rope made of untanned hides, works two carts, one of which descends empty on one inclined plane, while the other, loaded with cascalhão, is drawn to the top of the other, where it falls into a cradle, empties itself, and descends in its turn. At a work called Canjeca, formerly of great importance, about a mile up the river on the opposite side, there are three cylindrical engines for drawing the cascalhão, like those used in the mining country of Derbyshire, and also rail-ways over some un-even ground. This was the first and only machinery of consequence which I saw in the diamond district, and there appear many obstacles to the general introduction of it. Timber, when wanted of large size, has to be fetched a distance of one hundred miles at a very heavy expence; there are few persons competent to the construction of machines, and the workmen dislike to make them, fearing that this is only part of a general plan for superseding manual labour.

The stratum of cascalhão consists of the same materials with that in the gold district. On many parts, by the edge of the river, are large conglomerate masses of rounded pebbles cemented by oxide of iron, which sometimes envelop gold and diamonds. They calculate on getting as much cascalhão in the dry season as will occupy all their hands during the months which are more subject to rain. When carried from the bed of the river whence it is dug, it is laid in heaps containing apparently from five to fifteen tons each.

Water is conveyed from a distance, and is distributed to the various parts of the works by means of aqueducts, constructed with great ingenuity and skill. The method of washing for diamonds at this place is as follows: — A shed is erected in the form of a parallelogram, twenty-five or thirty yards long and about fifteen wide, consisting of upright posts which support a roof thatched with long grass. Down the middle of the area of this shed a current of water is conveyed through a canal covered with strong planks, on which the cascalhão is laid two or three feet thick. On the other side of the area is a flooring of planks, from four to five yards long, imbedded in clay, extending the whole length of the shed, and having a slope from the canal, of three or four inches to a yard. This flooring is divided into about twenty compartments or troughs, each about three feet wide, by means of planks placed on their edge. The upper ends of all these troughs (here called canoes) communicate with the canal, and are so formed that water is admitted into them between two planks that are about an inch separate. Through this opening the current falls about six inches into the trough, and may be directed to any part of it, or stopped at pleasure by means of a small quantity of clay. For instance, sometimes water is required only from one corner of the aperture, then the remaining part is stopped; sometimes it is wanted from the centre, then the extremes are stopped; and sometimes only a gentle rill is wanted, then the clay is applied accordingly. Along the lower ends of the troughs a small channel is dug to carry off the water.

On the heap of cascalhão, at equal distances, are placed three high chairs * for the officers or overseers. After they are seated, the negroes † enter the troughs, each provided with a rake of a peculiar form and short handle, with which he rakes into the trough about fifty or eighty pounds weight of cascalhão. The water being then let in upon it, the cascalhão is spread abroad and continually raked up to the head of the trough, so as to be kept in constant motion. This operation is performed for the space of a quarter of an hour; the water then begins to run clearer, having washed the earthy particles away, the gravel-like matter is raked up to the end of the trough; after the current flows away quite clear, the largest stones are thrown out, and afterwards those of inferior size, then the whole is examined with great care for diamonds ‡. When a negro finds one, he immediately stands upright and claps his hands, then extends them,

---

* In order to insure the vigilance of the overseers, these chairs are constructed without backs or any other support on which a person can recline.

† The negroes employed in these works are the property of individuals, who let them to hire at the daily rate of three vengtems of gold, equal to about eight-pence, Government supplying them with victuals. Every officer of the establishment is allowed the privilege of having a certain number of negroes employed.

‡ The negroes are constantly attending to the cascalhão from the very commencement of the washings, and frequently find diamonds before this last operation.

holding the gem between his fore-finger and thumb; an overseer receives it from him, and deposits it in a gamella or bowl, suspended from the centre of the structure, half full of water. In this vessel all the diamonds found in the course of the day are placed, and at the close of work are taken out and delivered to the principal officer, who, after they have been weighed, registers the particulars in a book kept for that purpose.

When a negro is so fortunate as to find a diamond of the weight of an octavo (17½ carats), much ceremony takes place; he is crowned with a wreath of flowers and carried in procession to the administrator, who gives him his freedom, by paying his owner for it. He also receives a present of new clothes, and is permitted to work on his own account. When a stone of eight or ten carats is found, the negro receives two new shirts, a complete new suit, with a hat and a handsome knife. For smaller stones of trivial amount proportionate premiums are given. During my stay at Tejuco a stone of 16½ carats was found: it was pleasing to see the anxious desire manifested by the officers that it might prove heavy enough to entitle the poor negro to his freedom, and when on being delivered and weighed, it proved only a carat short of the requisite weight, all seemed to sympathize in his disappointment.

Many precautions are taken to prevent the negroes from embezzling diamonds. Although they work in a bent position, and consequently never know whether the overseers are watching them or not, yet it is easy for them to omit gathering any which they see, and to place them in a corner of the trough for the purpose of secreting them at leisure hours, to prevent which they are frequently changed while the operation is going on. A word of command being given by the overseers, they instantly move into each other's troughs, so that no opportunity of collusion can take place. If a negro be suspected of having swallowed a diamond, he is confined in a strong room until the fact can be ascertained. Formerly the punishment inflicted on a negro for smuggling diamonds was confiscation of his person to the state : but it being thought too hard for the owner to suffer for the offence of his servant, the penalty has been commuted for personal imprisonment and chastisement. This is a much lighter punishment than that which their owners or any white man would suffer for a similar offence.

There is no particular regulation respecting the dress of the negroes : they work in the clothes most suitable to the nature of their employment, generally in a waistcoat and a pair of drawers, and not naked, as some travellers have stated. Their hours of labour are from a little before sun-rise until sun-set, half an hour being allowed for breakfast, and two hours at noon. While washing they change their posture as often as they please, which is very necessary, as the work requires them to place their feet on the edges of the trough, and to stoop considerably. This posture is particularly prejudicial to young growing negroes, as it renders them in-kneed. Four or five times during the day they all rest, when snuff, of which they are very fond, is given to them.

The negroes are formed into working parties, called troops, containing two hundred each, under the direction of an administrator and inferior officers. Each troop has a clergyman and a surgeon to attend it. With respect to the subsistence of the negroes, although the present governor has in some degree improved it by allowing a daily portion of fresh beef, which was not allowed by his predecessors, yet I am sorry to observe that it is still poor and scanty ; and in other respects they are more hardly dealt with than those of any other establishment which I visited : notwithstanding this, the owners are all anxious to get their negroes into the service, doubtless from sinister motives, of which more will be said hereafter.

The officers are liberally paid, and live in a style of considerable elegance, which a stranger would not be led to expect in so remote a place. Our tables were daily covered with a profusion of excellent viands, served up on fine Wedgewood ware, and the state of their household generally corresponded with this essential part of it.

G G

They were ever ready to assist me in my examination of the works, and freely gave me all the necessary information respecting them.

Having detailed the process of washing for diamonds, I proceed to a general description of the situations in which they are found. The flat pieces of ground on each side the river are equally rich throughout their extent, and hence the officers are enabled to calculate the value of an unworked place by comparison with the amount found on working in the part adjoining. These known places are left in reserve, and trial is made of more uncertain grounds. The following observation I often heard from the intendant: " That piece of ground" (speaking of an unworked flat by the side of the river) " will yield me ten thousand carats of diamonds whenever we shall be required to get them in the regular course of working, or when, on any particular occasion, an order from Government arrives, demanding an extraordinary and immediate supply."

The substances accompanying diamonds, and considered good indications of them, are bright bean-like iron ore, a slaty flint-like substance, approaching Lydian stone, of fine texture, black oxide of iron in great quantities, rounded bits of blue quartz, yellow crystal, and other materials entirely different from any thing known to be produced in the adjacent mountains. Diamonds are by no means peculiar to the beds of rivers or deep ravines ; they have been found in cavities and water-courses on the summits of the most lofty mountains.

I had some conversation with the officers respecting the matrix of the diamond, not a vestige of which could I trace. They informed me that they often found diamonds cemented in pudding-stone, accompanied with grains of gold, but that they always broke them out, as they could not enter them in the treasury, or weigh them with matter adhering to them. I obtained a mass of pudding-stone, apparently of very recent formation, cemented by ferruginous matter enveloping many grains of gold ; and likewise a few pounds weight of the cascalhão in its unwashed state.

Waterton:
Wanderings in South America

Charles Waterton, *Wanderings in South America, in the Years 1812, 16, 20 and 24. With Original Instructions for the Perfect Preservation of Birds, etc., for Cabinets of Natural History* (London: J. Mawman, 1825), pp. 15–29, 58–65, 174–80.

Charles Waterton (1782–65), a travelling naturalist, taxidermist and eccentric, was a member of an ancient Catholic family whose seat was at Walton Hall in Yorkshire, which he converted into the first bird sanctuary in Britain, erecting high walls around it and banning the use of guns within the precincts; his remains are interred in its grounds. In 1796–1800 he was educated at the Jesuit public school at Stoneyhurst, Lancashire. He proceeded to travel in Spain, then embarked on a visit to his family's sugar plantations in Demerara, Dutch Guyana (which became part of British Guyana in 1815). Between 1804 and 1813 he managed the estates and pursued his growing fascination with the fauna of South America. In 1812 he mounted his first expedition 'through the wilds of Demerara and Essequibo, a part of ci-devant Dutch Guiana', with the intention of collecting curare (or 'wourali'), a lethal poison used in hunting by the indigenous groups of the region, thought to be a possible cure for hydrophobia and other ailments. Life in the rainforest suited the eccentric and ascetic Yorkshireman. 'I never go encumbered with many clothes', he wrote; 'A thin flannel waistcoat under a check shirt, a pair of trousers and a hat were all my wardrobe: shoes and stockings I seldom had on … I eat moderately, and never drink wine, spirits, or fermented liquors in any climate. This abstemiousness has ever proved a faithful friend' (p. 121).

Nevertheless, a fever contracted on this expedition forced him to return to Britain, and in 1813 he declined an offer from Lord Bathurst to explore Madagascar. In March 1816 he embarked at Liverpool for Pernambuco on the coast of Brazil, proceeding on to Cayenne and Demerara once again, where he spent six months in the jungle. His third South American journey was made in 1820. Arriving in Guyana, he journeyed up the Demerara to the abandoned house of his friend Charles Edmonstone of Cardross, where he established a base for collecting natural specimens. Waterton, assisted by his friend the naturalist Sir Joseph Banks, had devised a new method of preserving animals. Instead of the normal procedure of mounting the dissected carcass on an internal frame, thereby impeding the natural shrinking of the animal's skin and resulting in grotesque distortion, he soaked it in an alcoholic solution of perchloride of mercury, to keep it moist, and then modelled the form from inside, allowing it to harden when finished. Stephen Bann has interpreted this process as analogous to the reconstructive rhetoric of Romantic historicism; perpetuating the impression of life 'precisely because he has accepted the fact of death: the carcass has had to be recognised as mere malleable material for the taxidermist to work upon' (Bann, *The Clothing of Clio: A Study of the Representation of History in Nineteenth-Century Britain and France* (Cambridge, 1984), p. 17). During his eleven-month sojourn in the jungle he collected 230 birds, two large land tortoises, five armadillos, two large serpents, a sloth, an antbear and a cayman, all of which were subjected to the new taxidermic treatment. Waterton was infuriated by the detention of his specimens by the customs office at Liverpool, wreaking his revenge on the officer concerned (a Mr Lushington) by employing his physiognomy as the model for a bizarre human face constructed out of the rump of a monkey, which he entitled 'The Nondescript'. This countenance appeared as the frontispiece to *Wanderings*.

After a final voyage to Canada, the US, the West Indies and Demerara in 1824, he published an account of all four journeys, to which was appended his essay 'On Preserving Birds for Cabinets of Natural History'. The book is perhaps the eccentric masterpiece of nineteenth-century travel writing about Latin America. Completely devoid of the Linnaean scientific terminology requisite in mainstream travel writing, Waterton evokes South American birds and animals in loving (and often morbid) detail, as it were from inside out, like his taxidermic specimens. *Wanderings* is written in an apostrophaic, Shandyan style, which eschews first-person narrative and is peppered with allusions to Latin authors. Waterton rejects the plain, descriptive style of conventional travelogue for rhetorical high colouring, seeking to bring his romantic adventures to life in the reader's imagination. The book was so successful that a large second edition was published in 1828, and it was warmly reviewed by Sydney Smith in the *Edinburgh Review* for February 1826. Smith's review opened with the memorable line, 'Mr Waterton is a Roman Catholic gentleman of Yorkshire, of good fortune, who, instead of passing his life at balls and assemblies, has preferred living with Indians and monkeys in the forests of Guiana'.

When he was forty-eight, Waterton married Anne Edmonstone, the seventeen-year-old daughter of his friend Charles Edmonstone, but she died the following year, leaving him a son, Edward. For the remainder of his life, Waterton led the life of a reclusive naturalist, arranging his specimens and doing the rounds of his bird sanctuary dressed in an old-fashioned swallowtail coat. He died at the age of eighty-three, still nursing his hatred of Protestants and Whigs, who, like the 'Hanoverian rats' which plagued his breeding nests, had overrun post-Reform Act England.

Courteous reader, here thou hast the outlines of an amazing landscape given thee; thou wilt see that the principal parts of it are but faintly traced, some of them scarcely visible at all, and that the shades are wholly wanting. If thy soul partakes of the ardent flame which the persevering Mungo Park's did, these outlines will be enough for thee: they will give thee some idea of what a noble country this is; and if thou hast but courage to set about giving the world a finished picture of it, neither materials to work on, nor colours to paint it in its true shades, will be wanting to thee. It may appear a difficult task at a distance; but look close at it, and it is nothing at all; provided thou hast but a quiet mind, little more is necessary, and the genius

which presides over these wilds will kindly help
thee through the rest. She will allow thee to
slay the fawn, and to cut down the mountain-
cabbage for thy support, and to select from every
part of her domain whatever may be necessary
for the work thou art about ; but having killed
a pair of doves in order to enable thee to give
mankind a true and proper description of them,
thou must not destroy a third through wanton-
ness, or to show what a good marksman thou art;
that would only blot the picture thou art finishing,
not colour it.

Though retired from the haunts of men, and
even without a friend with thee, thou wouldst not
find it solitary. The crowing of the hannaquoi
will sound in thine ears like the daybreak town
clock ; and the wren and the thrush will join with
thee in thy matin hymn to thy Creator, to thank
him for thy night's rest.

At noon the Genius will lead thee to the
troely, one leaf of which will defend thee from
both sun and rain. And if, in the cool of the
evening, thou hast been tempted to stray too far
from thy place of abode, and art deprived of light
to write down the information thou hast collected,
the fire-fly, which thou wilt see in almost every
bush around thee, will be thy candle. Hold it
over thy pocket-book, in any position which thou
knowest will not hurt it, and it will afford thee
ample light. And when thou hast done with it,

put it kindly back again on the next branch to thee. It will want no other reward for its services.

When in thy hammock, should the thought of thy little crosses and disappointments, in thy ups and downs through life, break in upon thee, and throw thee into a pensive mood, the owl will bear thee company. She will tell thee that hard has been her fate too ; and at intervals, " Whip-poor-Will," and " Willy come go," will take up the tale of sorrow. Ovid has told thee how the owl once boasted the human form, and lost it for a very small offence ; and were the poet alive now, he would inform thee, that " Whip-poor-Will," and " Willy come go," are the shades of those poor African and Indian slaves, who died worn out and brokenhearted. They wail and cry, " Whip-poor-Will," " Willy come go," all night long ; and often, when the moon shines, you see them sitting on the green turf, near the houses of those whose ancestors tore them from the bosom of their helpless families, which all probably perished through grief and want, after their support was gone.

About an hour above the rock of Saba, stands the habitation of an Indian, called Simon, on the top of a hill. The side next the river is almost perpendicular, and you may easily throw a stone over to the opposite bank. Here there was an opportunity of seeing man in his rudest state.

The Indians who frequented this habitation, though living in the midst of woods, bore evident marks of attention to their persons. Their hair was neatly collected, and tied up in a knot; their bodies fancifully painted red, and the paint was scented with hayawa. This gave them a gay and animated appearance. Some of them had on necklaces, composed of the teeth of wild boars slain in the chase; many wore rings, and others had an ornament on the left arm, midway betwixt the shoulder and the elbow. At the close of day, they regularly bathed in the river below; and the next morning seemed busy in renewing the faded colours of their faces.

One day there came into the hut a form which literally might be called the wild man of the woods. On entering, he laid down a ball of wax, which he had collected in the forest. His hammock was all ragged and torn; and his bow, though of good wood, was without any ornament or polish; "erubuit domino, cultior esse suo." His face was meagre, his looks forbidding, and his whole appearance neglected. His long black hair hung from his head in matted confusion; nor had his body, to all appearance, ever been painted. They gave him some cassava bread and boiled fish, which he ate voraciously, and soon after left the hut. As he went out, you could observe no traces in his countenance or demeanour, which indicated that he was in the least mindful of having been benefited by the society he was just leaving.

The Indians said that he had neither wife, nor child, nor friend. They had often tried to persuade him to come and live amongst them; but all was of no avail. He went roving on, plundering the wild bees of their honey, and picking up the fallen nuts and fruits of the forest. When he fell in with game, he procured fire from two sticks, and cooked it on the spot. When a hut happened to be in his way, he stepped in, and asked for something to eat, and then months elapsed ere they saw him again. They did not know what had caused him to be thus unsettled; he had been so for years; nor did they believe that even old age itself would change the habits of this poor, harmless, solitary wanderer.

From Simon's, the traveller may reach the large fall, with ease, in four days.

The first falls that he meets are merely rapids, scarce a stone appearing above the water in the rainy season; and those in the bed of the river, barely high enough to arrest the water's course, and by causing a bubbling, show that they are there.

With this small change of appearance in the stream, the stranger observes nothing new till he comes within eight or ten miles of the great fall. Each side of the river presents an uninterrupted range of wood, just as it did below. All the productions found betwixt the plantations and the rock Saba, are to be met with here.

From Simon's to the great fall, there are five habitations of the Indians. Two of them close to the river's side ; the other three a little way in the forest. These habitations consist of from four to eight huts, situated on about an acre of ground, which they have cleared from the surrounding woods. A few pappaw, cotton, and mountain cabbage-trees, are scattered round them.

At one of these habitations, a small quantity of the wourali poison was procured. It was in a little gourd. The Indian who had it, said that he had killed a number of wild hogs with it, and two tapirs. Appearances seemed to confirm what he said ; for on one side it had been nearly taken out to the bottom, at different times, which probably would not have been the case had the first or second trial failed.

Its strength was proved on a middle-sized dog. He was wounded in the thigh, in order that there might be no possibility of touching a vital part. In three or four minutes he began to be affected, smelt at every little thing on the ground around him, and looked wistfully at the wounded part. Soon after this he staggered, laid himself down, and never rose more. He barked once, though not as if in pain. His voice was low and weak ; and in a second attempt it quite failed him. He now put his head betwixt his fore legs, and raising it slowly again, he fell over on his side.   His eye immediately became fixed, and though his extremities every now and then shot convulsively, he never showed the least desire to raise up his head. His heart fluttered much from the time he laid down, and at intervals beat very strong; then stopped for a moment or two, and then beat again; and continued faintly beating several minutes after every other part of his body seemed dead.

In a quarter of an hour after he had received the poison he was quite motionless.

A few miles before you reach the great fall, and which, indeed, is the only one which can be called a fall, large balls of froth come floating past you. The river appears beautifully marked with streaks of foam, and on your nearer approach the stream is whitened all over.

At first, you behold the fall rushing down a bed of rocks, with a tremendous noise, divided into two foamy streams, which, at their junction again, form a small island covered with wood. Above this island, for a short space, there appears but one stream, all white with froth, and fretting and boiling amongst the huge rocks which obstruct its course.

Higher up it is seen dividing itself into a short channel or two, and trees grow on the rocks which caused its separation. The torrent, in many places, has eaten deep into the rocks, and split them into large fragments, by driving others against them.

The trees on the rocks are in bloom and vigour, though their roots are half bared, and many of them bruised and broken by the rushing waters.

This is the general appearance of the fall from the level of the water below, to where the river is smooth and quiet above. It must be remembered, that this is during the periodical rains. Probably, in the dry season, it puts on a very different appearance. There is no perpendicular fall of water of any consequence throughout it, but the dreadful roaring and rushing of the torrent, down a long, rocky, and moderately sloping channel, has a fine effect; and the stranger returns well pleased with what he has seen. No animal, nor craft of any kind, could stem this downward flood. In a few moments the first would be killed, the second dashed in pieces.

The Indians have a path alongside of it, through the forest, where prodigious crabwood trees grow. Up this path they drag their canoes, and launch them into the river above; and on their return, bring them down the same way.

About two hours below this fall, is the habitation of an Acoway chief called Sinkerman. At night you hear the roaring of the fall from it. It is pleasantly situated on the top of a sand-hill. At this place you have the finest view the river Demerara affords : three tiers of hills rise in slow gradation, one above the other, before you, and present a grand and magnificent scene, especially to him who has been accustomed to a level country.

Here, a little after midnight, on the first of May, was heard a most strange and unaccountable noise; it seemed as though several regiments were engaged, and musketry firing with great rapidity. The Indians, terrified beyond description, left their hammocks, and crowded all together, like sheep at the approach of the wolf. There were no soldiers within three or four hundred miles. Conjecture was of no avail, and all conversation next morning on the subject was as useless and unsatisfactory as the dead silence which succeeded to the noise.

He who wishes to reach the Macoushi country, had better send his canoe over land from Sinkerman's to the Essequibo.

There is a pretty good path, and meeting a creek about three quarters of the way, it eases the labour, and twelve Indians will arrive with it in the Essequibo in four days.

The traveller need not attend his canoe; there is a shorter and a better way. Half an hour below Sinkerman's he finds a little creek on the western bank of the Demerara. After proceeding about a couple of hundred yards up it, he leaves it, and pursues a west-north-west direction by land for the Essequibo. The path is good, though somewhat rugged with the roots of trees, and here and there obstructed by fallen ones; it extends more over level ground than otherwise. There are a few steep ascents and descents in it, with a little brook running at the bottom of them; but they are easily passed over, and the fallen trees serve for a bridge.

You may reach the Essequibo with ease in a day and a half; and so matted and interwoven are the tops of the trees above you, that the sun is not felt once all the way, saving where the space which a newly fallen tree occupied lets in his rays upon you. The forest contains an abundance of wild hogs, lobbas, acouries, powisses, maams, maroudis, and waracabas, for your nourishment, and there are plenty of leaves to cover a shed, whenever you are inclined to sleep.

The soil has three-fourths of sand in it, till you come within half an hour's walk of the Essequibo, where you find a red gravel and rocks. In this retired and solitary tract, nature's garb, to all appearance, has not been injured by fire, nor her productions broken in upon by the exterminating hand of man.

Here the finest green-heart grows, and wallaba, purple-heart, siloabali, sawari, buletre, tauronira, and mora, are met with in vast abundance, far and near, towering up in majestic grandeur, straight as pillars, sixty or seventy feet high, without a knot or branch.

Traveller, forget for a little while the idea thou hast of wandering farther on, and stop and look at this grand picture of vegetable nature; it is a reflection of the crowd thou hast lately been in, and though a silent monitor, it is not a less eloquent one on that account.—See that noble purple-heart before thee! Nature has been kind to it. Not a hole, not the least oozing from its trunk, to show that its best days are past. Vigorous in youthful blooming beauty, it stands the ornament of these sequestered wilds, and tacitly rebukes those base ones of thine own species, who have been hardy enough to deny the existence of Him who ordered it to flourish here.

Behold that one next to it!—Hark! how the hammerings of the red-headed woodpecker resound through its distempered boughs! See what a quantity of holes he has made in it, and how its bark is stained with the drops which trickle down from them. The lightning, too, has blasted one side of it. Nature looks pale and wan in its leaves, and her resources are nearly dried up in its extremities; its sap is tainted; a mortal sickness, slow as a consumption, and as sure in its consequences, has long since entered its frame, vitiating and destroying the wholesome juices there.

Step a few paces aside, and cast thine eye on that remnant of a mora behind it. Best part of its branches, once so high and ornamental, now lie on the ground in sad confusion, one upon the other, all shattered and fungus-grown, and a prey to millions of insects, which are busily employed in destroying them. One branch of it still looks healthy! Will it recover? No, it cannot; nature has already run her course, and that healthy-looking branch is only as a fallacious good symptom in him who is just about to die of a mortification when he feels no more pain, and fancies his distemper has left him; it is as the momentary gleam of a wintry sun's ray close to the western horizon.—See! while we are speaking a gust of wind has brought the tree to the ground, and made room for its successor.

Come further on, and examine that apparently luxuriant tauronira on thy right hand. It boasts a verdure not its own; they are false ornaments it wears; the bush-rope and bird-vines have clothed it from the root to its topmost branch. The succession of fruit which it hath borne, like good cheer in the houses of the great, has invited the birds to resort to it, and they have disseminated beautiful, though destructive, plants on its branches, which, like the distempers vice brings into the human frame, rob it of all its health and vigour; they have shortened its days, and probably in another year they will finally kill it, long before nature intended that it should die.

Ere thou leavest this interesting scene, look on the ground around thee, and see what every thing here below must come to.

Behold that newly fallen wallaba! The whirlwind has uprooted it in its prime, and it has brought down to the ground a dozen small ones in its fall. Its bark has already begun to drop off! And that heart of mora close by it is fast yielding, in spite of its firm, tough texture.

The tree which thou passedst but a little ago, and which perhaps has laid over yonder brook for years, can now hardly support itself, and in a few months more it will have fallen into the water.

Put thy foot on that large trunk thou seest to the left. It seems entire amid the surrounding fragments. Mere outward appearance, delusive phantom of what it once was! Tread on it, and like the fuss-ball, it will break into dust.

Sad and silent mementos to the giddy traveller as he wanders on! Prostrate remnants of vegetable nature, how incontestably ye prove what we must all at last come to, and how plain your mouldering ruins show that the firmest texture avails us naught when Heaven wills that we should cease to be!—

> " The cloud-capt towers, the gorgeous palaces,
> The solemn temples, the great globe itself,
> Yea, all which it inhabit, shall dissolve,
> And, like the baseless fabric of a vision,
> Leave not a wreck behind."

Cast thine eye around thee, and see the thousands of nature's productions. Take a view of them from the opening seed on the surface, sending a downward shoot, to the loftiest and the largest trees, rising up and blooming in wild luxuriance; some side by side, others separate; some curved and knotty, others straight as lances; all, in beautiful gradation, fulfilling the mandates they had received from heaven, and though condemned to die, still never failing to keep up their species till time shall be no more.

Reader, canst thou not be induced to dedicate a few months to the good of the public, and examine with thy scientific eye the productions which the vast and well-stored colony of Demerara presents to thee?

What an immense range of forest is there from the rock Saba to the great fall! and what an uninterrupted extent before thee from it to the banks of the Essequibo! No doubt, there is many a balsam and many a medicinal root yet to be discovered, and many a resin, gum, and oil yet unnoticed. Thy work would be a pleasing one, and thou mightest make several useful observations in it.

Would it be thought impertinent in thee to hazard a conjecture, that with the resources the government of Demerara has, stones might be conveyed from the rock Saba to Stabroek, to stem the equinoctial tides, which are for ever sweeping away the expensive wooden piles round the mounds of the fort? Or would the timber-merchant point at thee in passing by, and call thee a descendant of La Mancha's knight, because thou maintainest that the stones which form the rapids might be removed with little expense, and thus open the navigation to the wood-cutter from Stabroek to the great fall? Or wouldst thou be deemed enthusiastic or biassed, because thou givest it as thy opinion that the climate in these high lands is exceedingly wholesome, and the lands themselves capable of nourishing and maintaining any number of settlers? In thy dissertation on the Indians, thou mightest hint, that possibly they could be induced to help the new settlers a little; and that finding their labours well requited, it would be the means of their keeping up a constant communication with us, which probably might be the means of laying the first stone towards their christianity. They are a poor, harmless, inoffensive set of people, and their wandering and ill-provided way of living seems more to ask for pity from us, than to fill our heads with thoughts that they would be hostile to us.

What a noble field, kind reader, for thy experimental philosophy and speculations, for thy learning, for thy perseverance, for thy kind-heartedness, for every thing that is great and good within thee!

★   ★   ★   ★   ★

When a native of Macoushia goes in quest of feathered game or other birds, he seldom carries his bow and arrows. It is the blow-pipe he then uses. This extraordinary tube of death is, perhaps, one of the greatest natural curiosities of Guiana. It is not found in the country of the Macoushi. Those Indians tell you that it grows to the south-west of them, in the wilds which extend betwixt them and the Rio Negro. The reed must grow to an amazing length, as the part the Indians use is from ten to eleven feet long, and no tapering can be perceived in it, one end being as thick as the other. It is of a bright yellow colour, perfectly smooth both inside and out. It grows hollow ; nor is there the least appearance of a knot or joint throughout the whole extent. The natives call it Ourah. This, of itself, is too slender to answer the end of a blow-pipe ; but there is a species of palma, larger and stronger, and common in Guiana, and this the Indians make use of as a case, in which they put the ourah. It is brown, susceptible of a fine polish, and appears as if it had joints five or six inches from each other. It is called Samourah, and the pulp inside is easily extracted, by steeping it for a few days in water.

Thus the ourah and samourah, one within the other, form the blow-pipe of Guiana. The end which is applied to the mouth is tied round with a small silk grass cord, to prevent its splitting ; and the other end, which is apt to strike against the ground, is secured by the seed of the acuero fruit, cut horizontally through the middle, with a hole made in the end, through which is put the extremity of the blow-pipe. It is fastened on with string on the outside, and the inside is filled up with wild bees'-wax.

The arrow is from nine to ten inches long. It is made out of the leaf of a species of palm-tree, called Coucourite, hard and brittle, and pointed as sharp as a needle. About an inch of the pointed end is poisoned. The other end is burnt to make it still harder, and wild cotton is put round it for about an inch and a half. It requires considerable practice to put on this cotton well. It must just be large enough to fit the hollow of the tube, and taper off to nothing downwards. They tie it on with a thread of the silk grass, to prevent its slipping off the arrow.

The Indians have shown ingenuity in making a quiver to hold the arrows. It will contain from five to six hundred. It is generally from twelve to fourteen inches long, and in shape resembles a dice-box used at backgammon. The inside is

prettily done in basket work, with wood not unlike bamboo, and the outside has a coat of wax.
The cover is all of one piece, formed out of the
skin of the tapir. Round the centre there is
fastened a loop, large enough to admit the arm
and shoulder, from which it hangs when used.
To the rim is tied a little bunch of silk grass, and
half of the jaw-bone of the fish called pirai,
with which the Indian scrapes the point of his
arrow.

Before he puts the arrows into the quiver, he
links them together by two strings of cotton, one
string at each end, and then folds them round a
stick, which is nearly the length of the quiver.
The end of the stick, which is uppermost, is
guarded by two little pieces of wood crosswise,
with a hoop round their extremities, which appears something like a wheel; and this saves
the hand from being wounded when the quiver
is reversed, in order to let the bunch of arrows
drop out.

There is also attached to the quiver a little kind
of basket, to hold the wild cotton which is put on
the blunt end of the arrow. With a quiver of
poisoned arrows slung over his shoulder, and with
his blow-pipe in his hand, in the same position as
a soldier carries his musket, see the Macoushi
Indian advancing towards the forest in quest of
powises, maroudis, waracabas, and other feathered
game.

These generally sit high up in the tall and tufted trees, but still are not out of the Indian's reach; for his blow-pipe, at its greatest elevation, will send an arrow three hundred feet. Silent as midnight he steals under them, and so cautiously does he tread the ground, that the fallen leaves rustle not beneath his feet. His ears are open to the least sound, while his eye, keen as that of the lynx, is employed in finding out the game in the thickest shade. Often he imitates their cry, and decoys them from tree to tree, till they are within range of his tube. Then taking a poisoned arrow from his quiver, he puts it in the blow-pipe, and collects his breath for the fatal puff.

About two feet from the end through which he blows, there are fastened two teeth of the acouri, and these serve him for a sight. Silent and swift the arrow flies, and seldom fails to pierce the object at which it is sent. Sometimes the wounded bird remains in the same tree where it was shot, and in three minutes falls down at the Indian's feet. Should he take wing, his flight is of short duration, and the Indian, following the direction he has gone, is sure to find him dead.

It is natural to imagine that, when a slight wound only is inflicted, the game will make its escape. Far otherwise; the wourali poison almost instantaneously mixes with blood or water, so that if you wet your finger, and dash it along the poisoned arrow in the quickest manner possible, you are sure to carry off some of the poison. Though three minutes generally elapse before the convulsions come on in the wounded bird, still a stupor evidently takes place sooner, and this stupor manifests itself by an apparent unwillingness in the bird to move. This was very visible in a dying fowl.

Having procured a healthy full-grown one, a short piece of a poisoned blow-pipe arrow was broken off and run up into its thigh, as near as possible betwixt the skin and the flesh, in order that it might not be incommoded by the wound. For the first minute it walked about, but walked very slowly, and did not appear the least agitated. During the second minute it stood still, and began to peck the ground; and ere half another had elapsed, it frequently opened and shut its mouth. The tail had now dropped, and the wings almost touched the ground. By the termination of the third minute, it had sat down, scarce able to support its head, which nodded, and then recovered itself, and then nodded again, lower and lower every time, like that of a weary traveller slumbering in an erect position; the eyes alternately open and shut. The fourth minute brought on convulsions, and life and the fifth terminated together.

The flesh of the game is not in the least injured by the poison, nor does it appear to corrupt sooner than that killed by the gun or knife. The body of this fowl was kept for sixteen hours, in a climate damp and rainy, and within seven degrees of the equator; at the end of which time it had contracted no bad smell whatever, and there were no symptoms of putrefaction, saving that, just round the wound, the flesh appeared somewhat discoloured.

The Indian, on his return home, carefully suspends his blow-pipe from the top of his spiral roof; seldom placing it in an oblique position, lest it should receive a cast.

Here let the blow-pipe remain suspended, while you take a view of the arms which are made to slay the larger beasts of the forest.

When the Indian intends to chase the peccari, or surprise the deer, or rouse the tapir from his marshy retreat, he carries his bow and arrows, which are very different from the weapons already described.

The bow is generally from six to seven feet long, and strung with a cord, spun out of the silk grass. The forests of Guiana furnish many species of hard wood, tough and elastic, out of which beautiful and excellent bows are formed.

The arrows are from four to five feet in length, made of a yellow reed without a knot or joint. It is found in great plenty up and down throughout Guiana. A piece of hard wood, about nine inches long, is inserted into the end of the reed, and fastened with cotton well waxed. A square hole,

an inch deep, is then made in the end of this piece
of hard wood, done tight round with cotton to
keep it from splitting. Into this square hole is
fitted a spike of Coucourite wood, poisoned, and
which may be kept there, or taken out at pleasure. A joint of bamboo, about as thick as your
finger, is fitted on over the poisoned spike, to
prevent accidents and defend it from the rain, and
is taken off when the arrow is about to be used.
Lastly, two feathers are fastened on the other end
of the reed to steady it in its flight.

Besides his bow and arrows, the Indian carries
a little box made of bamboo, which holds a dozen
or fifteen poisoned spikes, six inches long. They
are poisoned in the following manner: a small
piece of wood is dipped in the poison, and with
this they give the spike a first coat. It is then
exposed to the sun or fire. After it is dry, it
receives another coat, and then dried again; after
this a third coat, and sometimes a fourth.

They take great care to put the poison on
thicker at the middle than at the sides, by which
means the spike retains the shape of a two-edged
sword. It is rather a tedious operation to make
one of these arrows complete; and as the Indian
is not famed for industry, except when pressed by
hunger, he has hit upon a plan of preserving his
arrows which deserves notice.

About a quarter of an inch above the part
where the Coucourite spike is fixed into the square

hole, he cuts it half through; and thus, when it has entered the animal, the weight of the arrow causes it to break off there, by which means the arrow falls to the ground uninjured; so that, should this be the only arrow he happens to have with him, and should another shot immediately occur, he has only to take another poisoned spike out of his little bamboo box, fit it on his arrow, and send it to its destination.

Thus armed with deadly poison, and hungry as the hyæna, he ranges through the forest in quest of the wild beasts' tract. No hound can act a surer part. Without clothes to fetter him, or shoes to bind his feet, he observes the footsteps of the game, where an European eye could not discern the smallest vestige. He pursues it through all its turns and windings, with astonishing perseverance, and success generally crowns his efforts. The animal, after receiving the poisoned arrow, seldom retreats two hundred paces before it drops.

We will now take a view of the Vampire. As there was a free entrance and exit to the vampire, in the loft where I slept, I had many a fine opportunity of paying attention to this nocturnal surgeon. He does not always live on blood.

When the moon shone bright, and the fruit of the banana-tree was ripe, I could see him approach and eat it. He would also bring into the loft, from the forest, a green round fruit, something like the wild guava, and about the size of a nutmeg. There was something also, in the blossom of the sawarri nut-tree, which was grateful to him; for on coming up Waratilla creek, in a moonlight night, I saw several vampires fluttering round the top of the sawarri tree, and every now and then the blossoms, which they had broken off, fell into the water. They certainly did not drop off naturally, for on examining several of them, they appeared quite fresh and blooming. So I concluded the vampires pulled them from the tree, either to get at the incipient fruit, or to catch the insects which often take up their abode in flowers.

The vampire, in general, measures about twenty-six inches from wing to wing extended, though I once killed one which measured thirty-two inches. He frequents old abandoned houses and hollow trees; and sometimes a cluster of them may be seen in the forest hanging head downwards from the branch of a tree.

Goldsmith seems to have been aware that the vampire hangs in clusters; for in the "Deserted Village," speaking of America, he says,—

" And matted woods, where birds forget to sing,
But silent bats in drowsy clusters cling."

The vampire has a curious membrane, which rises from the nose, and gives it a very singular appearance. It has been remarked before, that there are two species of vampire in Guiana, a larger and a smaller. The larger sucks men and other animals; the smaller seems to confine himself chiefly to birds. I learnt from a gentleman, high up in the river Demerara, that he was completely unsuccessful with his fowls, on account of the small vampire. He showed me some that had been sucked the night before, and they were scarcely able to walk.

Some years ago I went to the river Paumaron with a Scotch gentleman, by name Tarbet. We hung our hammocks in the thatched loft of a planter's house. Next morning I heard this gentleman muttering in his hammock, and now and then letting fall an imprecation or two, just about the time he ought to have been saying his morning prayers. "What is the matter, Sir," said I, softly; "is any thing amiss?" "What's the matter?" answered he surlily; "why, the vampires have been sucking me to death." As soon as there was light enough, I went to his hammock, and saw it much stained with blood. "There," said he, thrusting his foot out of the hammock, "see how these infernal imps have been drawing my life's blood." On examining his foot, I found the vampire had tapped his great toe: there was a wound somewhat less than that made by a leech; the blood was still oozing from it; I conjectured he might have lost from ten to twelve ounces of blood. Whilst examining it, I think I put him into a worse humour by remarking, that an European surgeon would not have been so generous as to have blooded him without making a charge. He looked up in my face, but did not say a word: I saw he was of opinion that I had better have spared this piece of ill-timed levity.

It was not the last punishment of this good gentleman in the river Paumaron. The next night he was doomed to undergo a kind of ordeal unknown in Europe. There is a species of large red ant in Guiana, sometimes called Ranger, sometimes Coushie. These ants march in millions through the country, in compact order, like a regiment of soldiers; they eat up every insect in their march; and if a house obstruct their route, they do not turn out of the way, but go quite through it. Though they sting cruelly when molested, the planter is not sorry to see them in his house; for it is but a passing visit, and they destroy every kind of insect vermin that had taken shelter under his roof.

Now, in the British plantations of Guiana, as well as in Europe, there is always a little temple dedicated to the goddess Cloacina. Our dinner had chiefly consisted of crabs, dressed in rich and different ways. Paumaron is famous for crabs, and strangers who go thither consider them the greatest luxury. The Scotch gentleman made a very capital dinner on crabs; but this change of diet was productive of unpleasant circumstances: he awoke in the night in that state in which Virgil describes Cæleno to have been, viz. " fædissima ventris proluvies." Up he got, to verify the remark,

"Serius aut citius, sedem properamus ad unam."

Now, unluckily for himself, and the nocturnal tranquillity of the planter's house, just at that unfortunate hour, the coushie ants were passing across the seat of Cloacina's temple; he had never dreamed of this; and so, turning his face to the door, he placed himself in the usual situation which the votaries of the goddess generally take. Had a lighted match dropped upon a pound of gunpowder, as he afterwards remarked, it could not have caused a greater recoil. Up he jumped, and forced his way out, roaring for help and for a light, for he was worried alive by ten thousand devils. The fact is, he had sat down upon an intervening body of coushie ants. Many of those which escaped being crushed to death, turned again; and, in revenge, stung the unintentional intruder most severely. The watchman had fallen asleep, and it was some time before a light could be procured, the fire having gone out; in the mean time, the poor gentleman was suffering an indescribable martyrdom, and would have found himself more at home in the Augean stable than in the planter's house.

I had often wished to have been once sucked by the vampire, in order that I might have it in my power to say it had really happened to me. There can be no pain in the operation, for the patient is always asleep when the vampire is sucking him; and as for the loss of a few ounces of blood, that would be a trifle in the long run. Many a night have I slept with my foot out of the hammock to tempt this winged surgeon, expecting that he would be there; but it was all in vain; the vampire never sucked me, and I could never account for his not doing so, for we were inhabitants of the same loft for months together.

The Armadillo is very common in these forests; he burrows in the sand-hills like a rabbit. As it often takes a considerable time to dig him out of his hole, it would be a long and laborious business to attack each hole indiscriminately without knowing whether the animal were there or not. To prevent disappointment, the Indians carefully examine the mouth of the hole, and put a short stick down it. Now if, on introducing the stick, a number of mosquitos come out, the Indians know to a certainty that the armadillo is in it: wherever there are no mosquitos in the hole, there is no armadillo. The Indian having satisfied himself that the armadillo is there, by the mosquitos which come out, he immediately cuts a long and slender stick, and introduces it

into the hole : he carefully observes the line the
stick takes, and then sinks a pit in the sand to
catch the end of it : this done, he puts it farther
into the hole, and digs another pit, and so on,
till at last he comes up with the armadillo, which
had been making itself a passage in the sand
till it had exhausted all its strength through pure
exertion.   I have been sometimes three quarters
of a day in digging out one armadillo, and obliged
to sink half a dozen pits, seven feet deep, before
I got up to it.   The Indians and negroes are
very fond of the flesh, but I considered it strong
and rank.

On laying hold of the armadillo you must be
cautious not to come in contact with his feet :
they are armed with sharp claws, and with them
he will inflict a severe wound in self-defence :
when not molested, he is very harmless and
innocent ; he would put you in mind of the hare
in Gay's fables, —

> " Whose care was never to offend,
> And every creature was her friend."

The armadillo swims well in time of need, but
does not go into the water by choice.   He is very
seldom seen abroad during the day ; and when
surprised, he is sure to be near the mouth of his
hole.   Every part of the armadillo is well protected by his shell, except his ears.   In life, this
shell is very limber, so that the animal is enabled
to go at full stretch, or roll himself up into a ball,

as occasion may require.

On inspecting the arrangement of the shell, it
puts you very much in mind of a coat of armour;
indeed it is a natural coat of armour to the armadillo, and being composed both of scale and bone,
it affords ample security, and has a pleasing
effect.

Often, when roving in the wilds, I would fall
in with the land tortoise; he too adds another to
the list of unoffending animals; he subsists on
the fallen fruits of the forest. When an enemy
approaches he never thinks of moving, but quietly
draws himself under his shell, and there awaits
his doom in patience: he only seems to have two
enemies who can do him any damage; one of
these is the boa constrictor: this snake swallows
the tortoise alive, shell and all. But a boa large
enough to do this is very scarce, and thus there
is not much to apprehend from that quarter; the
other enemy is man, who takes up the tortoise,
and carries him away. Man also is scarce in
these never-ending wilds, and the little depreda-
tions he may commit upon the tortoise will be
nothing, or a mere trifle. The tiger's teeth cannot
penetrate its shell, nor can a stroke of his paws
do it any damage. It is of so compact and strong
a nature, that there is a common saying, a London waggon might roll over it and not break it.

Hall:
Extracts from a Journal

Basil Hall, *Extracts from a Journal Written on the Coasts of Chili, Peru, and Mexico, in the Years 1820–21–22*, 2 vols (Edinburgh: Constable, 1824), vol. I, pp. 86–112; vol. II, pp. 264–70.

Basil Hall (1788–1844) was born into a landed Scottish family and educated at the Royal High School, Edinburgh, before entering the navy in 1802. Active service in the Napoleonic wars brought swift promotion, and in 1816 he accompanied Lord Amherst's embassy to China in command of the ten-gun brig *Lyra*. He published an account of the embassy and his exploration of the China Sea in his first travel book, *A Voyage of Discovery to the West Coast of Corea and the Great Loo-Choo Islands* (1818). Hall was made a Fellow of the Royal Society in March 1816. In May 1820 he was appointed captain of HMS *Conway*, a 26-gun frigate, with orders to sail for the South American station, join its commander Sir Thomas Hardy at the Rio de la Plata and sail with him around the Horn to Valparaiso in Chile. The next two years (1820–2) were spent cruising up and down the Pacific seaboard of South and North America during a period which saw the climax of the Chilean, Peruvian and Mexican wars of independence. In addition to his diplomatic duties described below, Hall conducted scientific surveys (his pendulum observations were published in the *Philosophical Transactions* in 1823) and made a number of excursions into the interior. Returning to England in early 1823, he published *Extracts from a Journal* the following year; the book was so successful that it rapidly went through several editions. The *Quarterly Review* praised Hall's 'manly, unaffected style, rough and racy', and his 'considerable skill and effect' in 'describ[ing] manners and scenery'. However, the young naturalist Charles Darwin, who read *Extracts* on board the *Beagle*, disagreed, complaining in his diary, 'it appears to me that all Capt Hall's beautiful descriptions require a little washing with a Neutral tint – it may partly destroy their charms, but I am afraid will add to their reality' (Darwin, *Diary*, p. 336). Hall became an established expert on South American affairs and in-house reviewer for the *Quarterly* and the *United Services Magazine*. In 1831–3 he edited an extensive collection entitled *Fragments of Voyages and Travels*, which was frequently reprinted. He went insane in 1842 and died in Haslar hospital two years later.

By the time Hall arrived in Valparaiso, Chile had gained independence after San Martín and Bernardo O'Higgins's defeat of the Spanish armies at the battle of Maipo in April 1818. Much of Peru, with the exception of Lima, had likewise been cleared of royalist forces. The collapse of Spanish control and the start of free commerce presented huge opportunities to the British merchants who flooded into Chile from 1818 onwards, and consular missions were established at Valparaiso, Coquimbo and Concepción. The commander-in-chief of the South American Squadron was the sole constituted British authority in the region, and the navy had the exacting task of defending British interests in the anarchic war zone. The ships of the squadron were distributed in those regions where the British presence was most significant: Buenos Aires, Valparaiso, Callao (the port of Lima) and San Blás in New Spain. In this diplomatic role Hall had the opportunity to meet the leaders of both political factions, and his book contains compelling eyewitness accounts of O'Higgins, the liberator San Martín, the Spanish viceroy General La Serna and the maverick British naval genius Lord Cochrane, admiral of the victorious Chilean fleet.

Hall's sympathy for the cause of independence is evident in both of the following excerpts, the first of which favourably compares the condition of republican Chile with royalist Lima. The traditional stocks-in-trade of traveller's reports of Peru, such as the description of the bullfight and the *saya y manto* costume of the Limena women, are here inflected with political nuances. Hall landed in Peru in February 1821, just a few months before San Martín entered Lima and declared independence on 28 July, so his portrait of Lima captures the final days of the old colonial regime. The second excerpt here is from the passage on the Mexican revolution added to the third edition of Hall's book in 1824. 'Circumstances have occurred', wrote Hall, 'to give an increased degree of interest to the affairs of Mexico' (vol. I, p. ix). Hall accurately indicates that Mexico had been 'twice revolutionised', first by a bloody popular uprising led by the *insurgentes* Miguel Hidalgo y Costilla and José María Morelos in 1810–15, and then by the propertied classes led by Augustín Iturbide in reaction to the liberal Spanish constitution of 1820. Iturbide's attempt to conciliate Mexican *criollos* and Spanish *peninsulares* was enshrined in the Plan de Iguala in February 1821, with its declaration that 'all inhabitants of New Spain, without any distinction between Europeans, Africans and Indians, are citizens of this monarchy, with access to all positions according to their merits and virtues'. In the second passage Hall represents the Plan de Iguala as a Quixotic venture which was doomed to failure. Iturbide's bid to establish a constitutional monarchy by crowning himself Emperor Agustín I in May 1822 was indeed short-lived. He was rapidly forced to abdicate in March 1823 in the face of a republican coup led by General Antonio López de Santa Anna, and fled into exile in London.

CHAPTER III.

PERU.

FIRST VISIT TO LIMA, WHILE PERU WAS STILL IN
POSSESSION OF THE SPANIARDS.

On the 5th of February 1821, after a passage
of nine days from Valparaiso, we anchored in the
Roads of Callao, the port of Lima, from which it
is distant about six miles.

At the time of our arrival, the state of Peru,
both domestic and political, was highly interesting, though differing in almost every particular
from that of Chili.

There is no circumstance which distinguishes
travels by land, from voyages by sea, more than
the different manner in which new countries are
brought under notice. On land the traveller is

so gradually introduced to new scenes, as scarcely to be aware that he has passed a frontier, for the manners of the adjacent countries often blend themselves insensibly into one another. When countries, on the other hand, are approached by sea, the case is different; for we are abruptly introduced, while the impressions of the country we have come from are fresh in our recollection, to a totally new set of objects, which we are thus enabled to compare with those we have left. Even when the two countries are in a great measure similarly circumstanced, as in the case of the different South American states, there will always be found a sufficient number of distinctions, arising out of climate and other local causes, to diversify the picture.

In Chili, as we have just seen, national independence had been for several years established, and a free and extensive commerce had, as a natural consequence, speedily sprung up; knowledge was gradually making its way; the moral and political bonds in which the minds of the people had been so long constrained were broken asunder; and the consequences of such freedom were rapidly developing themselves in a thousand shapes. In Peru, on the contrary, the word Independence was now heard for the first time; but as yet only in whispers, under the protection of San Martin's cannon. In Lima, where such free sentiments were still deemed treasonable, prejudice and error had established their head-quarters; and the obstinate bigotry with which old customs and opinions were adhered to, was rather strengthened than diminished by the apprehension of a total subversion of the whole system. The contrast between the two countries, Chili and Peru, as it met our eyes, was most striking; and if due justice could be done to the description of each, a pleasing inference would be drawn by every Englishman in favour of the popular side of the question.

The contrast between a country in a state of war, and one in a state of peace was, perhaps, never more strikingly displayed than upon this occasion : but, besides the interest arising out of such contrast, as applicable to the states of peace and war, the view was curious and instructive, as displaying the rapid effect produced by a change in the government of one of the two countries. As long as both were similarly administered, Peru had an infinite advantage over Chili in wealth and importance; but as soon as Chili became independent, she at once assumed the superiority.

We left Valparaiso harbour filled with shipping; its custom-house wharfs piled high with goods, too numerous and bulky for the old warehouses; the road between the port and the capital was always crowded with convoys of mules, loaded with every kind of foreign manufacture; while numerous ships were busy taking in cargoes of the wines, corn, and other articles, the growth of the country; and large sums of treasure were daily embarked for Europe, in return for goods already distributed over the interior. A spirit of inquiry and intelligence animated the whole society; schools were multiplied in every town; libraries established; and every encouragement given to literature and the arts : and as travelling was free, passports were unnecessary. In the manners, and even in the gait of every man, might be traced the air of conscious freedom and independence. In dress also a total change had very recently taken place, and from the same causes. The former uncouth, and almost savage costume of the ladies, and the slovenly cloaks worn by the men, had given way to the fashions of Europe : and although these may be deemed circumstances almost too minute to mention, they are not unimportant when connected with feelings of national pride, heretofore unknown. It is by these, and a multitude of other small changes, that these people are constantly reminded of their past compared with their present situation; and it is of essential use to their cause, that they should take delight in assimilating themselves, even in trifles, with other independent nations of the world.

No such changes, and no such sentiments, were as yet to be found in Peru. In the harbour of Callao, the shipping were crowded into a corner, encircled by gun-boats, close under the fort, and with a strong boom drawn round them. The custom-house was empty, and the door locked; no bales of goods rose in pyramids on the quays; no loaded mules covered the road from Callao to Lima; nor during the whole ascent was an individual to be seen, except, perhaps, a solitary courier galloping towards the fortress. In Lima itself the difference was as striking: jealousy and distrust of one another, and still more of strangers, filled every breast; disappointment and fear, aggravated by personal inconvenience and privation, broke up all agreeable society; rendering this once great, luxurious, and happy city, one of the most wretched places on earth.

Lima was not, however, on this account, the less interesting to a stranger: and although we often regretted not seeing it in its days of glory, we could not but esteem ourselves fortunate, in having an opportunity of witnessing the effect of a combination of circumstances, not likely to be met with again. The immediate cause of this unhappy state of things, was the spirit of independence which had recently burst forth in South America; and it may be remarked, that none of those free states have achieved their liberty without first running a similar course of suffering; a sort of ordeal to purify them from the contamination of their former degradation.

Lima, up to this period, had been exempted

from the sufferings of the countries by which she was surrounded. It is true there had been wars of a revolutionary character, in the interior of Peru; but their desolating effect had not till now reached the capital, the inhabitants of which went on in their usual style of splendid luxury, in thoughtless ease and security, till the enemy came and knocked at the " silver gates of the city of the kings," as Lima was proudly called in the days of her magnificence. San Martin's expedition took the Limenians quite by surprise; for they had always held Chili in contempt, as a mere appendage to Peru, from which no attack could be apprehended. The attack, however, was made, by land and by sea; and, while San Martin was making head steadily with his troops, drawing nearer and nearer to the capital, cutting off its supplies, and gaining over to his cause all the districts through which he passed; Lord Cochrane swept the sea of Spanish ships; blockaded the Peruvian ports; and carried off their finest frigate, from under the very guns of their strongest fort.

The violent irritation produced in Lima by

these operations of the enemy was quite natural; for the fortunes of the inhabitants, who had been accustomed for ages to revel in luxury and wealth, were now reduced to the lowest ebb; and the Spaniards, proud by birth and education, were cut to the soul by such humiliating reverses, of which these unaccustomed privations made them only the more sensible. As they were aware that Lord Cochrane and the greater part of his officers and crew were English, it was to be expected they would be jealous and distrustful of all Englishmen, however unconnected with the Chilians, or however circumspect in their conduct. A person professing neutrality is placed in an awkward situation, between two contending parties : his indifference is ascribed to ill-will—the slightest expression which escapes him in favour of the other party is resented as hostility—and any agreement, on a single point, is instantly seized upon as an indubitable proof of his friendly disposition.

To a mere traveller, this state of things might have been amusing enough ; but to us, who had a particular line of conduct to pursue, and a number of objects to attend to, it was frequently the source of considerable embarrassment. We were obliged to communicate occasionally with both parties, on business relative to commerce, and other matters affecting the British interests; and as the nature of the subject often required personal intercourse, we were inevitably led, at times, to a greater degree of apparent familiarity with one party, than the other could allow to be consistent with our professed neutrality. Each, however, in turn, invariably forgot this reflection, when the intercourse happened to lie with themselves: so that, to maintain our neutral character on these occasions, and not at the same time to give offence, required some address. With the Chilians, who were advancing, it was not so difficult as with the Spaniards, who stood in need of countenance: the Chilians also had good reason to believe that we wished them success on account of our trade; as well as from the sentiments known to be expressed on the subject in England. But with the Spaniards, who were sinking in the world, it was otherwise: nothing would satisfy them but a declaration of cordial adherence to their cause, and hatred to that of the Insurgents, as they, in the bitterness of their hearts, always called the Patriots.   At the same time they always affected to despise their enemies, and to be perfectly indifferent to our opinion; yet, with the perversest spirit of inconsistency, they occupied themselves in watching us, and misinterpreting all our actions and expressions to such a degree, that nothing was too extravagant to be told and believed in Lima respecting our breaches of neutrality. It was in vain, by a frank and open behaviour, to hope to escape suspicion; for it had become a sort of disease amongst the Spaniards to suspect the English; and its symptoms were aggravated every moment by the increasing distresses to which they were exposed. It will be easily conceived that, under such circumstances, we had not much enjoyment in visiting Lima, and that, situated as I was with many anxious duties to attend to, I could find little leisure to remark or to record peculiarities of society and manners.

Even when we did go into company, no great pleasure was to be derived from it; as the people had no leisure nor spirits to discuss any other topic than their own apprehensions and sufferings. The undisturbed quiet which they had so long enjoyed, made them only more sensible to the present evil; and all was doubt and despair. In former times, said the Limenians, our city was that in which pleasure held her court; wealth and ease were our attendants; enjoyment was our only business; and we dreamt of no evil but an earthquake. They had yet to learn that there are moral and political, as well as physical earthquakes, which, though they leave churches and dwellings undestroyed, may lay the whole fabric of society in ruins.

The Royalist army, in common with the people, as usual, referred every evil to the mismanagement of the executive government; and having decided, in their summary way, that the Viceroy was unfit to reign, they forthwith deposed him at the point of the bayonet; and raised one of their own Generals in his place. This strong measure had been carried into effect a few days before we arrived, and we found the city in considerable bustle, preparatory to the festivities usual on the installation of a new Viceroy. The soldiers, of course, were confident the change would immediately turn the fortunes of the day, and, even in the city, a faint hope for a moment animated the inhabitants: but most reflecting persons saw clearly, that these violent proceedings only betrayed to the enemy their own want of union and discipline.

As we were not, and, indeed, could not be competent judges of these proceedings, and were not accredited to any particular government or authority, we were always left free to take things as we found them, and to communicate with the person at the head of the government, for the time being, whoever he might be, and without inquiring how he got there.   It thus became my duty to pay my respects to the new Viceroy, General La Serna; as it would have been to have waited on his predecessor, General Pezuela, had I arrived a few days sooner.

The palace had a good deal the air of a native court in India; exhibiting the same intermixture of meanness and magnificence in style, which, while it displays the wealth and labour it has cost, betrays, at the same time, the want of taste and judgment in the design.   There was no keeping amongst the parts ; so that the shabby and the gorgeous were blended, and one was never sure that any thing pleasing would not be found contiguous to something offensive. The entrance was by a dirty court, like that of a stable-yard, communicating with a staircase, on the steps of which the soldiers of the guard, in ragged shabby uniforms, were lounging about, smoking their segars at their ease, and making way for no one. A long and narrow set of winding passages brought us to a suite of waiting rooms, filled with many weary supplicants, amongst whom the etiquette of precedence was not forgotten, the poorest and most hopeless being left in the outer apartments. In the room adjoining the audience chamber, we saw only the priesthood and military ; for, in these turbulent seasons, the value of a sword is estimated, at least at its due weight. Our interview, being merely ceremonial, was short, and led to nothing worth relating.

In the evening I was introduced to several families, all of which were more or less cast down by the circumstances of the day ; and their good breeding was hardly sufficient to conceal their suspicions of our neutrality.

Next morning we called upon the deposed Viceroy, rather as a civility than a duty, for his authority was utterly destroyed, and he had retired to his country-seat, called La Magdalene, not far from Lima. He was more dejected than we thought a haughty grandee ought to have been ; but he explained this to us, by saying, that he felt deeply for this lost country, which he foresaw would never prosper under such rebellious guidance. Instead, however, of his being afflicted at the change, it is probable he secretly rejoiced at his dismissal from the command. He had done his duty as long as he could, by making a respectable stand against the enemy ; and it was clear, that he must, ere long, have yielded up the capital, not so much to the superior force of San Martin's army, as to the overwhelming influence of public sentiment, the tide of which had decidedly turned, and was at this time flowing directly against the Spanish authority.

During the first few days, our thoughts were so much taken up with official duties, that little time was left for observing either the town or the society. We became every day more and more sensible of our precarious footing, and the necessity of observing the greatest circumspection in our intercourse with these jealous people. Living entirely on board ship, would at once have confirmed all their suspicions of our favouring the enemy, whose squadron was anchored in the outer Roads; while residing altogether at Lima might have been attributed to our wish to spy into the nakedness of the land. The course we did follow, of being at Lima, or at Callao, or on board, as circumstances required, though it did not exempt us from suspicion, was the best we could adopt; and we hoped, by caution and forbearance, to avoid giving cause of offence; but in this, as will be seen, we found ourselves much mistaken.

Being desirous of ascertaining, on all occasions, the real state of popular feeling, which generally developes itself at public meetings, I went to one of the bull-fights, given in honour of the new Viceroy's installation. It took place in an immense wooden amphitheatre, capable of holding, it was said, twenty thousand people. As we had been disappointed at Valparaiso by a sham bull-fight, we hoped here to witness an exhibition worthy of the mother country. But the resemblance was, I suspect, not less faulty, though in the opposite extreme; for the bulls were here put to death with so many unusual circumstances of cruelty, as not only to make it unlike the proper bull-fights, but to take away all pleasure in the spectacle from persons not habituated to such sights. These exhibitions have been described by so many travellers, that it is needless here to do more than advert to some circumstances peculiar to those of Lima.

After the bull had been repeatedly speared, and tormented by darts and fire-works, and was all streaming with blood, the matador, on a signal from the Viceroy, proceeded to dispatch him. Not being however sufficiently expert, he merely sheathed his sword in the animal's neck without the intended effect. The bull instantly took his revenge, by tossing the matador to a great height in the air, and he fell apparently dead in the arena. The audience applauded the bull, while the attendants carried off the matador. The bull next attacked a horseman, dismounted him, ripped up the horse's belly, and bore both him and his rider to the ground : the horse was not suffered to die in peace, but being raised on his legs, was urged, by whipping and goading, to move round the ring in a state too horrible to be described, but which afforded the spectators the greatest delight. The noble bull had thus succeeded in baffling his tormentors as long as fair means were used, when a cruel device was thought of to subdue him. A large curved instrument called a Luna was thrown at him, in such a way as to divide the hamstrings of the hind legs : such, however, were his strength and spirit, that he did not fall, but actually travelled along at a tolerable pace on his stumps,—a most horrible sight ! This was not all; for a man armed with a dagger now mounted the bull's back, and rode about for some minutes to the infinite delight of the spectators; who were thrown into ecstasies, and laughed and clapped their hands at every stab given to the miserable animal, not for the purpose of killing him, but to stimulate him to accelerate his pace;

at length, the poor beast, exhausted by loss of blood, fell down and died.

The greater number of the company, although females, seemed enchanted with the brutal scene passing under their eyes, and I looked round, in vain, for a single face that looked grave : every individual, indeed, seemed quite delighted. It was melancholy to observe a great proportion of children amongst the spectators ; from one of whom, a little girl, only eight years old, I learned that she had already been present at three bull-fights; the details of which she gave with great animation and pleasure, dwelling especially on such horrid circumstances as I have described. It would shock and disgust to no purpose to give a minute account of other instances of wanton cruelty, which, however, appeared to be the prin-cipal recommendation of these exhibitions. But it was impossible to help feeling, in spite of our much-talked-of neutrality, that any change which would put a stop to such proceedings was greatly to be wished. In every instance in South America, where the cause of independence has succeeded, two measures have been invariably adopted : one the abolition of the slave-trade, and as far as possible of slavery ; the other, the relinquishment of bull-fights. With respect to the slave question, most people think alike; but many hesitate as to the propriety of doing away the bull-fights, especially they who have witnessed them in Spain only, or who have never witnessed them at all ; but it is rare to hear any one condemn their abolition after having been present at those of Lima.

I heard a Chilian gentleman offer a curious theory on this subject. He declared that the Spaniards had systematically sought by these cruel shows, and other similar means, to degrade the taste of the Colonies, and thereby more easily to tyrannize over the inhabitants. The people, he said, first rendered utterly insensible to the feelings of others, by a constant familiarity with cruelty and injustice, soon became indifferent to the wrongs of their country, and in the end lost all motive to generous exertion in themselves.

An excellent old Spanish gentleman, of whom I shall have occasion to speak hereafter, stated,.

that these bull-fights were totally different from those exhibited in Spain : those of Lima, indeed, he could not bear to look at; nor had he ever met an Englishman who could be prevailed upon to visit the amphitheatre a second time. He ridiculed the theory of the Chilian above mentioned; though he acknowledged with shame that these scenes, horrible as they were, had always been encouraged by the Viceroys, and other Spanish rulers of the country.

In the evening I went in company with a young Spaniard to be introduced to a fine old nobleman, the Marquis of Montemiré, uncle of the Duke of San Carlos, who was for some time in England as minister from the Court of Madrid. He was eighty years of age, and appeared much broken down by the climate ; but still possessing in a remarkable degree the cheerfulness of youth : indeed, his thoughts and the turn of his expressions were so juvenile, that he wanted nothing but bodily strength to take an active part in the bustling scenes of the day.

At the Marquis's we met a heavy-looking elderly priest, who put a thousand idle questions to us respecting the news from Europe. In the course of this conversation, my malicious companion, in order to plague his reverend friend, whispered to me to say the Inquisition had been re-established in Spain. Accordingly, taking the first opportunity, I said something bearing this interpretation. The effect was amusing enough, for the old father, who it seems had been the chief inquisitor, clapped his hands, and, with a sparkling eye, shouted, " Bravo ! I thought it must be so !" but perceiving his young friend smiling, he first looked angry, and then laughed, calling him a sad " pícaro."—" Nevertheless," added he, in a lower tone, with his fist clenched, and his teeth closed, " though it be not yet re-established, it soon will."

Every thing connected with the recently abolished Inquisition is viewed at Lima with a degree of scorn and hatred, very remarkable in a city so crowded with clerical establishments ; and where the observances of the church form so great a part of the business of the people. But whatever be the cause of this unmeasured detestation, nothing can be more determined than it is ; and our portly friend, the ex-inquisitor, must I fear be content to follow the stream, and give up his chance of again tormenting his countrymen.

A story is told of this priest, however, which shows he was not quite hardened by the duties of his former office, but that he mingled his natural feelings with those proper to his calling, in a manner rather amiable for an inquisitor. Happening one day to visit a house where four or five Englishmen were dining, he joined in conversation with them; and was so much pleased with his company, that he turned round to a friend, and exclaimed, " Oh! what a pity it is that such fine rosy-looking, good young men, should all necessarily and inevitably go to the Devil!" (a los infiernos.)

The domestic manners of the society here differ from those of Chili, almost as much as the dresses. Instead of meeting at balls, concerts, and tertulias or parties, the women associate very little with one another; there are few dances, very little music, and, except at the bull-fights or the play, and sometimes in the country, the ladies seldom assemble together. But they are all extremely regular in their attendance upon mass; indeed, the women in these countries form the congregations almost exclusively. At the houses where we called in the morning, we usually found the ladies dressed very gaily to receive visitors; that is, male visitors, for we seldom met any but the ladies of the house on these occasions. In the evening, the same thing generally takes place; and our chance of meeting the gentlemen of the family, had we wished it, was always least at their own home.

In the cool part of the day, for about an hour and a half before sunset, the ladies walk abroad, dressed in a manner as far as I know unique, and certainly highly characteristic of the spot. This dress consists of two parts, one called the Saya, the other the Manto. The first is a petticoat, made to fit so tightly that, being at the same time quite elastic, the form of the limbs is rendered distinctly visible. The Manto, or cloak, is also a petticoat, but, instead of hanging about the heels, as all honest petticoats ought to do, it is drawn over the head, breast, and face; and is kept so close by the hands, which it also conceals, that no part of the body, except one eye, and sometimes only a small portion of one eye, is perceptible. A rich coloured handkerchief, or a silk band and tassel, are frequently tied round the waist, and hang nearly to the ground in front. A rosary, also, made of beads of ebony, with a small gold cross, is often fastened to the girdle, a little on one side; though in general it is suspended from the neck.

The effect of the whole is exceedingly striking; but whether its gracefulness—for, with the fine figure of the Lima women, and their very beautiful style of walking, this dress is eminently graceful—be sufficient to compensate for its indelicacy to an European eye, will depend much upon the stranger's taste, and his habits of judging of what he sees in foreign countries. Some travellers insist upon forcing every thing into comparison with what they have left at home, and condemn or approve, according as this unreasonable standard is receded from or adhered to. To us, who took all things as we found them, the Saya and Manto afforded much amusement, and, sometimes, not a little vexation. It happened occasionally, that we were spoken to in the streets by ladies, who appeared to know us well, but whom we could not discover, till some apparently trivial remark in company long afterwards betrayed the Tapadas, as they call themselves. Ladies of the first rank indulge in this amusement, and will wear the meanest Saya, or stoop to any contrivance to effect a thorough disguise. I myself knew two young ladies, who completely deceived their brother and me, although we were aware of their fondness for such pranks, and I had even some suspicions of them at the very time. Their superior dexterity, however, was more than a match for his discernment, or my suspicions; and so completely did they deceive our eyes, and mislead our thoughts, that we could scarcely believe our senses, when they at length chose to discover themselves.

Lima has been described as the " Heaven of women, the purgatory of men, and the hell of jackasses," and so, perhaps, it may be in times of peace; but the war had now broken down such distinctions, and all parties looked equally miserable; or, if any one had the advantage, it was the donkeys, who from the absence of all business were, for the first time in their lives, exempted from labour. The men were miserable from unwonted privation, apprehended loss of fortune, and wounded national pride. But the ladies, however annoyed by these circumstances, in common with the rest of the world, still maintained their prerogative of having their own way ; a right which, when acting in co-operation with the impenetrable disguise of the Saya and Manto, gave to manners a tone and character that may be imagined, but cannot well be described. Neither would it be fair for a passing and busy visitor, like myself, with his thoughts and attention occupied by other objects, to give general opinions upon the habits of a great city. But even had our opportunities and leisure been greater, the moment was singularly unpropitious, since scarcely any circumstance in society occupied its wonted place. Even in families, the effect of the times was deeply felt : a particular view of politics was adopted by one member, the opposite by another ; some acted from principle, some from interest, others from fear ; thus, sincerity and

confidence were banished, just at the moment
when the pressure of the war was most urgent,
and when a cordial union was the only safeguard
against the ruin and misery of the whole house.

Had my attention been less occupied in preserving a prudent and circumspect line of conduct, I might, undoubtedly, have noticed many
incidents, which, if properly described, would
have served to characterize the singular state of
Lima at the moment : but this being impossible,
I could only hope to catch occasionally some minute though sufficiently portentous symptoms of
the times.

★   ★   ★   ★   ★

In all companies, the conversation turned on
political topics ; and it was very curious to observe, amidst much prejudice and error in reason-
ing, and much exaggeration and misstatement of
facts, how justly every one felt on the occasion,

and with what delight they exercised the new privilege of speaking out; a privilege, it may be remarked, which is at once cause and effect : since we know, that, in former times, when no freedom of speech was permitted, the faculty of thinking to any purpose was equally repressed; a truth which, though a mere common-place, it is not, on that account, the less interesting to see confirmed in practice. At this time every one not only took a pride in saying what his opinions were, but seized every opportunity that occurred, or could be devised, to manifest his political sincerity. The borders of the ladies' shawls were wrought into patriotic mottos ; the tops of the newspapers and play-bills bore similar inscriptions ; patriotic words were set to all the old national airs ; and I saw a child one day munching a piece of gilt gingerbread, stamped with the word Independencia !

I am aware that all this bustle can prove but little ; and that nothing is more prostituted than this sort of verbal enthusiasm, which evaporates at the first show of opposition ; and certainly, taken singly, it would be of small moment in a political point of view, however amusing to witness on a great scale: but it is no bad accompaniment to successful action, and helps to keep alive the new-born spirit of independence, when other and more important causes are ready to give practical effect to the sentiment.

Patriotic exertions are always thought more highly of when viewed from a distance, than when examined closely. But, even in the eyes of those who are present, the interest which a show of patriotism excites is often at first of a very lively character. This dazzling effect, however, speedily goes off: the real characters and motives of the actors become so well known to us, that the fictitious representation of pure disinterested public spirit no longer pleases; and at last we see nothing in this revolutionary drama that is acted to the life, but the cruelty and the sorrow.

In the case of the Mexican Revolution, Iturbidé endeavoured to conciliate all parties, and tried, by various means, to unite the interests of the old Spaniards with those of the natives: but the result of the experiment shows how vain all such attempts are. It was, in fact, entirely contrary to the habits of the Spaniards, to form a solid friendship with the people over whom they had so long held absolute dominion : it was equally contrary to the feelings of the Americans to repose confidence in those who had never trusted them. It is due, however, to Iturbidé, to say, that by this idea of uniting the two heartily together, the blow which was sure to fall eventually on the heads of the Spaniards was deferred ; and more time was given for them to wind up their affairs, and render their fate as little severe as possible. If this was really the object, the device which Iturbidé fell upon was ingenious, and statesmanlike.*

But the poor Spaniards had a very difficult task to perform, and, upon the whole, they did not execute it well. For they could not bring themselves to make a sincere effort to deserve the good-will of the Americans, but viewed, with mor-

---

* *Note to the Third Edition.*—Since the Second Edition of this Work was printed, I have had the satisfaction of conversing with Iturbidé himself in London, and have been gratified by learning that, as far as his motives and conduct are concerned, he is perfectly satisfied with the accuracy of my statements.

tification and envy, the growing prosperity of the country, no longer exclusively theirs. They felt the foundation of their own fortunes gradually slipping from them; and having been habituated to the enjoyment of exclusive privileges, could not reconcile themselves to share their fortunes and long established rights, with their former dependents. Being conscious that these feelings rendered them unworthy of confidence, they naturally inferred, that in reality they were not trusted. In this frame of mind, they lived in constant dread of popular vengeance, and often gave way to terrors from causes insignificant, or imaginary. When they met together, they never failed to augment one another's fears, by repeating stories of the threats and insults they had met with; and spoke of the various symptoms of enmity on the part of the free Americans, who, they said, were only waiting for an opportunity to expel them from the country.

The correspondence also which they maintained with all parts of the interior contributed, in a remarkable degree, to heighten these feelings of alarm; since it was impossible to investigate every idle report which came from a distance. They were also absurdly unguarded in the terms which they used in speaking of the native inhabitants of the country. They delighted, for instance, in conversation to contrast their own " superior ilustracion" with the " ignorancia barbara" of the Mexicans; and if any one of us, who were in different parties, ventured to insinuate, that this ignorance of the natives might, perhaps, have been produced by the manner in which the country had been governed; and that, possibly, there might be much intellectual wealth among the inhabitants, though the mines, in which it was hid, had never been worked—they would turn fiercely upon us, and maintain, that the people of whom we spoke were incapable of being educated. If we further suggested that the experiment had never been fairly tried, they flatly denied the fact, and declared there was nothing in the laws which prevented a native from obtaining the same knowledge, wealth, and power as a Spaniard. But this is not to the purpose; for whatever the laws may have been, we know well what the actual practice was; and even where exceptions occurred,

the argument of the Spaniards was not strengthened : since, whenever a native did rise to wealth
or consequence, he became, from that instant,
virtually a Spaniard ; and derived his riches by
means of monopolies, at the expence of the country ; and as he obtained power, solely by becoming a servant of the government, he merely assisted in oppressing his countrymen, without the
possibility of serving them.

Graham:
Journal of a Voyage to Brazil

Maria Graham (Lady Callcott), *Journal of a Voyage to Brazil, and Residence there, during Part of the Years 1821, 22, 23* (London: John Murray, 1824), pp. 100–12, 135–7, 142–9, 292–6.

Maria Graham (1785–1842) was born near Cockermouth, the daughter of Rear Admiral George Dundas. As a young woman she mixed in the literary circle of Samuel Rogers, Thomas Campbell and the painter Thomas Lawrence, before accompanying her father to India in 1808. At Bombay she met and married Thomas Graham, a naval officer, and toured the subcontinent with him. In 1811 the couple returned to Britain, and in 1812 Maria published her first travel account, entitled *Journal of a Residence in India*, one of the most accomplished descriptions of the country published in the early nineteenth century. She followed this with *Letters from India* (1814), a general account of Indian society, history and mythology aimed at the general reader. In 1819 the Grahams toured Italy and the following year she published *Three Months in the Mountains East of Rome*. In July 1821 Thomas was appointed to the South American Squadron and the couple crossed the Atlantic on board the frigate *Doris*, arriving at Pernambuco in September. They remained in Brazil, residing in Pernambuco, Bàhia and Rio de Janiero, until March 1822, when Thomas was posted to Chile. He died, however, while his ship was rounding Cape Horn. After burying her husband, Maria took up residence in Valparaiso in May, where she was 'protected' by her fellow Scot Lord Cochrane, admiral of the Chilean fleet and future Earl of Dundonald. Here she met many of the leading lights of Chilean independence, including San Martín, who stayed in her cottage *en route* to exile in Europe. In March 1823 she returned to Brazil, possibly following Cochrane, who, frustrated with the Chilean government's failure to finance his navy, had transferred to the Brazilian service. She worked briefly as a tutor to the Brazilian Infanta María da Gloria, in 1826 crowned Queen of Portugal. She convalesced from a long illness and prepared her South American journals for publication. Her paper entitled 'An Account of the Effects of the Late Earthquake in Chili' was read to the Geological Society (it influenced Charles Lyell) and published in *Transactions of the Geological Society of London* (second series, vol. I (1824), p. 413). Graham took up her post in Brazil in July 1824, but her royal appointment was fraught with difficulties and she returned to England around the end of 1825. In 1827 Graham married again, this time to the painter Augustus Callcott, and her remaining years, including another Italian tour in 1828, were dedicated to art and writing about art. In 1831 she ruptured a blood vessel and became an invalid, but she lived on, publishing prolifically all the while under her new title of Lady Callcott, until 1842, when she died peacefully in her home at Kensington.

Graham visited Brazil during a climacteric period in its history. The Prince Regent Dom Pedro had converted to the cause of independence, in January 1822 assuming leadership of the Brazilian government; the following September, he proclaimed independence, declaring war on the Portuguese forces remaining in Brazil. Graham was eyewitness to these dramatic events through her friendship with Cochrane. Upon returning to England, Graham decided to narrate her South American adventures in two separate books. This was partly on the grounds that Spanish and Portuguese America were 'as different in climate and productions, as the inhabitants are in manners, society, institutions, and government' (p. iv) and deserved separate treatment, partly from a desire not to lose sight of public events in Brazil by narrating her two periods of residence in separate volumes. Her complete travelogue was published in 1824 by John Murray in the form of two books: *Journal of a Voyage to Brazil* and *Journal of a Residence in Chili, during the Year 1822 and a Voyage from Chili to Brazil in 1823*. The Brazilian volume, from which the present excerpts are taken, is introduced by a history of the new country, based largely on Robert Southey's *History of Brazil*. The two sections narrating her two periods of residence are connected 'by a notice of the public events of the year of her absence' (p. iv). The book is a sympathetic record of the Brazilian independence struggle, marked by Graham's moral indignation at many features of the colonial legacy, most notably the slave trade, which continued in Brazil until late in the nineteenth century. It is perhaps regrettable that she is sparing in her comments on the intrigues in the royal household to which she was personally privy, notably the intense rivalry between her employer Queen Leopoldina and Dom Pedro's beautiful and assertive Creole mistress Domitilia de Castro. In October 1824, after only a month's employment, Graham (the hapless Empress's only remaining friend) was dismissed from her post as governess to the Infanta by a cabal of palace servants who disliked her Scottish obsessions with fresh air, intellectuality and politeness. She was apparently outraged at the custom of the young Infanta having to take her bath in full view of all the palace servants and sentries, and sought unsuccessfully to abolish it. The excerpts published here represent Graham as an *'exploratrice sociale'* and female moralist, combining picturesque description of tropical landscape with a rather self-righteous condemnation of the domestic sloth of Creole women. Her account of María de Jesús, one of many female combatants in the independence wars, and her deeply ambivalent reaction to a group of Botocudo Indians in the final excerpt, typify her wide-ranging treatment of Brazilian society and manners.

The name of Pernambuco, which is that of the captainship, is now generally applied to the capital, which consists of two parts; 1st, the city of Olinda, which was founded by the Portuguese, under Duarte Coelho Pedreiro, about 1530 or 1540, and, as its name implies, on a beautiful spot, where moderate, but abrupt hills, a fine river, and thick wood, combine to charm the eye ; but the approach to it by sea must always have been difficult, if not dangerous : and, 2nd, the town of Recife de Pernambuco, or the Reef of Pernambuco, built by the Dutch, under Maurice of Nassau, and by them called Maurice Town. It is a singular spot, well fitted for trade; it is situated upon several sand banks, divided by salt water creeks and the mouth of two fresh water rivers, connected by three bridges, and divided into as many parts; Recife, properly so called, where are the castles of defence, and the dock-yard, and the traders; Sant Antonio, where are the government house, the two principal churches, one for the white and one for the black population; and Boa Vista, where the richer merchants, or more idle inhabitants, live among their gardens, and where convents, churches, and the bishop's palace, give an air of importance to the very neat town around them.

All this I knew before I landed, and thought I was pretty well prepared for Pernambuco. But no previous knowledge could do away the wonder with which one must enter that very extraordinary port. From the ship, which is anchored three miles from the town, we see that vessels lie within a reef on which the sea is perpetually breaking, but till I was actually within that reef, I had not the least idea of the nature of the harbour : the swell going ashore would have seemed tremendous, had we not been prepared for it, and made our passage of three miles a very long one. We approached the sandy beach between Recife and Olinda so nearly, that I thought we were going to land there ; when coming abreast of a tower on a rock, where the sea was breaking violently, we turned short round, and found ourselves within a marvellous natural break-water, heard the surf dashing without, and saw the spray, but we ourselves were sailing along smoothly and calmly, as if in a mill-pond. The rock of which the reef is formed, is said to be coral; but it is so coated with barnacle and limpet above barnacle and limpet, that I can see nothing but the remainder of these shells for many feet down, and as deep into the rock as our hammers will break. It extends from a good way to the northward of Paraiba to Olinda, where it sinks under water, and then rises abruptly at Recife, and runs on to Cape St. Augustine, where it is interrupted by the bold granite head, that shoots through it into the ocean: it then re-appears, and continues, interruptedly, towards the south. The breadth of the harbour here between the reef and the main land varies from a few fathoms to three quarters of a mile; the water is deep close to the rock, and there the vessels often moor. There is a bar at the entrance of the harbour, over which there is, in ordinary tides, sixteen feet water, so that ships of considerable burden lie here.* His Majesty's brig Alacrity lay some time within the reef; and two feet more water on the bar, would have enabled the Doris to have entered, though, as far as I have seen, there would be no room to turn about if she wished to go out again. The reef is certainly one of the wonders of the world; it is scarcely sixteen feet broad at top. It slopes off more rapidly than the Plymouth break-water, to a great depth on the outside, and is perpendicular within, to many fathoms. Here and there, a few inequalities at the top must formerly have annoyed the harbour in high tides or strong winds, but Count Maurice remedied this, by laying huge blocks of granite into the faulty places, and has thus rendered the top level, and the harbour safe at all times. The Count had intended to build warehouses along the reef, but his removal from the government prevented his doing so. A small fort near the entrance defends it, and indeed always must, so narrow and sudden is the pas-

---

* In 1816, under the governor, Monte Negro, the harbour was cleared and deepened, and particularly the bar.

sage. Near it, a light-house is in a fair way of being soon finished, at the very extremity of the reef, and these are the only two buildings on this extraordinary line of rock. We rowed up the harbour among vessels of all nations, with the town on one side, and the reef on the other, until we came to one of the wide creeks, over which the Dutch built a fine stone bridge, now in decay. We were a a good deal struck with the beauty of the scene; the buildings are pretty large, and white; the land low and sandy, spotted with bright green tufts of grass, and adorned with palm-trees. A few years ago a violent flood nearly destroyed the greater part of the centre of the bridge, yet the arches still serve to support light wooden galleries on each side of it, and the houses and gateways are still standing at either end. We landed pretty near the bridge, and were received by Colonel Patronhe, who apologised for the governor, who could not come to receive us, as he was in the council room.* The colonel conducted us to the government house, a very handsome building, with a square in front, and a tower, and we entered what had evidently been a splendid hall. The gilding and painting still remained on some parts of the ceiling and walls; but now it is occupied by horses standing ready saddled; soldiers armed, and ready to mount at a moment's warning; every thing on the alert; guns in front with lighted matches by them, and an air of bustle and importance among the soldiers, that excites a sort of sympathetic curiosity as to their possible and immediate destination. On going up stairs we found almost as much confusion: for the governor has hitherto lived in the very out-skirts of the town, and has but just come to the house in Sant Antonio, which was formerly the Jesuits' college, partly to be in the centre of business, and partly to secure his family, in case of accident, as the besiegers' out-posts are very near his

---

* The council or junta of provisional government consisted of ten members, of which Luiz do Rego was the head; they were drawing up an address to the inhabitants of Recife, assuring them of safety and protection; exulting in the advantage gained in the night, and asserting that there were plenty of provisions within the town; and encouraging them in the name of the king and cortes, to defend the city against the insurgents, who were of course branded with the names of enemies to the king and country.

former residence. I found Madame do Rego an agreeable, rather pretty woman, and speaking English like a native : for this she accounted, by informing me that her mother, the Viscondeça do Rio Seco, was an Irish woman. Nothing could be kinder and more flattering than her manner, and that of General do Rego's two daughters, whose air and manner are those of really well-bred women, and one of them is very handsome. After sitting some little time, refreshments were brought in, and shortly after, the governor himself appeared ; a fine military-looking man. He appeared ill, being still suffering from the effects of a wound he received some months ago, while walking through the town with a friend. It has since been ascertained, that the instigator of the crime was a certain Ouvidor (judge) whom he had displaced shortly after he assumed the government. The assassin fired twice ; Luiz do Rego received several shots and slugs in his body, but the most severe wound was in his left arm. His friend's life was for some time despaired of, but both are now nearly well. At the time the crime was committed, the perpetrator was seized more than once by some of the bye-standers ; but as often, a baker's basket was pushed in between him and whoever seized him ; he threw away his pistols and escaped.*

Having paid our visit, we proceeded to walk about the town. The streets are paved partly with blueish pebbles from the beach, partly with red or grey granite. The houses are three or four stories high, built of a whitish stone, and all are white-washed, with door-posts and window-frames of brown stone. The ground floor consists of shops, or lodging for the negroes, and stables : the floor above is generally appropriated to counting-houses and ware-rooms ; and the dwelling-house still higher, the kitchen being universally at the top, by which means the lower part of the house is kept cool. I was surprised to

---

* Luiz do Rego was not the first governor of Pernambuco who had been shot at. In 1710, when Sebastian de Castro, in conformity to his orders from Lisbon, had erected a pillar, and declared Recife a town, San Antonio da Recife, the Olindrians shot him on his walk to Boa Vista, in four places. The Ouvidor was one of the conspirators. The bishop had a share in this unchristian action. The object of the people of Olinda and of the assassin's party was, to confine Recife to its own parish, extending only to the Affogados on one side, and Fort Brun on the other.

find it so possible to walk out without inconvenience from the heat, so near the equator; but the constant sea-breeze, which sets in here every day at ten o'clock, preserves a temperature, under which it is at all times possible to take exercise. The hot time of day is from eight, when the land breeze fails, to ten. As we were to pass the stone bridge on our way back to the boat, which was ordered to meet us at the point of Recife, because the receding tide would have left it dry in the creek where we landed; we left it on one hand, and walked through Sant Antonio towards Boa Vista. When we came to the wooden bridge, 350 paces long, connecting it with Sant Antonio, we found that it had been cut through the middle, and is only now passable by means of two planks easily withdrawn, in case the besiegers should get possession of Boa Vista. Nothing can be prettier of its kind than the fresh green landscape, with its broad river winding through it, which is seen on each hand from the bridge, and the white buildings of the treasury and mint, the convents, and private houses, most of which have gardens. The verdure is delightful to an English eye; and I doubt not that the flat meadows, and slowly-flowing water, were particularly attractive to the Dutch founders of Recife. We walked back by the stone bridge, 280 paces long, as we intended; in vain did we look for shops; not one was open, the shopkeepers being all on military duty. They form the militia, and, as many of them are from Europe, and as they all expect to be plundered should the country Brazilians take the town by force, they are most zealous in their attendance as soldiers.

At each end of every street we found a light gun, and at the heads of the bridges two, with lighted matches by them, and at each post we were challenged by the guard. At the end of the stone bridge, at the ponte dos tres pontes*, next to Recife, the guards are more numerous and strict. In this quarter, the chief riches of the place are lodged, and that is the point most easily defended. It is very nearly surrounded with water, the houses are high, strongly built, and close together, the streets being very narrow, and the strong gateway at each end

* A little fort which defends the entrance to Recife.

of the bridge might secure time to demolish it entirely, and thus render that part of the town secure, except by the sand bank communicating with Olinda, and that is guarded by two considerable forts.

We had hardly gone fifty paces into Recife, when we were absolutely sickened by the first sight of a slave-market. It was the first time either the boys or I' had been in a slave-country ; and, however strong and poignant the feelings may be at home, when imagination pictures slavery, they are nothing compared to the staggering sight of a slave-market. It was thinly stocked, owing to the circumstances of the town ; which cause most of the owners of new slaves to keep them closely shut up in the depôts. Yet about fifty young creatures, boys and girls, with all the appearance of disease and famine consequent upon scanty food and long confinement in unwholesome places, were sitting and lying about among the filthiest animals in the streets. The sight sent us home to the ship with the heart-ache : and resolution, " not loud but deep," that nothing in our power should be considered too little, or too great, that can tend to abolish or to alleviate slavery,

27th. — I went on shore to-day to spend a few days with Miss S., the only English lady in the town. She is now living in her brother's town-house, where the office and warehouses are, because the country-house is within reach of the patriots. I do long to walk or ride out to the tempting green hills beyond the town ; but as that cannot be, I must content myself with what is within the lines. To-day, as we were coming in from Boa Vista, we met a family of Certanejos, who had brought provisions into the town some days ago, returning home to the Certam, or wild country of the interior. These Certanejos are a hardy, active set of men, mostly agriculturists. They bring corn and pulse, bacon and sweet-meats, to the sea-coast, hides and tallow also at times. But the sugar, cotton, and coffee, which form the staple exports of Pernambuco, require the warmer, richer lands, nearer the coast. Cotton is, however, brought from the Certam, but it is a precarious crop, depending entirely on the quantity of rain in the season ; and it sometimes does not rain in the Certam for two years. The party we met formed a very picturesque

P

groupe, the men clad in leather from head to foot, of which their light jerkin and close pantaloons are fitted as closely as the clothing on the Egina marbles, and have something of the same effect : the small round hat is in the form of Mercury's petasus ; and the shoes and gaiters of the greater number are excellently adapted to defend the legs and feet in riding through the thickets. The colour of all this is a fine tan brown. I was vexed that the woman of the party wore a dress evidently of French fashion: it spoiled the unity of the groupe. She was mounted behind the principal man, on one of the small active horses of the country ; several sumpter horses followed, laden with household goods and other things in exchange for their provisions: cloths, both woollen and cotton, coarse crockery, and other manufactured articles, especially knives, are what they chiefly take in barter; though I saw some furniture, with pretensions to elegance, among the stuff of the family I met. After the horses came a groupe of men, some walking and keeping pace with the amble of the beasts; others riding and carrying the children ; the procession being closed by a very stout good-looking man, smoking as he went along, and distinguished by a pair of green baize trowsers.

In the evening we rode out; whether it was because we had been so many weeks on board ship, and without horse-exercise, or because of the peculiar sweetness and freshness of evening after the sultry tropical day we had just passed, I know not, but I never enjoyed an hour in the open air so much. We rode out of the town by some pretty country-houses, called *silios*, to one of the outposts at Mondego, which was formerly the governor's residence. The tamarind, the silk-cotton tree *, and the palm, shaded us, and a thousand elegant shrubs adorned the garden walls. It is impossible to describe the fresh delicious feel of such an evening, giving repose and health after the fiery day. We were very sorry when obliged to return home ; but the sun was gone, there was no moon, and we were afraid that the guards at the various posts of defence might stop us. As we came back, we were challenged at every station ; but the words, *amigos ingresos* were our passport, and we got to Recife just as the evening hymn was singing, harshly and unmusically enough, by the

---

* Bombex pentandrium. *Jaquin.*

GATE & SLAVE MARKET AT PERNAMBUCO.

negroes and mulattoes in the streets ; but yet every thing that unites men in one common sentiment is interesting. The church doors were open, the altars illuminated, and the very slave felt that he was addressing the same Deity, by the same privilege with his master. It is an evening I can never forget.

28th. — This morning before breakfast, looking from the balcony of Mr. S.'s house, I saw a white woman, or rather fiend, beating a young negress, and twisting her arms cruelly while the poor creature screamed in agony, till our gentlemen interfered. Good God ! that such a traffic, such a practice as that of slavery, should exist. Near the house there are two or three depôts of slaves, all young ; in one, I saw an infant of about two years old, for sale. Provisions are now so scarce that no bit of animal food ever seasons the paste of man-dioc flour, which is the sustenance of slaves : and even of this, these poor children, by their projecting bones and hollow cheeks, show that they seldom get a sufficiency. Now, money also is so scarce, that a purchaser is not easily found, and one pang is added to slavery : the unavailing wish of finding a master! Scores of these poor creatures are seen at different corners of the streets, in all the listlessness of despair — and if an infant attempts to crawl from among them, in search of infantile amusement, a look of pity is all the sympathy he excites. Are the patriots wrong ? They have put arms into the hands of the *new* negroes, while the recollection of their own country, and of the slave-ship, and of the slave-market, is fresh in their memory.

I walked to-day to the market-place, where there is but little ; — beef scarce and dear, no mutton, a little poultry, and a few pigs, disgusting, because they feed in the streets where every thing is thrown, and where they and the dogs are the only scavengers. The blockade is so strict, that even the vegetables from the gentlemen's private gardens, two miles from the out-posts, are detained. No milk is to be had, bread of American flour is at least twice as dear as in England, and the cakes of mandioc baked with cocoa nut juice, too dear for the common people to afford a sufficiency even of them.

Fire-wood is extravagantly high, charcoal scarce. The negroes keep the markets: a few on their own account, more on that of their masters. The dress of the free negroes is like that of the creole Portuguese; a linen jacket and trowsers, or on days of ceremony one of cloth, and a straw hat, furnish forth either a black or a white gentleman. The women, in-doors, wear a kind of frock which leaves the bosom much exposed. When they walk out they wear either a cloak or mantle ; this cloak is often of the gayest colours ; shoes also, which are the mark of freedom, are to be seen of every hue, but black. Gold chains for the neck and arms, and gold ear-rings, with a flower in the hair, complete a Pernambucan woman's dress. The new negroes, men and women, have nothing but a cloth round their loins. When they are bought, it is usual to give the women a shift and petticoat, and the men at least trowsers, but this is very often omitted.

Yesterday the motley head-dresses of the Portuguese inhabitants were seen to great advantage, in a sally through the streets, made by a kind of supplementary militia to enforce the closing of all shop-doors, and the shutting up of all slaves, on an alarm that the enemy was attacking the town to the southward. The officer leading the party was indeed dressed *en militaire,* with a drawn sword in one hand, and a pistol in the other. Then followed a company that Falstaff would hardly have enlisted, armed in a suitable manner, with such caps and hats as became the variety of trades to which the wearers belonged, the rear being brought up by a most singular figure, with a small drum-shaped black cap on the very top of a stiff pale head, a long oil-skin cloak, and in his left hand a huge Toledo ready drawn, which he carried upright. The militia are better dressed, and are now employed in regular turn of duty with the royal troops, who are going over to the patriots daily.

Calling at the palace this forenoon, we learned that a hundred Indians are expected in the town, by way of assistance to the garrison. They wear their aboriginal dress, and are armed with slings, bows, and arrows. We are told their ideas of government consist in believing that implicit obedience is due both to king and priests. Brandy is the bribe for which they will do any thing; a dram of that liquor and a handful of mandioc flour being all the food they require when they come down to the port.

This evening, as there are no horses to be hired here, we borrowed some from our English and French friends, and rode to Olinda by the long sandy isthmus, which connects it with Recife. This is the isthmus fortified with a palisade, by Sir John Lancaster, during his stay at Recife, which he plundered. * The beach is defended by two castles, sufficiently strong when their situation is considered; on one side a furious surf breaking at their base, on the other a deep estuary and flat ground beyond, so that they cannot be commanded. The sand is partially covered by shrubs; one is very splendid with thick leaves and purple bell-shaped flowers; many are like those of the eastern world; many are quite new to me. I was surprised at the extreme beauty of Olinda, or rather of its remains, for it is now in a melancholy state of ruin. All the richer inhabitants have long settled in the lower town. The revenues of the bishopric being now claimed by the crown, and the monasteries suppressed for the most part, even the factitious splendour caused by the ecclesiastical courts and inhabitants is no more. The very college where the youths received some sort of education, however imperfect, is nearly ruined †, and there is scarcely a house of any size standing.

Olinda is placed on a few small hills, whose sides are in some directions broken down, so as to present the most abrupt and picturesque rock-scenery. These are embosomed in dark woods that seem coeval with the land itself: tufts of slender palms, here and there the broad head of an ancient mango, or the gigantic arms of the wide spreading silk-cotton tree, rise from out the rest in the near

---

* See Introduction, p. 20.

† This was the Jesuits' college founded under the administration of the admirable father Nobrega, and his companion De Gram. Here at eighteen years' old the celebrated Viera read lectures on rhetoric, and composed those commentaries on some of the classics, which were unfortunately lost in the course of the civil wars.

ground, and break the line of forest : amidst these, the convents, the cathedral, the bishop's palace, and the churches of noble, though not elegant architecture, are placed in stations which a Claude or a Poussin might have chosen for them ; some stand on the steep sides of rocks, some on lawns that slope gently to the sea-shore : their colour is grey or pale yellow, with reddish tiles, except here and there where a dome is adorned with porcelain tiles of white and blue.   Just as we reached the highest point of the town, looking across the woody bason round which the hills are grouped, the smoke from one of the outposts caught our sight.   The soldiers were standing or lying around, and their arms piled by them : they were just shadowed by tall trees behind, between whose trunks the scattered rays of the setting sun shed such a partial light as Salvator Rosa himself would not have disdained.   These same soldiers, how-ever, circumscribed our ride : we had intended to return by the inland road, but were not allowed to pass into it, as part, at least, lies without the posts, therefore we were obliged to return by the way we came.

At the spot where the present guard is placed, and where indeed a strong guard is peculiarly necessary, the river Bibiriba falls into the æstuary, which was formerly the port of Olinda.   A dam is built across with flood-gates which are occasionally opened ; and on the dam there is a very pretty open arcade, where the neighbouring inhabitants were accustomed in peaceable times to go in the evening, and eat, drink, and dance.   It is from this dam that all the good water used in Recife is daily conveyed in water-canoes, which come under the dam called the Varadouro, and are filled from twenty-three pipes, led so as to fill the canoes at once, without farther trouble. We saw seven-and-twenty of these little boats laden, paddle down the creek with the tide towards the town.   A single oar used rather as rudder than paddle guides the tank to the middle of the stream, where it floats to its destination.

The sun was low, long before we reached even the first of the two castles on our way back to the fort. The dogs had already begun their work of abomination. I saw one drag the arm of a negro from beneath the few inches of sand, which his master had caused to be thrown over his remains. It is on this beach that the measure of the insults dealt to the poor negroes is filled. When the negro dies, his fellow-slaves lay him on a plank, carry him to the beach, where beneath high-water mark they hoe a little sand over him ; but to the new negro even this mark of humanity is denied. He is tied to a pole, carried out in the evening and dropped upon the beach, where it is just possible the surf may bear him away. These things sent us home sad and spiritless, notwithstanding the agreeable scenes we had been riding among.

29th. The feast of St. Michael's has drawn out the Portuguese gentlewomen, of whom we had not yet seen one walking in the streets. The favourite dress seems to be black, with white shoes and white or coloured ribbons and flowers in the hair, with a mantle of lace or gauze, either black or white. We have seen a few priests too for the first time. I think the edict desiring them to keep within their convent walls, is in consequence of their being among the fomentors of the spirit of independence. The appropriation of so much of the church revenue by the court of Lisbon is of course unpopular among the clergy of the country ; and it is not difficult for them to represent, what indeed is truth, to the people, that the drawing of so much treasure from the country to support Lisbon, which can neither govern nor protect them now, is a rational ground of complaint. It is said, that the morals of the clergy here are most depraved. This is probably true. Men cut off by vows like those of the Roman clergy, from the active charities of social life, have only the resources of science and literature against their passions and vices. But here the very names of literature and science are almost unknown. The college and library of Olinda are in decay. There is not one book-seller in Pernambuco, and the population of its different parishes amounts to 70,000 souls ! A tolerably well written newspaper, of which I have not been able to procure the first number, was set up in

March, under the title of " Aurora Pernambucana," with the following motto from Camoens :

> Depois da procellosa tempestade,
> Nocturna sombra e sibilante vento,
> Tras a manha serena e claridade,
> Esperança de porto e salvamente :

alluding to the arrival of the news of the revolution in Portugal, on the 26th of that month, and the swearing of the governor, magistrates, &c. to adhere to the constitution as established by the Cortes. I am sorry to say that this only paper has been discontinued for the two last months, the editor having, as it seems, become a secretary of government, and having no longer time to superintend the press. *

Friday, 19*th.*—I accompanied Miss Pennell in a tour of visits to her Portuguese friends. As it is not their custom to visit or be visited in the forenoon, it was hardly fair to take a stranger to see them. However, my curiosity, at least, was gratified. In the first place, the houses, for the most part, are disgustingly dirty : the lower story usually consists of cells for the slaves, stabling &c. ; the staircases are narrow and dark ; and, at more than one house, we waited in a passage while the servants ran to open the doors and windows of the sitting-rooms, and to call their mistresses, who were enjoying their undress in their own apartments. When they appeared, I could scarcely believe that one half were gentlewomen. As they wear neither stay nor bodice, the figure becomes almost indecently slovenly, after very early youth ; and this is the more disgusting, as they are very thinly clad, wear no neck-handkerchiefs, and scarcely

---

* Not only has this paper been continued since, but others are now published in Recife.

any sleeves. Then, in this hot climate, it is unpleasant to see dark cottons and stuffs, without any white linen, near the skin. Hair black, ill combed, and dishevelled, or knotted unbecomingly, or still worse, *en papillote*, and the whole person having an unwashed appearance. When at any of the houses the bustle of opening the cob-webbed windows, and assembling the family was over, in two or three instances, the servants had to remove dishes of sugar, mandioc, and other provisions, which had been left in the best rooms to dry. There is usually a sofa at each end of the room, and to the right and left a long file of chairs, which look as if they never could be moved out of their place. Between the two sets of seats is a space, which, I am told, is often used for dancing ; and, in every house, I saw either a guitar or piano, and generally both. Prints and pictures, the latter the worst daubs I ever saw, decorate the walls pretty generally ; and there are, besides, crucifixes and other things of the kind. Some houses, however, are more neatly arranged; one, I think belonging to a captain of the navy, was papered, the floors laid with mat, and the tables ornamented with pretty porcelain, Indian and French . the lady too was neatly dressed in a French wrapper. Another house belonging to one of the judges was also clean, and of a more stately appearance than the rest, though the inhabitant was neither richer nor of higher rank. Glass chandeliers were suspended from the roof; handsome mirrors were intermixed with the prints and pictures. A good deal of handsome china was displayed round the room ; but the jars, as well as the chairs and tables, seemed to form an inseparable part of the walls. We were every where invited, after sitting a few moments on the sofa, to go to the balconies of the windows and enjoy the view and the breeze, or at least amuse ourselves with what was passing in the street. And yet they did not lack conversation : the principal topic, however, was praise of the beauty of Bahia; dress, children, and diseases, I think, made up the rest; and, to say the truth, their manner of talking on the latter subject is as disgusting as their dress, that is, in a morning: I am told they are different after dinner.

They marry very early, and soon lose their bloom.   I did not see one tolerably pretty woman to-day.   But then who is there that can bear so total a disguise as filth and untidiness spread over a woman?

★　　★　　★　　★　　★

Monday 22d.—This evening there was a large party, both Portuguese and English, at the consul's. In the well-dressed women I saw to-night, I had great difficulty in recognising the slatterns of the other morning. The senhoras were all dressed after the French fashion : corset, fichu, garniture, all was proper, and even elegant, and there was a great display of jewels.   Our English ladies, though quite of the second rate of even colonial gentility, however, bore away the prize of beauty and grace ; for after all, the clothes, however elegant, that are not worn habitually, can only embarrass and cramp the native movements ; and, as Mademoiselle Clairon remarks, " she who would " *act* a gentlewoman in public, must *be* one in private life."

The Portuguese men have all a mean look ; none appear to have any education beyond counting-house forms, and their whole time is, I believe, spent between trade and gambling : in the latter, the ladies partake largely after they are married. Before that happy period, when there is no evening dance, they surround the card tables, and with eager eyes follow the game, and long for the time when they too may mingle in it.   I scarcely wonder at this propensity. Without education, and consequently without the resources of mind, and in a climate where exercise out of doors is all but impossible, a stimulus must be had ; and gambling, from the sage to the savage, has always been resorted to, to quicken the current of life. On the present occasion, we feared the young people would have been disappointed of their dance, because the fiddlers, after waiting some time, went away, as they alleged, because they had not their tea early enough ; however, some of the ladies volunteered to play the piano, and the ball lasted till past midnight.

Tuesday, 23d. — I rode with Mr. Dance and Mr. Ricken along the banks of the lake, decidedly the most beautiful scenery in this beautiful country ; and then through wild groves, where all the splendours of Brazilian animal and vegetable life were displayed. The gaudy plumage of the birds, the brilliant hues of the insects, the size, and shape, and colour, and fragrance, of the flowers and shrubs, seen mostly for the first time, enchanted us, and rendered our little journey to the great pepper gardens, whither we were going, delightful. Every hedge is at this season gay with coffee blossom, but it is too early in the year for the pepper or the cotton to be in beauty. It is not many years since Francisco da Cunha and Menezes sent the pepper plant from Goa for these gardens, which were afterwards enlarged by him, when he became governor of Bahia. Plants were sent from hence to Pernambuco, which have succeeded in the botanical garden.

From the pepper gardens we rode on to a convent at the farther extremity of the town, and overlooking both the bays, above and below the peninsula of Bon fin, or N. S. da Monserrat It is called the Soledad, and the nuns are famous for their delicate sweetmeats, and for the manufacture of artificial flowers, formed of the feathers of the many-coloured birds of their country. I admired the white water-lily most, though the pomegranate flower, the carnation, and the rose are imitated with the greatest exactness. The price of all these things is exorbitant ; but the convents having lost much of their property since the revolution, the nuns are fain to make up by the produce of this petty industry, for the privations imposed on them by the reduction of their rents.

Wednesday, October 24th. — Mr. Pennell, his daughter, and a few other friends, joined us in an expedition to Itaparica*, a large island

* *Itapa* is the Indian name: the Portuguese termination, *Rica*, indicates the fertility of the island. On this island Francesco Pereira Coutinho, the first donatory, was killed by

that forms the western side of the Bay of All Saints. A shoal runs off
from it a long way to sea, and there are reefs of coral rocks on different
parts of its coast. The distance from the city to the nearest landing
place on the island is five miles and a half, which our boats' crews
rowed in less than two hours. We put in between two ledges of rock,
to a little jetty, belonging to the fazenda or factory of Aseoli, or Filis-
berti, both of whom were partners in Jerome Buonaparte's commercial
establishment here. There is no town on Itaparica; but there is a villa,
or village, with a fort on the Punto de Itaparica, which commands the
passage between it and the main land, and also the mouth of the river,
on which stands Nazareth da Farinha, so called from the abundance of
that article which it produces. There are also a great many fazendas,
which, with their establishment of slaves and cattle, may be considered
as so many hamlets. Each sugar farm, or ingenho, as the fazendas are
oftener called here, has its little community of slaves around it; and
in their huts something like the blessings of freedom are enjoyed, in
the family ties and charities they are not forbidden to enjoy. I went
into several of the huts, and found them cleaner and more comfortable than I expected; each contains four or five rooms, and each
room appeared to hold a family. These out-of-door slaves, belonging
to the great ingenhos, in general are better off than the slaves of
masters whose condition is nearer to their own, because, " The more
" the master is removed from us, in place and rank, the greater the
" liberty we enjoy; the less our actions are inspected and con-
" trouled; and the fainter that cruel comparison becomes betwixt
" our own subjection, and the freedom, or even dominion of another."
But, at best, the comforts of slaves must be precarious. Here it is
not uncommon to give a slave his freedom, when he is too old or too
infirm to work; that is, to turn him out of doors to beg or starve.
A few days ago, as a party of gentlemen were returning from a *pic
nic,* they found a poor negro woman lying in a dying state, by the

---

the savages. He had founded his city near the watering place called Villa Velha, by what
is now the fort of Gamboa, and not far from the habitation of the adventurer Caramura.
The first Christian settlement formed here was in 1561, when the Jesuits founded an Aldea,
and collected and humanised some of the natives.

side of the road. The English gentlemen applied to their Portuguese companions to speak to her, and comfort her, as thinking she
would understand them better; but they said, " Oh, 'tis only a black :
let us ride on," and so they did without further notice. The poor
creature, who was a dismissed slave, was carried to the English hospital, where she died in two days. Her diseases were age and
hunger.* The slaves I saw here working in the distillery, appear
thin, and I should say over-worked; but, I am told, that it is only in
the distilling months that they appear so, and that at other seasons
they are as fat and cheerful as those in the city, which is saying a
great deal. They have a little church and burying-ground here, and
as they see their little lot the lot of all, are more contented than I
thought a slave could be.

Sugar is the principal product of Itaparica; but the greater part of
the poultry, vegetables, and fruit, consumed in Bahia, are also from the
island, and lime is made here in considerable quantities from the ma-
drepores and corals found on the beach. This island used to furnish the
neighbourhood with horses. When the English fleet and army stopped
here, on the way to the Cape of Good Hope, the horses for the
cavalry regiments were procured here. However, there is nothing
remarkable in Itaparica but its fertility; the landscape is the same in
character with that of Bahia, though in humbler style; but it is fresh
and green, and pleasing. After dining in a palm-grove, and walking
about till we were tired, we re-embarked to return; but the tide was
unfavourable; we drifted among the rocks, where Coutinho, the first
founder of the colony of Bahia, was wrecked and afterwards murdered by the natives, and we were in consequence four hours in returning home.

26th, 27th, 28th, passed in pleasant enough intercourse with our

* " The custom of exposing old, useless, or sick slaves, in an island of the Tyber, there
" to starve, seems to have been pretty common in Rome; and whoever recovered, after
" being so exposed, had his liberty given him, by an edict of the Emperor Claudius;
" where it was likewise forbid to *kill any slave, merely for old age or sickness.*" — " We
" may imagine what others would practise, when it was the professed maxim of the elder
" Cato, to sell his superannuated slaves for any price, rather than maintain a useless
" burden." — *Discourses of the Populousness of Ancient Nations.*

U

countrymen, though neither of us were well enough to go much on shore, therefore our friends came to us.   There are eighteen English mercantile houses established at Bahia, two French, and two German. The English trade is principally carried on with Liverpool, which supplies manufactured goods and salt, in exchange for sugars, rums, tobaccos, cottons, very little coffee, and molasses.   Lately, sugars have been shipped, on English account, for Hamburgh to a great extent, and I believe part of the returns are in German or Prussian woollen-cloths.   The province of Bahia, by its neglect of manufactures, is quite dependent on commerce.   But the distance from the sea of the province of Minas Geraes, has induced the inhabitants to weave not only enough coarse cotton cloths for home consumption, but even to become an article of trade with the other captaincies.

In the province of Esperitu Santo, cotton sail-cloth is made; but the chief trade of this place is *slaving*.   This year no less than seventy-six slave-ships have sailed, without reckoning the smugglers in that line.

Sunday 28th. — Mr. Pennell had kindly fixed to-day for giving us a party in the country, and accordingly some of our young people were to go and assist in putting up tents, &c.; but a miscalculation of tide and time, and a mistake as to the practicability of landing on part of the beach beyond the light-house, occasioned a variety of adventures and accidents, without which I have always heard no fête champêtre could be perfect.   However that may be, our party was a pleasant one.   Instead of the tents, we made use of a country-house called the Roça, where beauty of situation, and neatness in itself and garden, made up for whatever we might have thought romantic in the tents, had they been erected.   It is the fashion to pave the courts of the country-houses here with dark pebbles, and to form in the pavement a sort of mosaic with milk-white shells.   The gardens are laid out in alleys, something in the oriental taste.   The millions of ants, which often in the course of a single night leave the best-clothed orange-tree bare both of leaves and flowers, render it necessary to surround each tree with a little stucco wall, or rather canal, in which there is water, till they are strong enough to recover if attacked by the ants. In the garden at Roça, every shrub of value, either for fruit or beauty, was so fenced, and there were seats, and water channels, and porcelain flowerpots, that made me almost think myself in the East. But there is a newness in every thing here, a want of interest on account of what has been, that is most sensibly felt. At most, we can only go back to the naked savage who devoured his prisoner, and adorned himself with bones and feathers here. In the East, imagination is at liberty to expatiate on past grandeur, wisdom, and politeness. Monuments of art and of science meet us at every step : *here*, every thing, nature herself, wears an air of newness, and the Europeans, so evidently foreign to the climate, and their African slaves, repugnant to every wholesome feeling, show too plainly that they are intruders, ever to be in harmony with the scene. However, Roça is beautiful, and all those grave thoughts did not prevent us from delighting in the fair prospect of

" Hill and valley, fountain and fresh shade;"

nor enjoying the scent of oleander, jasmine, tuberose, and rose, although they are adopted, not native children of the soil.

Of the Portuguese society here I know so very little, that it would be presumptuous to give an opinion of it. I have met with two or three well-informed men of the world, and some lively conversable women ; but none of either sex that at all reminded me of the well-educated men and women of Europe. Here the state of general education is so low, that more than common talent and desire of knowledge is requisite to attain any; therefore the clever men are acute, and sometimes a little vain, feeling themselves so much above their fellow-citizens, and the portion of book-learning is small. Of those who read on political subjects, most are disciples of Voltaire, and they outgo his doctrines on politics, and equal his indecency as to religion ; hence to sober people who have seen through the European revolutions, their discourses are sometimes disgusting. The Portuguese seldom dine with each other ; when they do, it is on some great occasion, to justify a splendid feast : they meet every evening either at the play, or in private houses, and in the last case gamble very deeply. The English society is just such as one may expect. A few merchants, not of the first order, whose thoughts are engrossed by sugars and cottons, to the utter exclusion of all public matters that do not bear directly on their private trade, and of all matters of general science or information. Not one knew the name of the plants around his own door; not one is acquainted with the country ten miles beyond St. Salvador's; not one could tell me even the situation of the fine red clay, of which the only manufacture, pottery, here is made: in short, I was completely out of patience with these incurious money-makers. I was perhaps unjust to my countrymen : I dare say there are many who *could* have told me these things, but I am sure none *did* tell me, and equally sure that I asked information of all I met with. But a woman is not, I believe, considered as privileged to know any thing by these commercial personages. The English are, however, hospitable and sociable among each other. They often dine together: the ladies love music and dancing, and some of the men gamble as much as the Portuguese. Upon the whole, society is at a low, very low scale here among the English. Good eating and good drinking they contrive to have, for the flesh, fish, and fowl are good ; fruits and vegetables various and excellent, and bread of the finest. Their slaves, for the English are all served by slaves, indeed, eat a sort of porridge of mandioc meal with small squares of jerked beef stirred into it, or, as their greatest luxury, stewed caravansas ; and this is likewise the principal food of the lower classes even of the free inhabitants. In the fruit season, pumpkins, jackfruit, cocoa-nut, and melons, nearly take place of the mandioc. The huts of the poor are formed of upright poles, with branches of trees wattled between, and covered and lined either with cocoa-leaf mats, or clay ; the roofs are also thatched. The better houses are built either of a fine blue stone, quarried on the beach of Victoria, or of brick. They are all white-washed : where the floor is not laid with wood, a fine red brick, six to nine inches square, and three in thickness, is used, and they are roofed with round red tiles. The houses are generally of one story high, with a room or two above by way of a look-out house.

Under the house is generally a sort of cellar, in which the slaves live ; and really I have sometimes wondered that human beings could exist in such.

★   ★   ★   ★   ★

August 29th. — To-day I received a visit from Dona Maria de Jesus, the young woman who has lately distinguished herself in the war of the Reconcave. Her dress is that of a soldier of one of the Emperor's battalions, with the addition of a tartan kilt, which she told me she had adopted from a picture representing a highlander, as the most feminine military dress. What would the Gordons and Mac Donalds say to this ? The "garb of old Gaul," chosen as a womanish attire ! — Her father is a Portuguese, named Gonsalvez de Almeida, and possesses a farm on the Rio do Pex, in the parish of San José, in the Certaŏ, about forty leagues in-land from Cachoeira. Her mother was also a Portuguese ; yet the young woman's features, especially her eyes and forehead, have the strongest characteristics of the Indians. Her father has another daughter by the same wife ; since whose death he has married again, and the new wife and the young children have made home not very comfortable to Dona Mariá de Jesus. The farm of the Rio do Pex is chiefly a cattle farm, but the possessor seldom knows or counts his numbers. Senhor Gonsalvez, besides his cattle, raises some cotton ; but as the Certaŏ is sometimes a whole year without rain, the quantity is uncertain. In wet years he may sell 400 arobas, at from four to five milrees ; in dry seasons he can scarcely collect above sixty or seventy arobas, which may fetch from six to seven milrees. His farm employs twenty-six slaves.

The women of the interior spin and weave for their household, and they also embroider very beautifully. The young women learn the use of fire-arms, as their brothers do, either to shoot game or defend themselves from the wild Indians.

Dona Maria told me several particulars concerning the country, and more concerning her own adventures. It appears, that early in the late war of the Reconcave, emissaries had traversed the country

Drawn by Augustus Earl   Engraved by Edwd Finden

DOÑA MARIA DE JESUS.

London Published by Longman &c. & J. Murray 13 March 1824

in all directions, to raise patriot recruits; that one of these had arrived at her father's house one day about dinner time; that her father had invited him in, and that after their meal he began to talk on the subject of his visit. He represented the greatness and the riches of Brazil, and the happiness to which it might attain if independent. He set forth the long and oppressive tyranny of Portugal; and the meanness of submitting to be ruled by so poor and degraded a country. He talked long and eloquently of the services Don Pedro had rendered to Brazil; of his virtues, and those of the Empress: so that at the last, said the girl, " I felt my heart burning in my " breast." Her father, however, had none of her enthusiasm of character. He is old, and said he neither could join the army himself, nor had he a son to send thither; and as to giving a slave for the ranks, what interest had a slave to fight for the independence of Brazil? He should wait in patience the result of the war, and be a peaceable subject to the winner. Dona Maria stole from home to the house of her own sister, who was married, and lived at a little distance. She recapitulated the whole of the stranger's discourse, and said she wished she was a man, that she might join the patriots. " Nay," said the sister, " if I had not a husband and children, for one half of what you say I would join the ranks for the Emperor." This was enough. Maria received some clothes belonging to her sister's husband to equip her; and as her father was then about to go to Cachoeira to dispose of some cottons, she resolved to take the opportunity of riding after him, near enough for protection in case of accident on the road, and far enough off to escape detection. At length being in sight of Cachoeira, she stopped; and going off the road, equipped herself in male attire, and entered the town. This was on Friday. By Sunday she had managed matters so well, that she had entered the regiment of artillery, and had mounted guard. She was too slight, however, for that service, and exchanged into the infantry, where she now is. She was sent hither, I believe, with despatches, and to be presented to the Emperor, who has given her an ensign's commission and the order of the cross, the decoration of which he himself fixed on her jacket.

She is illiterate, but clever. Her understanding is quick, and her perceptions keen. I think, with education she might have been a remarkable person. She is not particularly masculine in her appearance, and her manners are gentle and cheerful. She has not contracted any thing coarse or vulgar in her camp life, and I believe that no imputation has ever been substantiated against her modesty. One thing is certain, that her sex never was known until her father applied to her commanding officer to seek her.

There is nothing very peculiar in her manners at table, excepting that she eats farinha with her eggs at breakfast and her fish at dinner, instead of bread, and smokes a segar after each meal; but she is very temperate.

Sept. 8th, 1823. — I went with Mr. Hoste and Mr. Hately, of His Majesty's ship Briton, to Praya Grande, to see a party of Botocudo Indians, who are now there on a visit. As it is desired to civilise these people by every possible means, whenever they manifest a wish to visit the neighbourhood of the city, they are always encouraged and received kindly, fed to their hearts' content, and given clothes, and such trinkets and ornaments as they value. We saw about six men, and ten women, with some young children. The faces are rather square, with very high cheek-bones, and low contracted foreheads. Some of the young women are really pretty, of a light copper-colour, which glows all over when they blush; and two of the young men were decidedly handsome, with very dark eyes, (the usual colour of the eyes is hazel,) and aquiline noses; the rest were so disfigured by the holes cut in their lower lips and their ears to receive their barbarous ornaments, that we could scarcely tell what they were like. I had understood that the privilege of thus beautifying the face was reserved for the men *, but the women of this party

---

* See Southy's Brazil, for the manners of the Tupayas. I am not sufficiently acquainted with the filiation of the Indian tribes, to know what relation the Botocudos bear to the Tupayas.

were equally disfigured. We purchased from one of the men a mouth-piece, measuring an inch and a half in diameter. The ornaments used by these people are pieces of wood perfectly circular, which are inserted into the slit of the lip or ear, like a button, and are extremely frightful, especially when they are eating. It gives the mouth the appearance of an ape's; and the peculiar mumping it occasions is so hideously unnatural, that it gives credit to, if it did not originally suggest, the stories of their cannibalism.* The mouth is still more ugly without the lip-piece, the teeth appearing, and saliva running through.

When we entered the room where the savages are lodged, most of them were lying in mats on the floor; some on their faces, and some on their backs. Three of the women were suckling their infants, and these were dressed only in coarse cotton petticoats; the rest of the females had cotton frocks, the men shirts and trousers, given them on their arrival here. As they are usually naked in the woods, their garments seemed to sit uneasily on them : their usual motions seemed slow and lazy ; but when roused, there was a springy activity hardly fitting a human being, in all they did. They begged for money ; and when we took out a few vintems, the women crowded round me, and pinched me gently to attract my attention. They had learned a few words of Portuguese, which they addressed to us, but discoursed together in their own tongue, which seemed like a series of half-articulate sounds.

---

* Perhaps all the Indians may have been so far cannibals, as to taste of the flesh of prisoners taken in battle, or victims offered to the gods; but I cannot believe that any ever fed habitually on human flesh, for many reasons. But their traducers had their reasons for inventing and propagating the most atrocious falsehoods, as a sort of excuse for their own barbarity in hunting and making slaves of them. These practices, indeed, were so wicked, and so notorious, that in 1537, the Dominican Frey Domingos de Becançoo, provincial of the order in Mexico, sent Frey Domingos de Menaja to Rome to plead the cause of the Indians before Paul III.; who having heard *both sides*, pronounced that " The " Indians of America are men of rational soul, of the same nature and species as all " others, capable of the sacraments of the holy church, and consequently free by nature, " and lords of their own actions."

They had brought some of their bows and arrows with them of the rudest construction. The bow is of hard wood, with only two notches for the string. The arrows are of cane ; some are pointed only with hard wood, others with a flat bit of cane tied with bark to the end of the hard wood : these arrows are five feet long ; and I saw one of them penetrate several inches into the trunk of a tree, when shot by an Indian from his bow. I purchased one bow and two arrows. Most of these people had their hair closely clipped, excepting a tuft on the fore part of the head; and the men, who had slit their lips, had also pulled out their beards. The two handsome lads had cut their hair; but they had neither cut their lips nor pulled their beards. I tried to learn if this was a step towards civilisation, or if it was only that they had not reached the age when the ceremony of lip-slit-ting, &c. is practised, the interpreter attending them not being able to explain any thing but what concerns their commonest wants and actions.

Bullock:
Six Months' Residence in Mexico

William Bullock, *Six Months' Residence and Travels in Mexico* (London, 1824), pp. 123–34, 343–75.

William Bullock was born in Sheffield some time in the 1770s, and via his early training as an artist and showman came to found the Liverpool Museum in 1800. In 1805 he published a *Companion* to the museum, which proudly emphasised the Linnaean organisation of the natural history exhibits. In 1810 he moved his collection to London, commissioning the Egyptian Hall, Piccadilly (designed by the architect Peter Robinson and modelled on the Temple of Hot-hot at Dendera), as the seat of his new London Museum. His new premises opened in 1812. Bullock's success as a museologist lay in his ability to combine a sensational and exotic presentation with an educational rationale that appealed to the artisan autodidact as well as the 'polite' visitor: the London Museum rapidly became one of the most successful 'Shows of London'. In 1819 Bullock sold his permanent collection and dedicated the Egyptian Hall to the more lucrative business of temporary exhibitions, principally on exotic themes. In May 1821, he curated Giovanni Belzoni's Egyptian Exhibition, centred on a replica of the tomb of Seti I, which Belzoni had excavated at Thebes. A successful Lapp exhibition, complete with reindeer and a family of Saami people, capitalised on public interest in the Arctic expeditions of Ross and Parry.

In early 1823 Bullock travelled to newly independent Mexico on a semi-official mission, carrying samples of British manufactures and copies of Ackermann's *Repository of Arts, Literature, Fashions* to stimulate the Mexican market for British goods. Both Bullock and his brother George, a successful cabinet-maker, had close business links with the Saxon-born Ackermann, and William travelled on a ship chartered by the Rhenish Company of Merchants. He arrived at Vera Cruz in August, and made his way via Jalapa and Puebla to Mexico City, calling on future president General Antonio López de Santa Anna *en route*. Bullock spent only six months in Mexico, filling his time with business negotiations and meetings with politicians, merchants and men of science. Like Humboldt in 1803–4, he made several expeditions to other parts of the country, particularly to the mining district of Temascaltepec. On a second visit he took possession of the Del Bada silver mine, which had been presented to him by the republican leader Lucas Alamán. The country's rich mining industry had been ruined in the war of independence, and Alamán eagerly threw open the door to wealthy foreigners, whom he encouraged to become joint proprietors. By 1827 there were seven British, one German and two American companies in Mexico, with a total foreign investment of about twelve million dollars. But the bubble soon burst, and Bullock found himself proprietor of a mine which, for all its picturesque location, had no silver vein.

However, his time had not however been entirely wasted. Bullock observed, noted, drew and collected, returning to England with a huge collection of natural history specimens, pre-Hispanic antiquities and codices, as well as casts of the Aztec calendar stone and other monuments. In a bid to attract much-needed British investment to the Mexican mines, in spring 1824 he opened an exhibition entitled 'Mexico Ancient and Modern' in the Egyptian Hall. 'Modern Mexico' was represented by a panorama of Mexico City, complete with an Indian hut surrounded by agaves and other objects of botanical, zoological and ethnological interest. Visitors chatted with José Cayetano Ponce de León, an indigenous Mexican from Texcoco who had agreed to accompany Bullock on the long journey back to England. 'Ancient Mexico' contained Bullock's casts of the Aztec calendar and stone of sacrifices. Later in 1824 John Murray published his travel account, *Six Months' Residence and Travels in Mexico*; such was public demand that the entire first edition of 1,500 copies was bought up by London booksellers on the day of publication. Both exhibition and book capitalised on massive public interest in the new republic and the fact that accurate information about Mexico was scarce, mainly limited to Humboldt's *Political Essay on New Spain* (1809). Bullock's book is written in the egotistical, Pickwickian style of a travelling salesman/showman, barely disguising the commercial motivation which underlies its author's curiosity about Mexico. Although Bullock's initial reaction to Mexico City is one of disappointment, his attention is quickly alerted to its commercial possibilities. In the second passage he portrays the mountain landscapes of Temascaltepec in glowingly picturesque terms, representing the region's indigenous inhabitants as courteous and industrious, inviting British entrepreneurs and investors to regenerate Mexico after centuries of misrule. Bullock's enthusiasm for Mexico seems to have fluctuated as much as the shares in the ill-fated mining industry. In 1826 Captain Lyon, author of *Journal of a Residence in Mexico* (1828) and representative of a rival mining company, reported of Bullock that 'he now finds how mistaken he was in the grand ideas which he had formed of Mexico … against which and its whole population he rails most unmercifully'. Moving on to Cincinnati, Bullock unsuccessfully attempted to establish a model city called Hygeia, but eventually returned to London, where he died in 1849.

CHAPTER VIII.

City of Mexico.—Surrounding Country.—Its Streets.—
Houses.—Plaza Major Government House.—The Account
of the City by the Writers of the Seventeenth Century.

NOTHING around gives any idea of the
magnificent city to which you are approaching; all is dreary silence and miserable solitude.   And can this, I thought to
myself, be Mexico?—have I then for such
a place left my home and all that is dear
to me, whilst " half the world intervenes
between me" and the comforts of England? what have I gained in exchange!
We arrived at the barriers, and, passing
through a part of the shabby-looking troops
that surrounded the city, entered the
suburbs, which were mean and dirty, the

people inhabiting them covered with rags, or only wrapped in a blanket. So great was my disappointment, that I could scarcely bring myself to believe that I was in the capital of New Spain, the great mart of the precious metals, whence they flow to all parts of the habitable world:—a few minutes more, however, brought us into the city, and whatever I had seen of regularity and largeness of streets, size and grandeur of churches and houses, was here surpassed, and I felt repaid for all the dangers and troubles I had undergone. Many of the streets are nearly two miles in length, perfectly level and straight, and with the ends terminating in the view of the mountains that surround the valley. Most of the houses are of the same height, generally three stories, highly decorated, and ornamented with two rows of balconies of wrought iron, painted or gilt, and some of bronze. The stories are very lofty, the apartments being from fifteen to twenty feet high. The first or ground-floor is entered by a pair of large folding gates, ornamented with bronze, often thirty feet in height. These lead into the court-yard, surrounded by the house, filled with trees and flowers, producing a very pretty effect, and having a gallery to each floor, offering so many separate promenades under shelter from the sun and rain. The lower apartments are generally occupied by the porter and other servants; the floor above is often let off; but the highest, which is the principal, is occupied by the family themselves, having a separate stone staircase of great magnificence leading to it. Nothing can be better calculated than these residences for the delightful climate, in a country where change of temperature is scarcely known, where perennial spring reigns, where fire-places are never seen, and where it is scarcely necessary to have glass windows to exclude the night air from the bed-rooms. All that is requisite is a strong roof against the heavy rains that occur at certain seasons, and lofty rooms to afford a free circulation of the air; and nothing can be better adapted for this purpose than the style of architecture introduced by the Spaniards into Mexico.

The fronts of the houses are in general white, crimson, brown, or light green, painted in distemper, and having a pleasing appearance; and the dryness of the atmosphere is such, that they retain their beauty unimpaired many years. Many of these fronts have inscriptions upon them taken from Scripture, or stanzas addressed to the Saviour or his divine Mother.

Numbers too are entirely covered with glazed porcelain, in a variety of elegant designs and patterns, often with subjects from scriptural history, giving the whole a rich, and mosaic appearance, quite different from any thing of the kind in Europe. The walls of their great staircases are frequently covered in the same manner, and mixed with a profusion of gilding, which, in contrast with the blue and white porcelain, has a really splendid effect. I am inclined to think that this mode of ornament was borrowed from the Moorish palaces and mosques existing in Spain at the time of the discovery of Mexico, and introduced into this city and Puebla de los Angeles, when the wealth of the mines of the New World was such as to render it impracticable for the proprietors to spend their immense revenues in household expenses, equipages, or servants.

The porcelain was probably the manufacture of Holland and the Netherlands, then under the Spanish yoke. The walls of several of the churches are finished in the same manner. The roofs are all nearly flat, and bricked, and many of them are covered with flowers, affording a pleasant place of resort in a fine evening, as the prospect is delightful, and the air refreshing and uncontaminated by smoke. Owing to this species of ornament, the city, seen from an elevation, presents a far more beautiful appearance than those of Europe, where the red-tiled and deformed roofs, and shapeless stacks of chimnies, are the principal features in the prospect. Indeed, no place I ever saw affords so many interesting points for a panoramic view, independently of its own intrinsic beauty, its interesting architecture, its houses with their light balconies, covered parterres of shrubs and flowers,—its situation in the grand valley of Mexico, with its sea-like lakes, sur-

rounded by snow-capped volcanic mountains, the highest in New Spain. But the
furniture and internal decorations of most
of the houses ill accord with their external appearances. The closing of the
mines, the expulsion of the rich Spanish
families, and sixteen years of revolutionary
warfare, with all the concomitant miseries,
have wrought a melancholy alteration in
the fortunes of individuals, and in the general state of the country: and in this
the capital bears no inconsiderable share.
The superb tables, chandeliers, and other
articles of furniture, of solid silver, the
magnificent mirrors and pictures, framed
in the same precious metal, have now
passed through the mint, and in the shape
of dollars are circulating over Europe and
Asia; and families whose incomes have
exceeded half a million per annum can

now scarcely procure the means of a scanty existence.

But I hope that these times are nearly at an end, and that the period is arriving when Mexico will again exalt her head among the greatest cities of the world, a rank to which she is entitled from her own intrinsic beauty, and as the capital of one of the finest portions of the globe. The liberality and wisdom of her counsellors, under the new order of things, will enable her to break the trammels in which she has so long been confined, that intelligent strangers may be induced to visit her, and bring with them the arts and manufactures, the improved machinery and great chymical knowledge of Europe; and in return she can amply repay them by again diffusing through the world her immense mineral wealth.

The Plaza Major, or grand square of Mexico, is one of the finest that exists. The east side is occupied by the grand cathedral, and segrario, or parish church; the north by the splendid palace of the Viceroy; the south by a fine row of houses, the centre of which is the palace built by Cortez, and now called the Casa de Stada; the west has a range of buildings with a piazza in front, consisting of many good shops, some public offices, granaries, &c.

About the centre of the square is a fine equestrian statue of Charles V., erected by a Spanish artist, Sig. Tolsa, in Mexico, about twenty years since, and highly creditable to his talents. It is doubtless the finest specimen of casting in the New World, and would not disgrace the labour of Michael Angelo, Cellini, or John of Bologna. On my arrival the Ex-Emperor had erected a temporary amphitheatre of great size for the purpose of giving bull-fights; and this statue, which formed the centre of the arrena, was enclosed in a large globe of paper surmounted by a figure of fame.

The pleasing effect of the grand square is much injured by the admission of a trumpery building called the Parian, a kind of market or bazaar, held principally I believe by the Spanish shopkeepers. This erection is a disgrace to the taste of the government which permitted it to spoil one of the noblest squares they have, but the revenues it brings to the city are at present so necessary that its speedy removal is hopeless.

The palace, or government-house, is a truly magnificent building. It is nearly square, its front measuring several hundred feet. In its interior are four large square courts, over which most of the public offices are distributed, as well as the prison, the mint, barracks, botanic garden, &c.

The existing state of this city exhibits only a shadow of the grandeur it had once attained. The period of its greatest splendour, wealth, and luxury, may be placed within one century from its conquest by Cortez. The present internal decorations but ill accord with the magnificent houses and palaces on which thousands have been lavished, and prove at once the poverty of the present Mexicans and the wealth of their ancestors. The massive silver tables, staircases, and chandeliers, &c. &c. have all disappeared. The profusion of jewels and the extravagant equipages are no longer to be seen in the streets, and the *ensemble* even of people of the highest rank of the present day reminds us in nothing of the authenticated descriptions of the inhabitants of the same place by writers two centuries ago.

★   ★   ★   ★   ★

HAVING received an invitation from Mr. Smith Wilcox, the American Consul-General, to visit the silver mine about thirty leagues from Mexico, on which he was then, at considerable expense, erecting a steam-engine, for the purpose of clearing it of the water which had prevented it from being worked for several years;—on the 24th of April I accompanied that gentleman, his nephew, and the proprietor of the mine. We left the city after breakfast, in a carriage drawn by seven mules, and travelled by the side of the great aqueduct which bounds the road on one side, whilst the other is separated from the swampy meadows reclaimed from the lake by a deep ditch, the bank of which is planted with large trees somewhat resembling our poplars. At a league's distance we passed the fine palace or castle of Chepultepec, built by the Viceroy Galvez at an immense expense, and lately occupied by the Ex-Emperor: it stands on a remarkable hill, or rather rock, and commands a most beautiful view of the city and surrounding country. About two miles farther lies the village of Tacubaya, finely situated on the first rising ground, principally com-posed of the beautiful houses, villas, and superb gardens, of the nobility and rich citizens of the capital. A little above this place, not far from the Bishop's Palace, is the noblest view of the city, but even from hence no idea of its extent could be formed by a stranger, as the site is so flat that little more than its profile can be seen. It is from the top of its cathedral, or from its grand streets, crossing each other at right angles, that an estimate of the size and splendour of Mexico can be made. We now ascended by a tolerable road for nearly ten miles to an hacienda, where we stopped to dine, the road to it affording nothing very interesting, and in some places appearing barren and burnt up. At this spot rises the fine stream of water which forms the principal supply for the capital, to which it is carried, at great cost, by means of the aqueduct. We continued to ascend till within a short distance of Lerma, when, (having crossed the mountains that surround the valley of Mexico,) we descended into the plain or valley in which that place and the city of Tolucca stand. On reaching the town we found the entrance closed for the night, but after some detention procured admission from the

Governor, and reached the Posada about eight in the evening.

Lerma is a regularly built town, but consists principally of small houses: it appears never to have been finished.

We left it soon after daylight, and, passing the end of a lake which looks as if it had formerly been much larger, crossed the fine plain, covered by rich meadows and considerable farms, in high cultivation. In two hours we reached Tolucca, a distance of twelve miles, to breakfast.

This, like most of the Mexican cities, is handsome, and regularly built. Its exterior presents an appearance of prosperity I had not observed in other places: the houses had a new and fresh appearance, and, what I had not seen before, several new buildings were constructing. It has considerable manufactories of soap and candles; the best hams and sausages in New Spain are said to be cured here; we observed several manufactories of them, and admired again their fine breed of hogs.

We left Tolucca in the coach, and proceeded about two leagues farther, where the road for wheel-carriages ceases. Here having procured horses and mules for the whole party, which had been augmented by the addition of several persons going to the mine, (among them a Yorkshire blacksmith,) we ascended about a league, and then entered an extensive wood, which crowned the Cordillera, on the west side of the Table-land of Mexico. This was by much the most beautiful scene I had witnessed in America;—abounding with trees of the noblest form and loftiest height, most of them entirely new to me, but among them oaks and pines, whose size and luxuriance eclipsed any thing seen in the Alps or in Norway! We still continued to rise, and in one elevated open place caught the last view of the mountains that surround the vale of Mexico: on our left lay the volcano of Tolucca, covered with perpetual snow; and shortly after we reached a defile in the mountain, and began to descend towards the Pacific ocean.

The scenery was now inexpressibly grand. The ground, being broken into abrupt hills, afforded many openings, through which the tops of the immense forests below were seen to the greatest advantage. In many places, for a considerable distance, our path was shaded by trees of an amazing height, so close as almost to exclude the light,—on emerging suddenly from which the most enchanting prospects were spread beneath our feet; the summits of gigantic volcanos, receding like steps beneath us, seemed to lead the eye to the

waters of the Pacific, to which the moun-
tain-torrents we passed were hastening.
The descent now became very steep, so
that in many places we were obliged to
alight from our mules, and proceed, with
cautious steps, over broken masses of basalt
and other volcanic substances, where not
a trace of the labour of man was visible,
or any circumstances that could remind
us of being in an inhabited country;
except occasionally meeting small groups
of Indians, carrying the productions of their
little farms to the market of Tolucca, or
even as far as Mexico. From these simple
people the unprotected traveller has nothing
to fear; they are the most courteous, gentle,
and unoffending creatures in existence, and
never pass, without saluting, a stranger.
Their burthens consisted generally of fruit,
fowls, turkeys, mats, shingles of wood for
roofs of houses, and sometimes of charcoal.

They generally had their wives and daughters with them;—clean, modest-looking women, carrying heavy burthens exclusive of the children usually fastened on their backs. After a descent of several hours through this ever-varying and sublime scenery, to the effect of which a thunderstorm added much majesty, we arrived at a small plain, surrounded on all sides by pine-capped mountains. In the centre of this, in the midst of highly cultivated ground, rose the neat little Indian church and village of St. Miguel de los Ranchos, placed in one of the most delightful situations and lovely climates in the world. On the mountain we might almost have complained of cold, but the descent had brought us into a temperature resembling the finest parts of Europe, and our approach to the village just before sunset brought home strongly to our recollection.

Our path lay through corn fields, orchards, and gardens. Apples, pears, and peaches, almost obstructed our way; and fields of potatoes and beans in blossom might, but for the swarthy and thinly clothed inhabitants, who gazed with surprise at our advance, and the luxuriance of the Nopal or the great American Aloe, in full bloom, have made us fancy ourselves in England. We rode up to the church, and on dismounting presently found ourselves surrounded by numbers of men and boys, all eager to render us any assistance in their power. A small room adjoining this edifice, called the comunidad, provided by Government for the reception of strangers, was pointed out to us as our residence for the night; where having spread our mattresses on the floor, and given the Indians directions for the suppers of ourselves and horses, we walked out to examine the church. It was the eve of the feast of St. Mark, or, as the Indians who accompanied us called him, Nostras Boueno Amigo (our good friend).

The church was gaudily ornamented with pictures and statues, and had that day been dressed with fruits, flowers, palm blossoms, &c., disposed in arches, chaplets, and a variety of other pretty devices, in honour of their patron.

Opposite the door, under a venerable cedar, of great size, was a small temple and altar, decorated in a similar manner, with the addition of several human skulls, quite clean, and as white as ivory. Round the great tree some men were employed in splitting pieces of candle-wood, a species of pine which contains a considerable quantity of resin, and which, being lighted, burns with a clear flame like a candle.

I rambled through the village and the surrounding plantations of the maguey or aloe: many of the plants were then producing the pulque. Night was approaching, and I hastened my pace, to reach our lodging, when the bell suddenly tolled in a quick manner, and in an instant the churchyard was brilliantly illuminated by the flame of eight piles of the candle-wood, prepared for that purpose; the effect was heightened, by its being quite unexpected. On my entering the church-yard four men discharged a flight of rockets, which was instantly answered by a similar salute from every house in the place: this was the commencement of the fete for the following day. In a quarter of an hour the bonfires were extinguished, and the church doors closed; and we retired to our place of rest to take the homely supper provided for us by our new friends, which had been prepared in a house in the village. Our meal was not finished when a message requested our speedy attendance in the church: on entering we found it illuminated, and crowded by numbers of persons, of both sexes. Dancing, with singular Indian ceremonies, had commenced in front of the altar, which to my astonishment I immediately recognised to be of the same nature as those in use before the introduction of Christianity. The actors consisted of five men and three women, grotesquely but richly dressed, in the fashion of the time of Montezuma. One young man, meant to personate that monarch, wore a high crown, from which rose a plume of red feathers. The first part of the drama consisted of the representation of a warrior taking leave of his family preparatory to going to battle;—a man and woman danced in front of the altar, and clearly expressed the parting scene, and knelt down and solemnly prayed for the success of his undertaking. The next act commenced with two warriors, superbly dressed; one, a Mexican, was distinguished by the superior height of his head-dress, and by a piece of crimson silk suspended from his shoulders: after dancing some time, a mock fight began, which, after various evolutions, terminated of course in the Mexican taking his enemy prisoner, and dragging him by his hair into the presence of his sovereign; when the dance was resumed, and the vanquished frequently implored mercy, both from his conqueror and the monarch. The various parts were admirably performed:—no pantomime could be better, and I almost expected to see the captive sacrificed to the gods. The audience seemed pleased with our attendance, except one old man, who appeared to think we had seen too much; he was a little elevated with pulque, but some of the younger ones carried him out. In dancing, the women accompanied their motions and the music with a slight instrument in the right hand; it was a rattle, made of a small gourd ornamented with silver bells, and had a pleasing effect. I tried to buy one of these, but they refused to part with it. One old man seemed to act in a threefold capacity :—he was fiddler, or leader of the band; master of the ceremonies; and, if I mistake not, represented the high priest. He wore a white dress, over which were placed wreaths of small green leaves—and he apparently regulated the whole performance of the drama. On one occasion, when the royal Montezuma received the homage of his prisoner, the monarch remained standing, which being contrary to the etiquette of his court, he was gently reminded of the error by getting a smart stroke on the cheek with the fiddlestick of the high priest; on which his majesty immediately squatted, and received with propriety the address of his general and the supplication of his prisoner.

Soon after this we left the church and retired to rest, but were shortly afterwards serenaded at our residence; the party wished for admission, but Mr. Wilcox being indisposed, we refused to open our door. About midnight we heard them again at their revels, when a flight of rockets concluded their devotions till morning.

We were still eighteen miles from the mine, at which it was desirable we should arrive early ; we therefore left the village before day, some of the people having remained all night with our horses. They wished much to detain us, to see their fete, and I felt regret at not staying. Our road lay through the numerous little farms belonging to the town, which extends a considerable distance. All was as silent as death, except the stream that runs through this peaceful vale; and the moon shone without a cloud as we passed through the plantations and gardens of these happy children of nature, who here cultivate their native soil without the interruption of a single white face, and seem scarcely to feel or even know their humiliating situation. Half an hour's easy ride brought us again to the woods, and to a repetition of the same magnificent scenery as that of the day before. In some places, the height of the trees and closeness of the foliage over our heads were such as to make it absolutely dark, although the moon still shone with the greatest splendour. Our path was in some places dif-cult, and we had again to ascend towards the mountain-regions. About sunrise we reached a more open and cultivated country, and travelled near a rapid river, whose banks were covered with fields of wheat and maize—the prospect from hence is as rich as any part of Devonshire. Our narrow path, in many places, was so overgrown with vegetation as to be almost impassable. Among the fruits that presented themselves was our common blackberry, in greater perfection than in Europe; and once or twice we gathered very good strawberries. We now reached a sterile sandy district, and passed a few barren hills, which had, in some places, been worn by torrents into a variety of the most extraordinary forms: leaving these, we descended into a fine country, and entered the mining district of Themascaltepec, which a few years since produced a considerable portion of the precious metal exported to Europe. A mile of steep and difficult descent brought us to the town. from which the district is named, most romantically situated in a deep valley, near the junction of three rapid mountain-streams, on the only spot sufficiently level for the purpose.

Themascaltepec contains about one thousand inhabitants. It is now in a state of decay; most of the haciendas for preparing the silver ore are in ruins, and the expensive water-courses, which formerly turned the ponderous machinery for pounding the ore, are now neglected, and concealed by the thick vegetation with which they are overgrown.

The appearance of so many strangers in this retired little town excited some surprise among its inhabitants. I was the first Englishman that ever visited it. We were hospitably received at the house of Don Jose Benitas, where Mr. Wilcox was met by Mr. Goulde, his American engineer, and many of the people whom he had brought from the United States for the purpose of erecting the steam-engine then putting up at his mine, distant within a mile of the town.

After partaking of a good Spanish breakfast, for which our long ride gave us an excellent appetite, we remounted our horses and rode thither. The road or path had been improved at much expense by Mr. Wilcox, but still it is such as few persons accustomed to English turnpikes would choose to venture upon on horseback: but surely nothing can exceed it in point of romantic scenery, or in the luxuriance and variety of the vegetation, which in some places renders it difficult of passage. The mine is situated in a valley, through which a small stream winds, till it falls into the river at the bottom of the town.

We found the works in considerable forwardness, and part of the machinery for the steam-engine, which had been brought from Vera Cruz to Tolucca on waggons, and afterwards through the woods by means of rude wooden carriages built on the spot, assisted by Indians and oxen, lying near it.

A shed of great magnitude, in the form of a cross, and as large as a cathedral, had been very ably constructed, and roofed with shingles, under the direction of Don Jose Benitas, with the aid of Indians only; and without the use of iron, being lashed firmly together with thongs of raw hides. It is intended to cover the engine, and the various work-shops, as well as the mouth of the mine; and to protect the workmen from the sun and rain. The erection of roofs of this magnitude in England would have been an enormous expense, and exercised the talents of an able architect.

The Indian workmen, like all uninformed people, are strongly prejudiced in favour of their own customs; and the Europeans who have taken mines in Mexico will have much to contend with before they can bring them to work under their directions. They are indeed particularly averse to innovation. A common wheelbarrow is much too complex a machine to be used in removing the rubbish from the mine; and Mr. Wilcox was obliged to submit to two men dragging about half as much earth on a raw hide as one could have removed with ease on a barrow. A saw for cutting planks they had never seen till we arrived. Its operation astonished them. They thought it impossible that more than one plank could be made from a tree: yet, by kind usage, and by respecting their prejudices, I have no doubt they will gradually be brought to know the superiority of our Mechanics and to obey their directions; but it must be effected by degrees, and with caution: compulsive measures must never be resorted to, and the workmen sent out must be particularly cautioned not to interfere in their religious prejudices.

We returned to dinner, and in the evening rambled along the banks of one of the numerous streams that unite near this place, and form a considerable river, which empties itself into the Pacific ocean.

The situation of Themascaltepec is the most delightful that can be imagined: its temperature is rather warmer than that of the capital, but I never found it unpleasant, and there is scarcely a vegetable production that might not be cultivated here in perfection.

I know of no more desirable place for human residence: it wants only the re-establishment of the mines or manufactories, to make. it again what it has been, the source and mart of abundance and riches. The various remains of haciendas, and of smelting and amalgamation houses, on the banks of its rapid streams, attest its former consequence; and if ever commercial en-terprise, and the employment of British capital should be established in Mexico, no place I have seen can be better adapted for the purpose, as, independent of its other ad-vantages, any quantity of machinery could be worked by its waters, and the neigh-bouring woods could furnish an inexhaust-ible supply of fuel.

Sunday being market-day, the town was crowded with Indians, who brought with them great quantities of fruit, and other vegetable productions of the Tierra Caliente; among which were two or three kinds of raw cotton, and a quantity of sugar, in cakes, resembling bee's wax.

At the house of Don Jose Benitas was a meeting of Indians, to settle a contract for timber for the mine. The contractors, with three alcaldes, or chief magistrates of the villages, known by their silver-headed sticks, came to meet Mr. Wilcox, to arrange this important affair, and it was not done without much serious debating, and many long speeches, which the alcaldes delivered in a most deliberate and solemn manner.

In the evening we attended an itinerant kind of theatrical exhibition, consisting of interludes, rope-dancing, tumbling, &c. Some of the feats were exactly the same as those performed before Cortez, on his first arrival; and such as I have not seen in Europe. A fellow placed himself on the ground, raised his bare feet, and received on them a beam of wood, eight feet long, and eight inches thick, which he threw several times into the air, catching it again on the soles of his feet; he then caused it to spin round like the fly of a jack,—when, changing his manner of striking it, he made it turn lengthways, with great velocity throwing it from one foot to the other, so that the bells fastened to the ends of it kept time to the music. After amusing us awhile in this way, he rested a few minutes, when two boys were suspended to the ends of the beam, which he again balanced and threw with them into the air, receiving them altogether on his feet. They were then put into rotatory motion, and turned with such violence, that one of the lads fainted: this put an end to the exhibition, which was attended by some of the first people in the place, who provided their own seats, though some families had only a mat spread on the ground.

Ices, dulces, &c. were served during the time of exhibition. The place was illuminated by two fires of candle-wood, raised about seven feet from the ground.

The company seemed highly delighted, and the behaviour of the lower classes was very orderly, although there was no lack of mirth, as the Indian who enacted the clown performed his part in a manner which would not have disgraced Grimaldi himself. His comical remarks excited the most boisterous merriment, in which I was obliged to join at my own expense, as he made several pointed allusions to a stranger who had arrived at Themascaltepec from the other side of the world, to feast on humming birds, beetles, butterflies, and lizards.

The following day our party rode to an amalgamation house, the only one of consequence now in operation, about two miles up the river, on the bank of which it is situated. The superintendent showed us the whole process of extracting the silver from the ore, which gives employment to a great number of people, principally Indians. The ore, which was brought from a mine at some miles' distance, by mules, is of a yellowish clay colour, and not very rich: it is of that kind distinguished here by the name of colorado. It is first pounded by large heavy stampers, worked by water, and sifted through hides pierced with small holes, to answer the purpose of sieves; the powdered ore is next carried into a large flagged apartment, and piled in heaps of a ton or more in each, and then mixed with salt, sulphate of iron, lime, vegetable ashes, &c. A quantity of mercury in proportion to the calculated quantity of the silver, is added, and suffered to remain some time, the whole being turned or worked together by Indians treading it with their feet. When they suppose the mercury has entirely united with the ore, it is put into vats, over which a stream of water passes: the amalgamated ore is then stirred up, and the earthy part carried off by the stream, and the mercury, incorporated with silver, remains at the bottom. The silver is afterwards separated from the quicksilver by means of fire, with a considerable loss. It has been proved by experiments made lately in Cornwall on ore sent from Mexico for the purpose, that the same or nearly the same process used in smelting tin may, with considerable advantage, be applied to the more valuable metal.

Having obtained specimens of the ore, in its different stages of preparation, and the various processes used being explained, we rode through a very rich valley to Upper Themascaltepec, a small town of not very inviting appearance, about four miles from the lower town, and returned by another route to Mr. Wilcox's mine. The ride was altogether through a fertile country, and the farms and cottages presented an appearance of comfort not always seen. We killed several new birds, among which was a species of thrush, of a deep lead colour, whose note is not surpassed by any of that musical family which inhabit Europe.

I shot several humming birds in the

garden of the house in which we lived—a pomegranate tree in blossom was much frequented by them, and afforded me many opportunities of observing their manners.

The rocks round the town abound with an elegant species of lizard, of a dark blue and orange colour. I unfortunately engaged a boy to catch me half a dozen, for which I gave him a quarter of a dollar : he spread the report of this through the town, and the next day all the idle fellows of the place beset my lodgings with strings of lizards—the whole neighbourhood seemed to have been ransacked for them.

The appearance of the fire-flies in the evenings is very beautiful, and, to an European, surprising. Soon after sunset the air is filled with small luminous floating sparks, shooting in every direction, and vanishing in an instant. This was the first place

where I had seen them in great abundance, but my attempts to take them were
unsuccessful.

The evenings spent in these regions in
the open air are more delightful than
those of the finest parts of Italy; and
the appearance of the sides of the mountains round the town at this time was
highly picturesque at night, as it was
near the termination of the dry season,
when it is the custom to burn the low
brushwood and dry vegetables, to improve
and clear the ground for a new crop.
They were generally fired at night, when
the sides of the hills became a blaze, which
spread with rapidity, and resembled the
burning lava of a volcano, surrounding the
town for many miles with moving sheets
of flame.

Mr. Wilcox having finished the business
on which he came, we left this pleasant

place about noon, arrived at St. Miguel early in the evening, and experienced the same attention from the Indian inhabitants as before. I had furnished myself with a few segars for them, and they seem always gratified with any little attention from Europeans. Some horses, the property of travellers, had lately been carried off from the village, and they placed a strong guard over ours for their security. Many of them were at our door before daylight, to offer their assistance.

We left them early, intending to reach Lerma that night, but in ascending a very steep part of the road my saddle slipped off the horse, by which means I received a severe fall, and it was with difficulty I could reach Tolucca; where having been bled, and rested till the next day, we proceeded to Lerma, and the following evening entered Mexico, much pleased with the magnificent country through which we had passed, and the simple people who inhabit it.

Head:
Rough Notes

Francis Bond Head, *Rough Notes Taken during Some Rapid Journeys across the Pampas and among the Andes* (London: John Murray, 1826), pp. 14–24, 42–53, 111–26.

Captain Francis Bond Head (1793–1875) was descended from a Portuguese Jewish family named Méndez and educated at Rochester Grammar School and the Royal Military Academy (RMA) Woolwich, being commissioned as a lieutenant in the Royal Engineers in 1811. After serving as both a wartime and a peacetime soldier (he was apparently present at the battle of Waterloo), Head retired from the army in 1825 on half pay in order to take up the post of manager of the Rio de la Plata Mining Association, with a salary of £1,200 per annum. In the same year he departed for South America with a party of Cornish miners to work the mines under the concession of the newly independent government of the United Provinces of La Plata. Setting out from Buenos Aires, Head crossed the Pampas with a small party of miners, a French assayer and a surveyor, bound first for the gold mines of San Luis, and then for the silver mines of Uspallata in the province of Mendoza, a thousand miles from Buenos Aires. Upon arrival at Uspallata after an exhausting journey, however, Head was shattered to discover that the mines had already been allocated to a rival company. Leaving his party at Mendoza, he raced back to Buenos Aires, only to be instructed once again to return to Chile. Meeting up with his party, Head crossed the Andes to Santiago, unsuccessfully prospecting hundreds of miles of the roughest mountain territory in the search for mines. Thwarted, he returned to Buenos Aires once again, paid off his German miners and returned to England with the Cornish party. The directors of the company, who had spent £6,000 on this abortive venture, were incensed and laid the blame on Head, attempting to withdraw his salary. In an effort to clear his name, he published *Rough Notes*, which described his rapid transcontinental journeys and blamed the failure of the mining enterprise on European ignorance of South America, which his book set out to redress. Head became something of an expert on South American affairs, even attempting to introduce the lasso into service in the British cavalry. In 1830 he published a biography of the Abyssinian explorer James Bruce, and in 1835 his career took a distinguished turn when he was offered the lieutenant-governorship of Upper Canada, with the promise of a baronetcy. After his successful incumbency of this office during a difficult period, he returned to Britain and in 1867 was elected to the Privy Council. He died on his estate at Croydon in 1875, aged eighty-two.

Nicknamed 'Galloping Head' for the rapidity of the travels described in *Rough Notes*, Head excused his haste on the plausible grounds that he had left a large party of miners idly waiting for him in Buenos Aires, so that 'for upward of 6,000 miles I can truly declare that I was riding against Time' (p. viii). Part of the rhetorical appeal of Head's book lay in the fact that it was based on 'a few rough notes, describing anything which interested or amused me ... they are necessarily in that incoherent, unconnected state which makes them, I am fully aware, but little suited to meet the critical eye of the public' (p. x). But as Mary Louise Pratt has indicated in her discussion of the travel narratives of the 'capitalist vanguard' in post-independence South America, Head reversed the standard account of the Pampas as a bleak, inhospitable region, expressing 'a wild, unmitigated enthusiasm for free-wheeling pampa life ... his account stands out among those of the business emissaries for its critical perspective on Euroexpansionism and its relativizing perspective on culture' (Pratt, *Imperial Eyes: Studies in Travel Writing and Transculturation* (London, 1992), pp. 153–4). Pratt's point is illustrated in the first and third excerpts selected here, romanticising Gaucho life and expressing sympathy for the plight of the Pampas Indians. Head's account in this respect compares favourably with Charles Darwin's remarks on the Pampas Indians in the *Journal of Researches*.

The situation of the Gaucho is naturally independent of the political troubles which engross the
attention of the inhabitants of the towns. The
population or number of these Gauchos is very
small, and at great distances from each other:
they are scattered here and there over the face of
the country. Many of these people are descended
from the best families in Spain; they possess good-
manners, and often very noble sentiments: the life
they lead is very interesting—they generally in-

habit the hut in which they were born, and in which their fathers and grandfathers lived before them, although it appears to a stranger to possess few of the allurements of *dulce domum*. The huts are built in the same simple form; for although luxury has ten thousand plans and elevations for the frail abode of its more frail tenant, yet the hut in all countries is the same, and therefore there is no difference between that of the South American Gaucho, and the Highlander of Scotland, excepting that the former is built of mud, and covered with long yellow grass, while the other is formed of stones, and thatched with heather. The materials of both are the immediate produce of the soil, and both are so blended in colour with the face of the country, that it is often difficult to distinguish them; and as the pace at which one gallops in South America is rapid, and the country flat, one scarcely discovers the dwelling before one is at the door. The corral is about fifty or one hundred yards from the hut, and is a circle of about thirty yards in diameter, enclosed by a number of strong rough posts, the ends of which are struck into the ground. Upon these posts are generally a number of idle-looking vultures or hawks *, and the ground around the hut and corral is covered with bones and carcasses of horses, bullocks' horns, wool, &c., which give it the smell and appearance of an ill-kept dog-kennel in England.

The hut consists generally of one room, in which all the family live, boys, girls, men, women, and children, all huddled together. The kitchen is a detached shed a few yards off: there are always holes, both in the walls and in the roof of the hut, which one at first considers as singular marks of the indolence of the people. In the summer this

---

* The hawks are very tame, and they are seldom to be seen except at the huts; but occasionally they have followed me for many leagues, keeping just before me, and with their round black eyes gazing intently on my face, which I fancied attracted their notice from being burnt by the sun, and I literally often thought they were a little inclined to taste it. They are constantly in the habit of attacking the horses and mules who have sore backs; and I have often observed these birds hovering about six inches above them. It is curious to compare the countenance of the two animals. The hawk, with his head bent downwards, and his eye earnestly fixed upon the wound: the mule with his back crouched down, his ears lying back, whisking his tail, afraid to eat, and apparently not knowing whether to rear or kick.

abode is so filled with fleas and binchucas, (which are bugs as large as black beetles,) that the whole family sleep on the ground in front of their dwelling; and when the traveller arrives at night, and after unsaddling his horse walks among this sleeping community, he may place the saddle or recado on which he is to sleep close to the companion most suited to his fancy:—an admirer of innocence may lie down by the side of a sleeping infant; a melancholy man may slumber near an old black woman; and one who admires the fairer beauties of creation, may very demurely lay his head on his saddle, within a few inches of the idol he adores. However, there is nothing to assist the judgment but the bare feet and ancles of all the slumbering group, for their heads and bodies are covered and disguised by the skin and poncho which cover them.

In winter the people sleep in the hut, and the scene is a very singular one. As soon as the traveller's supper is ready, the great iron spit on which the beef has been roasted is brought into the hut, and the point is struck into the ground: the Gaucho then offers his guest the skeleton of a horse's head, and he and several of the family, on similar seats,

sit round the spit, from which with their long
knives they cut very large mouthfuls*. The hut
is lighted by a feeble lamp, made of bullock's tallow; and it is warmed by a fire of charcoal: on the
walls of the hut are hung, upon bones, two or three
bridles and spurs, and several lassos and balls: on
the ground are several dark-looking heaps, which one
can never clearly distinguish; on sitting down upon
these when tired, I have often heard a child scream
underneath me, and have occasionally been mildly
asked by a young woman, what I wanted?—at
other times up has jumped an immense dog! While
I was once warming my hands at the fire of charcoal,
seated on a horse's head, looking at the black roof
in a reverie, and fancying I was quite by myself, I
felt something touch me, and saw two naked black
children leaning over the charcoal in the attitude of
two toads: they had crept out from under some of

---

* When first I lived with the Gauchos, I could not conceive
how they possibly managed to eat so quickly meat which I
found so unusually tough, but an old Gaucho told me it was
because I did not know what parts to select, and he immediately
cut me a large piece which was quite tender. I always afterwards begged the Gauchos to help me, and they generally
smiled at my having discovered the secret.

the ponchos, and I afterwards found that many other persons, as well some as hens sitting upon eggs, were also in the hut. In sleeping in these huts, the cock has often hopped upon my back to crow in the morning; however, as soon as it is daylight, everybody gets up.

The life of the Gaucho is very interesting, and resembles that beautiful description which Horace gives of the progress of a young eagle:—

> Olim juventas et patrius vigor
> Nido laborum propulit inscium,
> Vernique jam nimbis remotis
> Insolitos docuêre nisus
> Venti paventem; mox in ovilia
> Demisit hostem vividus impetus,
> Nunc in reluctantes dracones
> Egit amor dapis, atque pugnæ.

Born in the rude hut, the infant Gaucho receives little attention, but is left to swing from the roof in a bullock's hide, the corners of which are drawn towards each other by four strips of hide. In the first year of his life he crawls about without clothes, and I have more than once seen a mother give a child of this age a sharp knife, a foot long, to play with. As soon as he walks, his infantine amusements are those which prepare him for the occupations of his future life: with a lasso made of twine he tries to catch little birds, or the dogs, as they walk in and out of the hut. By the time he is four years old he is on horseback, and immediately becomes useful by assisting to drive the cattle into the corral. The manner in which these children ride is quite extraordinary: if a horse tries to escape from the flock which are driven towards the corral, I have frequently seen a child pursue him, overtake him, and then bring him back, flogging him the whole way; in vain the creature tries to dodge and escape from him, for the child turns with him, and always keeps close to him; and it is a curious fact, which I have often observed, that a mounted horse is always able to overtake a loose one.

His amusements and his occupations soon become more manly—careless of the biscacheros (the holes of an animal called the biscacho) which undermine the plains, and which are very dangerous, he gallops after the ostrich, the gama, the lion, and the tiger; he catches them with his balls: and with his lasso he daily assists in catching the wild cattle, and in dragging them to the hut either for slaughter, or to be marked. He breaks in the young horses in the manner which I have described, and in these occupations is often away from his hut many days, changing his horse as soon as the animal is tired, and sleeping on the ground. As his constant food is beef and water, his constitution is so strong that he is able to endure great fatigue; and the distances he will ride, and the number of hours that he will remain on horseback, would hardly be credited. The unrestrained freedom of such a life he fully appreciates; and, unacquainted with subjection of any sort, his mind is often filled with sentiments of liberty which are as noble as they are harmless, although they of course partake of the wild habits of his life. Vain is the endeavour to explain to him the luxuries and blessings of a more civilized life; his ideas are, that the noblest effort of man is to raise himself off the ground and ride instead of walk—that no rich garments or variety of food can atone for the want of a horse—and that the print of the human foot on the ground is in his mind the symbol of uncivilization.

The Gaucho has by many people been accused of

indolence; those who visit his hut find him at the door with his arms folded, and his poncho thrown over his left shoulder like a Spanish cloak; his hut is in holes, and would evidently be made more comfortable by a few hours' labour: in a beautiful climate, he is without fruit or vegetables; surrounded by cattle, he is often without milk; he lives without bread, and he has no food but beef and water, and therefore those who contrast his life with that of the English peasant accuse him of indolence; but the comparison is inapplicable, and the accusation unjust; and any one who will live with the Gaucho, and will follow him through his exertions, will find that he is any thing but indolent, and his surprise will be that he is able to continue a life of so much fatigue. It is true that the Gaucho has no luxuries, but the great feature of his character is, that he is a person without wants: accustomed constantly to live in the open air, and to sleep on the ground, he does not consider that a few holes in his hut deprive it of its comfort. It is not that he does not like the taste of milk, but he prefers being without it to the every-day occupation of going in search of it. He might, it is true, make cheese, and sell it for money, but if he has got a good saddle and good spurs, he does not consider that money has much value: in fact, he is contented with his lot; and when one reflects that, in the increasing series of human luxuries, there is no point that produces contentment, one cannot but feel that there is perhaps as much philosophy as folly in the Gaucho's determination to exist without wants; and the life he leads is certainly more noble than if he was slaving from morning till night to get other food for his body or other garments to cover it. It is true he is of little service to the great cause of civilization, which it is the duty of every rational being to promote; but an humble individual, living by himself in a boundless plain, cannot introduce into the vast uninhabited regions which surround him either arts or sciences: he may, therefore, without blame be permitted to leave them as he found them, and as they must remain, until population, which will create wants, devises the means of supplying them.

The character of the Gaucho is often very estimable; he is always hospitable—at his hut the traveller will always find a friendly welcome, and he will often be received with a natural dignity of manner which is very remarkable, and which he scarcely expects to meet with in such a miserable-looking hovel. On entering the hut, the Gaucho has constantly risen to offer me his seat, which I have declined, and many compliments and bows have passed, until I have accepted his offer, which is the skeleton of a horse's head. It is curious to see them invariably take off their hats to each other as they enter into a room which has no window, a bullock's hide for a door, and but little roof.

The habits of the women are very curious: they have literally nothing to do; the great plains which surround them offer them no motive to walk, they seldom ride, and *their* lives certainly are very indolent and inactive. They have all, however, families, whether married or not; and once when I inquired of a young woman employed in nursing a very pretty child, who was the father of the " creatura," she replied, Quien sabe?

★   ★   ★   ★   ★

MODE OF TRAVELLING.

THERE are two ways of travelling across the Pampas, in a carriage, or on horseback. The carriages are without springs, either of wood or iron, but they are very ingeniously slung on hide-ropes, which make them quite easy enough. There are two sorts of carriages, a long vehicle on four wheels, like a van (with a door behind), which is drawn by four or six horses, and which can carry eight people; and a smaller carriage on two wheels, of about half the length, which is usually drawn by three horses.

When I first went across the Pampas, I purchased for my party a large carriage, and also an enormous, two-wheeled, covered cart, which carried about twenty-five hundred weight of miners' tools, &c. I engaged a capataz (head-man), and he hired for me a number of peons, who were to receive thirty or forty dollars each for driving the vehicles to Mendoza.

The day before we started, the capataz came to me for some money to purchase hides, in order to prepare the carriages in the usual way.   The hides were soaked, and then cut into long strips, about three-quarters of an inch broad, and the pole, as also almost all the wood-work of the carriage, were firmly bound with the wet hide, which, when dry, shrunk into a band almost as hard as iron.   The spokes of the wheels, and, very much to our astonishment, the fellies or the circumference of the wheels were similarly bound, so that they actually travelled on the hide.   We all declared it would be cut before it got over the pavement of Buenos Aires, but it went perfectly sound for seven hundred miles, and was then only cut by some sharp granite rocks over which we were obliged to drive.

With respect to provisions, we were told (truly enough) that there is little to be had on the Pampas but beef and water ; and a quantity of provisions, with cherry brandy, &c. &c., was collected by the party, some of whom, I believe, fancied that I was going to take them, not to El Dorado, but to " that undiscovered country from which no traveller returns;" however, when we were ready to start, one of them found out that the loaves and fishes, the canteen, &c., were all left out (whether by accident or design, it matters not), and they then all cheerfully consented to " rough it," which is really the only way to travel without vexation in any country.   We took some brandy and tea with us, but so destitute were we of other luxuries, that the first day we had nothing to drink our tea out of but egg-shells.

As it had been reported to the government of Buenos-Ayres, that the Pampa Indians had invaded the country through which we had to pass, the minister was kind enough to give me an order to a Commandant who was on the road with troops, for assistance if required ; and besides this, we purchased a dozen muskets, some pistols, and sabres, which were slung to the roof of the carriage.

As it is customary to pay the peons half their money in advance, and as men who have been paid in advance have in all countries a number of thirsty friends, it is very difficult to collect all the drivers. Ours were of all colours, black, white, and red; and they were as wild a looking crew as ever was assembled. We had six horses in the carriage, six in the cart, each of which was ridden by a peon, and I, with one of the party, rode.

The travelling across the Pampas a distance of more than nine hundred miles is really a very astonishing effort. The country, as before described, is flat, with no road but a track, which is constantly changed. The huts, which are termed posts, are at different distances, but upon an average, about twenty miles from each other; and in travelling with carriages, it is necessary to send a man on before, to request the Gauchos to collect their horses.

The manner in which the peons drive is quite extraordinary. The country being in a complete state of nature, is intersected with streams, rivulets, and even rivers, with pontanas (marshes), &c., through which it is absolutely necessary to drive. In one instance the carriage, strange as it may seem, goes through a lake, which of course is not deep. The banks of the rivulets are often very precipitous, and I constantly remarked that we drove over and through places which in Europe any military officer would, I believe, without hesitation report as impassable.

The mode in which the horses are harnessed is admirably adapted to this sort of rough driving. They draw by the saddle instead of the collar, and having only one trace instead of two, they are able, on rough ground, to take advantage of every firm spot; where the ground will only once bear, every peon takes his own path, and the horses' limbs are all free and unconstrained.

In order to harness or unharness, the peons have only to hook and unhook the lasso which is fixed to their saddle; and this is so simple and easy, that we constantly observed when the carriage stopped, that before any one of us could jump out of it, the peons had unhooked, and were out of our sight to catch fresh horses in the corral.

In a gallop, if any thing was dropped by one of the peons, he would unhook, gallop back, and overtake the carriage without its stopping for him. I often thought how admirably in practice this mode of driving would suit the particular duties of that noble branch of our army, the Horse Artillery.

The rate at which the horses travel (if there are

enough of them) is quite surprising. Our cart, although laden with twenty-five hundred weight of tools, kept up with the carriage at a hand-gallop. Very often, as the two vehicles were going at this pace, some of the peons, who were always in high spirits, would scream out, " Ah mi patron !" and then all shriek and gallop with the carriage after me; and very frequently I was unable to ride away from them.

But strange as the account of this sort of driving may sound, the secret would be discovered by any one who could see the horses arrive. In England, horses are never seen in such a state; the spurs, heels, and legs of the peons are literally bathed with blood, and from the sides of the horses the blood is constantly flowing rather than dropping.

After this description, in justice to myself, I must say, that it is impossible to prevent it. The horses cannot trot, and it is impossible to draw the line between cantering and galloping, or, in merely passing through the country, to alter the system of riding, which all over the Pampas is cruel.

The peons are capital horsemen, and several times we saw them at a gallop throw the rein on the horse's neck, take from one pocket a bag of loose tobacco, and with a piece of paper, or a leaf of the Indian corn, make a segar, and then take out a flint and steel and light it.

The post-huts are from twelve to thirty-six miles, and in one instance fifty-four miles, from each other; and as it would be impossible to drag a carriage these distances at a gallop, relays of horses are sent on with the carriage, and are sometimes changed five times in a stage.

It is scarcely possible to conceive a wilder sight than our carriage and covered cart, as I often saw them *, galloping over the trackless plain, and preceded or followed by a troop of from thirty to seventy wild horses, all loose and galloping, driven by a Gaucho and his son, and sometimes by a couple of children. The picture seems to correspond

---

* I was one day observing them, instead of looking before me, when my horse fell in a biscachero, and rolled over upon my arm. It was so crushed that it made me very faint; but before I could get into my saddle, the carriages were almost out of sight, and while the sky was still looking green from the pain I was enduring, I was obliged to ride after them, and I believe I had seven miles to gallop as hard as my horse could go, before I could overtake the carriage to give up my horse.

with the danger which positively exists in passing through uninhabited regions, which are so often invaded by the merciless Indians.

*   *   *   *   *

In riding across the Pampas, it is generally the custom to take an attendant, and people often wait to accompany some carriage ; or else, if they are in condition, ride with the courier, who gets to Mendoza in twelve or thirteen days.   In case travellers wish to carry a bed and two small portmanteaus, they are placed upon one horse, which is either driven on before, or, by a halter, tied to the postilion's saddle.

The most independent way of travelling is without baggage, and without an attendant.   In this case, the traveller starts from Buenos Aires or Mendoza with a postilion, who is changed at every post. He has to saddle his own horses, and to sleep at night upon the ground on his saddle ; and as he is unable to carry any provisions, he must throw himself completely on the feeble resources of the country, and live on little else than beef and water.

It is of course a hard life ; but it is so delightfully independent, and if one is in good riding condition, so rapid a mode of travelling, that I twice chose it, and would always prefer it; but I recommend no one to attempt it, unless he is in good health and condition.

When I first crossed the Pampas, I went with a carriage, and although I had been accustomed to riding all my life, I could not at all ride with the peons, and after galloping five or six hours was obliged to get into the carriage; but after I had been riding for three or four months, and had lived upon beef and water, I found myself in a condition which I can only describe by saying that I felt no exertion could kill me.   Although I constantly arrived so completely exhausted that I could not speak, yet a few hours' sleep upon my saddle, on the ground, always so completely restored me, that for a week I could daily be upon my horse before sunrise, could ride till two or three hours after sunset, and have really tired ten and twelve horses a day.   This will explain the immense distances which people in South America are said to ride, which I am confident could only be done on beef and water.

At first, the constant galloping confuses the head,

and I have often been so giddy when I dismounted
that I could scarcely stand; but the system, by degrees, gets accustomed to it, and it then becomes
the most delightful life which one can possibly
enjoy. It is delightful from its variety, and
from the natural mode of reflecting which it en-
courages—for, in the grey of the morning, while
the air is still frosty and fresh, while the cattle are
looking wild and scared, and while the whole face
of Nature has the appearance of youth and innocence, one indulges in those feelings and speculations in which, right or wrong, it is so agreeable to
err; but the heat of the day, and the fatigue of
the body, gradually bring the mind to reason ;
before the sun has set many opinions are corrected,
and, as in the evening of life, one looks back with
calm regret upon the past follies of the morning.

In riding across the Pampas with a constant
succession of Gauchos, I often observed that the
children and the old men rode quicker than the
young men. The children have no judgment, but
they are so light, and always in such high spirits,
that they skim over the ground very quickly. The
old grey-headed Gaucho is a good horseman, with

great judgment, and although his pace is not quite so rapid as the children's, yet, from being constant and uniform, he arrives at his goal nearly in the same time. In riding with the young men, I found that the pace was unavoidably influenced by their passions, and by the subject on which we happened to converse; and when we got to the post, I constantly found that, somehow or other, time had been lost.

In crossing the Pampas it is absolutely necessary to be armed, as there are many robbers or salteadores, particularly in the desolate province of Santa Fé.

The object of these people is of course money, and I therefore always rode so badly dressed, and so well armed, that although I once passed through them with no one but a child as a postilion, they thought it not worth their while to attack me. I always carried two brace of detonating pistols in a belt, and a short detonating double-barrelled gun in my hand. I made it a rule never to be an instant without my arms, and to cock both barrels of my gun whenever I met any Gauchos.

With respect to the Indians, a person riding can

use no precaution, but must just run the gauntlet, and take his chance, which, if calculated, is a good one.

If he fall in with them, he may be tortured and killed, but it is very improbable that he should happen to find them on the road ; however, they are so cunning, and ride so quick, and the country is so uninhabited, that it is impossible to gain any information about them : besides this, the people are so alarmed, and there are so many constant reports concerning them, that it becomes useless to attend to any, and I believe it is just as safe to ride towards the spot at which one hears they are, as to turn back.

The greatest danger in riding alone across the Pampas, is the constant falls which the horses get in the holes of the biscachos. I calculated, that, upon an average, my horse fell with me in a gallop once in every three hundred miles; and although, from the ground being very soft, I was never seriously hurt, yet previous to starting one cannot help feeling what a forlorn situation it would be, to break a limb, or dislocate a joint, so many hundred miles from any sort of assistance.

★ ★ ★ ★ ★

THE PAMPAS INDIANS.

WHEN one compares the relative size of America with the rest of the world, it is singular to reflect on the history of those fellow-creatures who are the aborigines of the land; and after viewing the wealth and beauty of so interesting a country, it is painful to consider what the sufferings of the Indians have been, and still may be. Whatever may be their physical or moral character, whether more or less puny in body or in mind than the inhabitants of the old world, still they are the human beings placed there by the Almighty; the country belonged to them, and they are therefore entitled to the regard of every man who has religion enough to believe that God has made nothing in vain, or whose mind is just enough to respect the persons and the rights of his fellow-creatures.

A fair description of the Indians I believe does not exist. The Spaniards, on the discovery of the country, exterminated a large proportion of this

unfortunate race; the rest they considered as beasts
of burden, and during their short intervals of repose, the priests were ordered to explain to them,
that their vast country belonged to the Pope at
Rome.   The Indians, unable to comprehend this
claim, and sinking under the burdens which they
were doomed to carry, died in great numbers.   It
was therefore convenient to vote that they were im-
becile both in body and mind; the vote was se-
conded by the greedy voice of avarice, and carried
by the artifices of the designing, and the careless
indolence of those who had no interest in the question : it became a statement which historians have
now recorded.

But although the inquiry has been thus lulled to
rest, and is now the plausible excuse for our total
ignorance on the subject, ought not the state of
man in America to be infinitely more interesting
than descriptions of its mines, its mountains, &c.
&c. &c.

During my gallop in America, I had little time
or opportunity to see many of the Indians; yet
from what I did hear and see of them, I sincerely
believe they are as fine a set of men as ever existed

under the circumstances in which they are placed. In the mines I have seen them using tools which our miners declared they had not strength to work with, and carrying burdens which no man in England could support; and I appeal to those travellers who have been carried over the snow on their backs, whether they were able to have returned the compliment, and if not, what can be more grotesque than the figure of a civilized man riding upon the shoulders of a fellow-creature whose physical strength he has ventured to despise?

The Indians of whom I heard the most were those who inhabit the vast unknown plains of the Pampas, and who are all horsemen, or rather pass their lives on horseback. The life they lead is singularly interesting. In spite of the climate, which is burning hot in summer, and freezing in winter, these brave men, who have never yet been subdued, are entirely naked, and have not even a covering for their head.

They live together in tribes, each of which is governed by a Cacique, but they have no fixed place of residence. Where the pasture is good there are they to be found, until it is consumed by their horses, and they then instantly move to a more verdant spot. They have neither bread, fruit, nor vegetables, but they subsist entirely on the flesh of their mares, which they never ride; and the only luxury in which they indulge, is that of washing their hair in mare's blood.

The occupation of their lives is war, which they consider is their noble and most natural employment; and they declare that the proudest attitude of the human figure is when, bending over his horse, man is riding at his enemy. The principal weapon which they use is a spear eighteen feet long; they manage it with great dexterity, and are able to give it a tremulous motion which has often shaken the sword from the hand of their European adversaries.

From being constantly on horseback, the Indians can scarely walk. This may seem singular, but from their infancy they are unaccustomed to it. Living in a boundless plain, it may easily be conceived, that all their occupations and amusements must necessarily be on horseback, and from riding so many hours the legs become weak, which naturally gives a disinclination to an exertion which every day becomes more fatiguing; besides, the pace at which they can skim over the plains on horseback is so swift, in comparison to the rate they could crawl on foot, that the latter must seem a cheerless exertion.

As a military nation they are much to be admired, and their system of warfare is more noble and perfect in its nature than that of any nation in the world. When they assemble, either to attack their enemies, or to invade the country of the Christians, with whom they are now at war, they collect large troops of horses and mares, and then uttering the wild shriek of war, they start at a gallop. As soon as the horses they ride are tired, they vault upon the bare backs of fresh ones, keeping their best until they positively see their enemies. The whole country affords pasture to their horses, and whenever they choose to stop, they have only to kill some mares. The ground is the bed on which from their infancy they have always slept, and they therefore meet their enemies with light hearts and full stomachs, the only advantages which they think men ought to desire.

How different this style of warfare is to the march of an army of our brave but limping, footsore men, crawling in the rain through muddy lanes, bending under their packs, while in their rear the mules, and forage, and packsaddles, and baggage, and waggons, and women—bullocks lying on the ground unable to proceed, &c. &c., form a scene of despair and confusion which must always attend the army that walks instead of rides, and that eats cows* instead of horses. How impossible would it be for an European army to contend with such an aerial force. As well might it attempt to drive the swallows from the country, as to harm these naked warriors.

A large body of these Indians twice crossed my path, as I was riding from Buenos Aires to Mendoza and back again. They had just had an engagement with the Rio Plata troops, who killed several of them, and these were lying naked and dead on the plain not far from the road. Several of the Gauchos, who were engaged, told me that the Indians had fought most gallantly, but that all their horses were tired, or they could never have been attacked : the Gauchos, who themselves

* On a long march it seldom happens that the bullocks are able to keep up with the men.

ride so beautifully, all declare that it is impossible
to ride with an Indian, for that the Indians' horses
are better than theirs, and also that they have such
a way of urging on their horses by their cries, and
by a peculiar motion of their bodies, that even if
they were to change horses, the Indians would beat
them.   The Gauchos all seemed to dread very
much the Indians' spears.   They said that some of
the Indians charged without either bridle or saddle,
and that in some instances they were hanging almost
under the bellies of their horses, and shrieking, so
that the horses were afraid to face them.   As the
Indians' horses got tired, they were met by fresh
troops, and a great number of them were killed.

To people accustomed to the cold passions of
England, it would be impossible to describe the
savage, inveterate, furious hatred which exists
between the Gauchos and the Indians.   The latter
invade the country for the ecstatic pleasure of mur-
dering the Christians, and in the contests which
take place between them mercy is unknown.   Before I was quite aware of these feelings, I was
galloping with a very fine-looking Gaucho, who
had been fighting with the Indians, and after

listening to his report of the killed and wounded, I happened, very simply, to ask him, how many prisoners they had taken? The man replied by a look which I shall never forget—he clenched his teeth, opened his lips, and then sawing his fingers across his bare throat for a quarter of a minute, bending towards me, with his spurs striking into his horse's side, he said, in a sort of low, choking voice, " Se matan todos," (we kill them all.)   But this fate is what the Indian firmly expects, and from his earliest youth he is prepared to endure not only death, but tortures, if the fortune of war should throw him alive among his enemies; and yet how many there are who accuse the Indians of that imbecility of mind which in war bears the name of cowardice.   The usual cause for this accusation is, that the Indians have almost always been known to fly from fire-arms.

When first America was discovered, the Spaniards were regarded by the Indians as divinities, and perhaps there was nothing which tended to give them this distinction, more than their possessing weapons, which, resembling the lightning and the thunder of Heaven, sent death among them in a manner which they could not avoid or comprehend ; and although the Christians are no longer considered as divine, yet the Indians are so little accustomed to, or understood the nature of fire-arms, that it is natural to suppose the danger of these weapons is greater in their minds than the reality.

Accustomed to war among themselves with the lance, it is a danger also that they have not learnt to encounter; and it is well known that men can learn to meet danger, and that they become familiar with its face, when, if the mask be changed, and it appear with unusual features, they again view it with terror.   But even supposing that the Indians have no superstitious fear of fire-arms, but merely consider their positive effects,—is it not natural that they should fear them?   In Europe, or in England, what will people, with sticks in their hands, do against men who have fire-arms?   Why exactly what the naked Indians have been accused of doing—run away.—And who would not run away?

But the life which the Indian leads must satisfy any unprejudiced person that he must necessarily possess high courage.   His profession is War, his food is simple, and his body is in that state of health and vigour, that he can rise naked from the plain on which he has slept, and proudly look upon his image which the white frost has marked out upon the grass without inconvenience. What can we " men in buckram" say to this ?

The life of such a people must certainly be very interesting, and I always regretted very much that I had not time to throw off my clothes and pay a visit to some of the tribes, which I should otherwise certainly have done, as, with proper precautions, there would have been little to fear ; for it would have been curious to have seen the young sporting about the plains in such a state of wild nature, and to have listened to the sentiments and opinions of the old; and I would gladly have shivered through the cold nights, and have lived upon mare's flesh in the day, to have been a visitor among them.

From individuals who had lived many years with them, I was informed that the religion of the Pampas Indians is very complicated. They believe in good spirits and bad ones, and they pray to both. If any of their friends die before they have reached the natural term of life, (which is very

unusual,) they consider that some enemy has prevailed upon the evil spirit to kill their friend, and
they assemble to determine who this enemy can be.
They then denounce vengeance against him. These
disputes have very fatal consequences, and have
the political effect of alienating the tribes from one
another, and of preventing that combination among
the Indians which might make them much more
dreaded by the Christians.

They believe in a future state, to which they
conceive they will be transferred as soon as they
die. They expect that they will then be constantly
drunk, and that they will always be hunting; and
as the Indians gallop over their plains at night,
they will point with their spears to constellations
in the Heavens, which they say are the figures of
their Ancestors, who, reeling in the Firmament, are
mounted upon horses swifter than the wind, and
are hunting ostriches.

They bury their dead, but at the grave they
kill several of their best horses, as they believe that
their friend would otherwise have nothing to ride.
Their marriages are very simple. The couple to
be married, as soon as the sun sets, are made to lie

on the ground with their heads towards the west. They are then covered with the skin of a horse, and as soon as the sun rises at their feet, they are pronounced to be married *.

The Indians are very fond of any sort of intoxicating liquor, and when they are at peace with Mendoza, and some of the other provinces, they often bring skins of ostriches, hides, &c., to exchange for knives, spurs, and liquor.

The day of their arrival they generally get drunk, but before they indulge in this amusement, they deliberately deliver up to their Cacique their knives, and any other weapons they possess, as they are fully aware that they will quarrel as soon as the wine gets into their heads. They then drink till they can hardly see, and fight, and scratch, and bite, for the rest of the evening. The following day they devote to selling their goods, for they never will part with them on the day on which they resolve to be tipsy, as they say that in that state they would be unable to dispose of them to advantage.

* I believe this would almost be a legal marriage in Scotland.

They will not sell their skins for money, which they declare is of no use, but exchange them for knives, spurs, maté, sugar, &c. They refuse to buy by weight, which they do not understand; so they mark out upon a skin how much is to be covered with sugar, or anything of the sort which they desire to receive in barter for their property. After their business is concluded, they generally devote another day to Bacchus, and when they have got nearly sober, they mount their horses, and with a loose rein, and with their new spurs, they stagger and gallop away to their wild plains.

Without describing any more of their customs, which I repeat only from hearsay, I must only again lament that the history of these people is not better known; for, from many facts which I heard concerning them, I really believe that they, as well as the Araucana Indians, possess many brave and estimable qualities. It is singular, however, to think how mutually they and the inhabitants of the old world are unacquainted with each other. These untamed soldiers know nothing of the governments, customs, habits, wants, luxuries, virtues, or follies, of our civilised world, and what does the civilised world know of them? It votes them savages *et voilà tout ;* but as soon as fire-arms shall get into the hands of these brave naked men, they will tumble into the political scale as suddenly as if they had fallen from the moon ; and while the civilized world is watching the puny contests of Spaniards who were born in the old world, against their children who were born in the new one, and is arguing the cause of dependence *versus* independence, which in reality is but a quibble, the men that the ground belongs to will appear, and we shall then wonder how it is that we never felt for them, or cared for them, or hardly knew that they existed.

It may to many appear improbable that they should be ever able to overturn any of the feeble governments which at present exist; yet these men, without fire-arms, and with nothing in their hands but the lance, which is literally a reed, were twice within fifty leagues of Buenos Aires while I was in the country, and the Montaneros went among them while I was at San Luis, to offer to arm them. Besides this, the experience and history of the old world instruct us that the rise and fall of nations is a subject far beyond the scrutiny of man, and that, for reasons which we are unable to comprehend, the wild and despised tribes of our own world have often rushed from the polar towards the equatorial regions, and like the atmosphere from the north, have chilled and checked the luxury of the south; and therefore, however ill it may suit our politics to calculate upon such an event as the union of the Araucana and Pampas Indians, who can venture to say that the hour may not be decreed, when these men, mounted upon the descendants of the very horses which were brought over the Atlantic to oppress their forefathers, may rush from the cold region to which they have been driven, and with irresistible fury proclaim to the guilty conscience of our civilised world, that the hour of retribution has arrived; that the sins of the fathers are visited upon the children; that the descendants of Europeans are in their turn trampled under foot, and, in agony and torture, in vain are asking mercy from the *naked Indians?*

What a lesson this dreadful picture would afford!

However, it is neither my profession nor my wish to moralise; but it is impossible for a solitary individual to pass over the magnificent regions of America, without respecting the fellow-creatures who were placed there by the Almighty.

*　　*　　*　　*　　*

Proctor:
Journey across the Cordilleras of the Andes

Robert Proctor, *Narrative of a Journey across the Cordilleras of the Andes, and of a Residence in Lima, and Other Parts of Peru in the Years 1823 and 1824* (London: Constable, 1825), pp. 301–16.

Robert Proctor embarked from England on the brig *Cherub* for Buenos Aires on 8 December 1822. He travelled, in his own words, as 'agent for the contractors, to obtain the ratification of the loan by the government and congress, and to draw for the amount upon London' (p. 131). He was entrusted with the important commission of securing the £1,200,000 loan taken out by the Peruvian government to finance part of the enormous cost of liberating the country from Spanish rule, and to bridge the massive trade gap caused by the decline of the Peruvian economy in a period of war and instability. The main contemporary selling point of Proctor's narrative was its account of Peru and of the political anarchy surrounding the Peruvians' belated independence struggle against Spanish rule. Proctor's role as agent for the loan gave him access to prominent political figures and permitted him to cast new light on some of the machinations behind the public events of independence. He hinted that 'less is known regarding [Peru] and its inhabitants than any of the other independent states' of South America. At another level, the book is also an exciting record of the long journey Proctor undertook with his wife, infant son and three servants from Buenos Aires across the Pampas to the province of Mendoza, where he was welcomed by San Martín himself. After visiting the silver mines at Uspallata (to be prospected a couple of years later by a disappointed Francis Head), Proctor crossed the Andes to Chile, where he had an audience with the director of the new junta, General Ramon Freire, as well the recently deposed Bernardo O'Higgins, whom he found confined as 'a kind of state-prisoner'. He memorably described the latter as 'short in stature and corpulent, and his face reminds me of the portraits of Oliver Cromwell' (p. 108). Making his way to the crime-ridden port of Valparaiso, teeming with 'the lowest description' of English smugglers and adventurers, he boarded a ship for Peru on 13 May 1823, and arrived in Lima with letters of introduction to the Scottish merchant and loan broker John Parish Robertson, as well as to the leaders of the newly independent government.

In the event, the period of Proctor's sojourn in Peru coincided with a political crisis in which the advances made by the Chilean-backed independence movement suffered severe setbacks; for in the words of John Lynch, Peru was indeed 'the problem child of the American revolution' (Lynch, *The Spanish American Revolutions 1808–1826* (New York, 1986), p. 267). In the first place, congress dragged its feet in ratifying the British loan in order to impede the military-backed executive government headed by José de la Riva Agüero, which had been foisted on them in February 1823. The divisions within Peru's government led to the recapture of Lima by Spanish forces in June of the same year, just after Proctor had finally been notified of the ratification of the loan by congress. Amidst panic in Lima, vividly described in his book, the president and congress fled to Trujillo, where they anxiously awaited the arrival of Simón Bolívar's army to oust the royalists, whilst Proctor and his family took refuge amongst the British merchant ships at Callao. Proctor proceeded to Trujillo to negotiate with Riva Agüero, who had split with congress. The latter quickly reconstituted itself in Lima after the Spanish withdrew, appointing a new president, Torre Tagle, whom Riva Agüero refused to recognise. The Peru evoked in Proctor's book is thus split into two zones, occupied in the south by the Spaniards and in the north afflicted by civil war between the two *independista* factions of Torre Tagle and Riva Agüero. Bolívar arrived in Lima on 1 September 1823 and was immediately invested with supreme authority. Riva Agüero defected to the royalists but was deposed by a mutiny. At this point (December) Proctor set out from Lima on an expedition to visit the Pasco mines, as described in the following excerpt. The unsettled state of the country and the atmosphere of intrigue and suspicion are everywhere evident in his narrative, and the presence of *montenero* bands and Spanish forces in Pasco eventually forced Proctor to abandon his journey. Nevertheless his description of the indigenous society of highland Peru and the vertical ecology of the Andes makes striking reading, as the Indians struggled to get on with their everyday lives in the face of political turmoil. In February 1824 Argentinian and Chilean troops in Callao mutinied for arrears of pay, and handed over the fortress to royalist forces; Lima was shortly to follow. 'Peru is a chamber of horrors', complained the frustrated Bolívar, but the Venezuelan liberator was soon to triumph over the royalists at the battles of Junín and Ayacucho in December 1824. Amidst the confusion, however, Proctor had already made good his escape from Callao and managed to return to England in one piece, where he published this vivid account of his adventures the following year.

CHAPTER XXXIX.

Journey to the mines of Pasco—Party of Los Inocentes—Murders and robberies by them—The mines of Canta—Cocota—Peruvian scenery, and inhabitants—Chicha.

On the 13th December, having made the necessary arrangements by getting warm clothing, &c., I started with a native who acted as my guide and companion, and a led mule to carry our small stock of baggage and comforts. We left Lima about three o'clock in the afternoon, having to go six leagues that night. For some distance our path lay along the foot of the mountains by the road to Chancay, until about two leagues from the city, we reached the encampment occupied by the Spanish army, while San Martin lay at Huaura : as my companion had served as an officer in that army, he could point out the different stations, and the advantages of the position. At this spot the mountains approached very close to the sea, so as to leave a smaller space to be defended, than if the valley had been wider. In the centre of the encampment was a rising ground, on which the royalists had mounted their artillery, forming a battery of twelve pieces, and the embrasures were still visible. In advance was a long wide plain, through which passed the road to Chancay.   The *tapias* had here all been levelled, as well that the artillery might be able to play with effect upon an enemy, as that the cavalry might act without obstruction.

At this point the Pasco road branches to the right, skirting the arid mountains, while on the left we saw some very fine cultivated estates ; but the houses and buildings upon them had been allowed to go to ruin.

Soon afterwards we overtook two fellow travellers, a soldier and his lady, belonging to a party at a short distance, with the " horses of the state," grazing free of expense, on a plantation, the proprietor of which was no doubt sufficiently paid by the honour thus done him.   Our new friend belonged to the Chilian *Inocentes*, the corps commanded by General Miller in Upper Peru, the exploits of which I have already celebrated, and certainly they were good specimens of the body to which they were attached.   The gentleman carried the carcass of a sheep, hanging on each side of his saddle, which he was conveying to his friends.   The lady was sitting astride on her horse, and amused me exceedingly by the account she gave of the recent campaign, and of the plunder she had obtained.   She was dressed quite *à la militaire*, and managed her horse with admirable skill. This lawless band had been playing their old game on the road by robbing the Indians as they brought down small quantities of silver to the city, and as we went through a narrow pass between the hills, our two companions showed us some blood on the sand, which they said was that of a traveller murdered the day before. I told them plainly, as our best security, that any one attempting to rob us would meet with as good a resistance as we could make, and at the same time I took care that they should see my pistols. Ere long we arrived at the estate where the whole body rested, and we parted with mutual civilities.

We passed on our road the remains of several Indian towns, generally on the tops or sides of the hills. We were now joined by an elderly man known to my companion, and who invited us to sleep at his house near the road, which offer we accepted.

The old *godo*, for so he proved to be, lived at a good estate, at the end of a valley, terminating among the hills : his house was a miserable dirty *chacra*, surrounded by the cane huts of the slaves, and by different *corrales*, with mud walls for the various kinds of stock : close by was the thrashing-floor, a round circular yard, paved with small pebbles. Having turned our mules into one of these enclosures, and supplied them with a bundle or two of lucern, we followed our host into a small room, where he had a bed for himself when he came to visit his plantation.

During the preparation of the *chupe* for supper, he amused us with a statement of his losses by the patriots, which he estimated at 70,000 dollars, by different robberies and exactions, and every turn of his conversation, when comparing the old state of things with the new, " his excellency the viceroy" was continually in his mouth. His *capitas*, or bailiff, was a curious old fellow, and formed a good match for the master. The discontented royalist, however, hospitably offered me the use of his bed, which I of course declined, preferring to wrap myself up in my cloak on my saddle in an outer room with the baggage. In answer to a question I put to the old bailiff, whether there were any fleas in the house, his dry answer was, *Si señor hembra y macho,* " Yes, Sir, male and female."

We were up early the next morning, and breakfasted on chocolate, having taken the necessary apparatus with us, and boiling it with ignited spirit. We then started; the bailiff was sent with us to shew us into the *Camino Real,* or King's Road, which we had deviated from a little in order to sleep at the old gentleman's dwelling. The bailiff, while accompanying us, gave a most feeling description of the stinginess of our host, and declared that he had lived a dog's life all the time he had been in his service.

After leaving him we entered the dry mountainous country, and at a considerable height above the valley, we passed an *acequia,* or small canal, originally cut by the Indians along the sides of the hills to conduct water to some distant spot. The effect of this stream, contrasted with the bare face of the mountains, was very pleasant : it was bordered by very tall luxuriant canes, which grew immediately at the edge of the water, and marked its winding course for many miles. We soon came into a deep stony valley or channel, between two ranges of barren rocky eminences, called the *Rio Seco*, "dry river," of the same description as those mentioned in my journey to Truxillo. The sun's vertical rays here shot down upon our heads with great power, and, being reflected by the hard arid ground, the heat was almost intolerable : the journey, therefore, for three or four leagues was very toilsome to man and beast. We at last came to a very steep hill, celebrated in that part of the country for being the resort of banditti, and they certainly could not choose a more convenient situation, as the path was here contracted to a narrow pass, and the robbers could see several miles each way, so as to be at once secure of their prey, and from the surprise of enemies. My companion told me that he and some others were travelling this road on a former occasion, with a considerable quantity of dollars in their possession, when, arriving near the summit, they saw a body of men stationary on the top of the hill. They concluded that they must certainly be robbers, and the party halted to recruit their forces by other travellers, who were coming up behind, when it was unanimously agreed that they would not be robbed tamely. They therefore, like good generals, left their baggage in the rear, and the whole party advanced up the hill in battle array. When they reached the top the robbers proved to be only travellers like themselves, regaling after the fatigues of the road : the baggage was accordingly sent for, the stock of provisions was opened, and the rest of the day was spent in merriment on the spot.

From our lofty situation we could see as it were immediately below us a pretty green valley, but we were nearly two hours before we reached it, the eye being much deceived as to the distance. A few leagues on this side of Pasco, a stream issues from the Cordillera, to which others unite themselves, and, when it passes Canta, it assumes the name of the river of Canta, being there a considerable torrent: it empties itself into the sea at Chancay, fourteen leagues from Lima, fertilizing in its course a very cheerful country. The whole valley or *quebrada* through which this river runs is one of the prettiest that can be imagined : it is closely shut in, in many situations, by high ranges of bare rugged rocks, which leave little more space at the bottom than is sufficient for the torrent. In other places the water is ingeniously carried along the sides of the hills in small channels, neatly formed of earth and stones; for wherever the soil will admit of cultivation, the natives irrigate it. For this purpose, the sides of the mountains are laid out in steps or terraces, though with a considerable declivity, each plantation having a wall at the bottom of it, to prevent the soil from being washed entirely away. In these little, and often precipitous fields, the most luxuriant lucern is grown intermixed with plats of Indian corn, all contrasting beautifully with the high barren mountains in the vicinity.

The mule-track along the face of these hills generally skirted one of these fertilizing streams, and even the bubbling sound of the water, passing over the stony bottom of the channel, seemed to cool us as we proceeded in the heat of the day. The valley was well inhabited : small Indian villages were scattered along the road, often in the most delightful and picturesque situations, and overshadowed by fruit trees of a kind which will not thrive near the coast. I was now in the midst of Peruvian scenery, and among its inhabitants, unmixed with whites or negroes; and I saw both country and people, probably with very little difference from their condition in the innocent and happy times of the Incas.

Our first entrance into this aboriginal *quebrada,* if I may so call it, was at the small village of Cocoto, which consists of a few unconnected *ranchos.* Continuing to wind up the woods, we passed a beautiful cascade which, leaping over a precipice, fell as much as an hundred yards in perpendicular height into the valley. Further on we reached a solitary church, famous as the reported birth-place of Santa Rosa, the Peruvian saint, to whom the edifice was dedicated. We were benighted before we reached our *pascana* or pasture, but we were well repaid for the additional danger of travelling in these precipitous roads by the solemn and grand effect of the moon-light upon vast craggy eminences, obscured only at short intervals by flying clouds. On approaching Yasso we were greeted by the loud barking of the dogs always kept by the Indians, and we soon arrived at the village, containing half a dozen huts, where we put up for the night. We spread our beds, consisting of our

326 Travels, Explorations and Empires: Volume 7

saddles and blankets, in a small field of lucern, and made our mules fast, according to the method of the country, to a strong weed which grows among it.

I had observed to-day that many of the cottages had boughs hung up at the doors as a sign to travellers that *chicha* was sold in the rancho. *Chicha* is the national drink of the Indians, and I was informed that it is made of Indian corn chewed by the women, and then fermented. The liquor, thus produced, is more like our beer than any thing else, and is by no means an unpalatable drink. The natives are so much addicted to it, that many of them, while they can procure it, are in a continual state of intoxication.

Having made our supper to-night of *chupe* and broiled mutton, and having taken a good draught of *chicha* to keep out the cold night air, we rolled ourselves up in our blankets; but we passed a bad night, as the mules frequently broke loose, and we were obliged to get up to make them fast again.

CHAPTER XL.

Yasso, and its situation—Rainy season in the Andes—Lobrojillo
—Entrance of the Spaniards into Pasco, and abandonment of
the journey—Manners of the inhabitants—Cultivation of potatoes—Chase of the Vacuña.

In the morning I was somewhat benumbed by the
cold and the heavy dew.   At day-light I found that
the little village of Yasso was placed in a most romantic situation, with its green fields and fruit-trees
almost overhanging the torrent, which rushed along,
dashing its white foam against the large fragments
of rock that obstructed its course.   The scene was
rendered more picturesque by the ruins of a large
building, which had the appearance of the remains
of a Gothic edifice, but I found, on inquiry, that it
had been only an *ingenio*, or smelting furnace for
silver : it was in decay, as the mine to which it belonged, after a time, was discovered to be not worth
working.

The whole of the mountainous country in which
we were enclosed is full of minerals, and we passed
a chain of hills of ironstone, and all the water that
issued from them was of a rusty colour, and the taste
strongly chalybeate.   Towards Canta, the capital of

the province, the hills on each side of the valley were higher, while we continued winding up the mule-track, like that in the Cordillera between Buenos Ayres and Chili, cut on the bare face of the hills, or sometimes along the edges of the torrents. I observed in many places small towns, perched like eagles' nests at the top of some elevation, at such a giddy height, that the inhabitants, moving about the lofty ridges above us, seemed mere pigmies. In addition to the beautiful and luxuriant irrigated valleys I have described, wherever there was sufficient depth of soil on the face of the mountains, the ancient Indians had cultivated the spot, and made small enclosures to keep the mould from being washed down. Whole mountains are seen thus laid out, and they give a good idea of the industry and population of the early inhabitants. In these patches they grew, and indeed still partially grow, potatoes, barley, maize, and wheat, trusting to the rainy season for the fruit of their labours. The rains in the Andes begin generally in December, and the mountains almost immediately become clothed with pasture and wild flowers. At the time I was passing over this country, the rainy season had commenced in the higher regions of the Cordillera; but it had not reached as far as Canta. The distant roll of the thunder was nevertheless heard, re-echoed by the mountains, and the river was swollen and red with the soil brought down by the innumerable streams which joined it before its arrival at Canta.

Soon after leaving Yasso this morning, we crossed

the river by a rustic bridge, stretched from one rock to another, where they projected into the torrent and made the channel narrower. This bridge was formed of two long pieces of timber, and they were bound together by ropes of the fibres of aloe leaves ; upon these were laid large quantities of other leaves, and altogether they made a secure though vibrating bridge of three or four feet broad. The banks of the river were generally fringed with tall canes, prickly pears, and aloes, with their lofty flowers, running up sometimes to the height of more than twenty feet. Having travelled for about a mile up a most dangerous road of rude steps, cut or worn in the side of the rocky hills, we descended again towards the torrent, and finding a pretty little grass-plat, shaded by trees on the bank of the river, we boiled our chocolate, and stretched at length on the ground, contemplated at leisure the sublime scenery of the Andes, and watched the labours of the Indians, whom we observed on the surrounding eminences preparing their lands, in order to sow them after the first fall of rain.

We this morning met a Montonero soldier, who told us, to our surprise, that the royalists were in Pasco. This man was an Indian from Reyes, a town between Pasco and Xauja : he was dressed in a coarse yellow jacket and high cap, with long trowsers reaching far below his boots. We did not like the expression of his countenance, and suspected that he meant us no good : at last he fairly told us he thought we were *godos* hastening to join the Spaniards, and nothing, for a long time, could convince him of the contrary. He asked me, however, the person's house to whom we were going in Lobrojillo, and when I mentioned it, he said all was right, as the man happened to be a captain of Montoneros. Finding, therefore, that he had no pretence for plundering us, as we were good patriots, he inquired what we had to sell: we told him that we were only travelling to gratify curiosity, and he proceeded to beg for every thing we had brought with us.

About half a mile before we arrived at Lobrojillo, we again crossed the torrent by a curious natural bridge formed of two large granite rocks, which seemed to have fallen over it, their tops resting against each other, and affording a secure road without any assistance from art.

Lobrojillo is an Indian town, consisting of about 100 thatched huts, built round a square on the banks of the river, and encompassed by a small valley of irrigated land. On inquiring for Casquero, the man to whom I carried a letter of introduction, there being no inns on the road, I learnt that his house was a little way out of the town. My host was a short thick *Mestizo*, or half Indian and half European, and was a captain of a troop of Montoneros belonging to Canta and the neighbourhood. Though a man of some consequence in the place, he lived like the Indians, in a mud cottage, or rather in a range of mud buildings thatched with straw, and built round a yard. He confirmed the unpleasant news that the Spaniards had entered Pasco, and advised me by no means to attempt to proceed, as independently of the Spaniards having possession of Pasco, the road to it was occupied by bands of Montoneros, who had been of the party of Riva Aguero, and had not yet submitted to Bolivar. They consisted very much of Indians, who knew little or nothing of Spanish, and he stated them to be very barbarous and cruel. Under these circumstances it would have been madness to have persevered, and as this valley led to no other point, I was obliged to be satisfied with what I had already seen, and to collect all the information I could obtain respecting the county on the other side the Cordillera, which I had intended to have visited.

Canta is situated on a dry plain about a mile from Lobrojillo, and two or three leagues from the foot of the summit of the Andes in that quarter. It is a large town, but has a miserable appearance from a distance, being more like a large group of barns than houses. The inhabitants were complaining very much of the backwardness of the rains, and that the cattle were starving for want of pasture. The town itself looked the more uncomfortable for this reason. The inhabitants are chiefly Indians, of a more robust and hardy race than those of the coast, but having the same softness of manners, and the same innocent and melancholy expression of countenance. Their dress is almost entirely of their own manufacture. The men wear small coarse *ponchos*, and underneath jackets and breeches of cloth, with worsted stockings knitted by the females, and shoes of raw hide, drawn tight over the foot by a thong,

which goes all round. The men's hats are coarse
beaver. The women are dressed much in the same
way as those of the coast, and all are evidently of
one race, though climate and employment have rendered the native inhabitants near the sea somewhat
different in their appearance and habits.

The Indians of the interior are a very active and
hardy set of people, and are particularly famous for
long journeys on foot, which they perform with surprising speed. The road to Pasco from Lima is fifty
leagues, and it is performed by animals in four or
five days, while an Indian *propio*, or courier on foot,
will go the distance in three days, by cutting over
the tops of the mountains, accompanied merely by
his dog, and walking with a long staff. They can
endure hunger as well as fatigue, and with a small
bag of *cancha*, and another of *coca*, they travel
for days without requiring any other sustenance.
Cancha is made of a sweet kind of maize which
grows in the Sierra, parched and ground small by
rolling a round stone on a flat one; it is very
nourishing and agreeable to the palate, and is eaten
as a powder. *Coca* is the dried leaf of a tree which
they chew like tobacco, mixing it with lime: it has
the double advantage of preventing hunger, and of
being a strong stimulant. As the Spanish army is
composed, in a great measure, of these Indians, it will
in some measure account for the length and rapidity
of its marches through dreadful roads, and over
apparently impassable mountains.

I have before mentioned that the agriculture of

the Sierra is confined principally to maize, wheat, barley, and potatoes. This latter vegetable grows to the greatest perfection in the Sierra, of which recent inquiries have shown it to be a native. There are three kinds of it in Peru: the first is a bright yellow, the second blue, and the third white; and all three are of the size and shape of what we call champions, and are the best I have ever eaten, though the yellow is perhaps to be preferred. Most of the little plats of ground cultivated by the Indians are dug by the hand with a clumsy kind of spade fixed at the end of a long handle: it is then broken to pieces by hoes; but I also saw a team of oxen at work ploughing in a low situation on the banks of the river.

Besides their woollen manufactures of coarse cloth, worsted stockings, and *ponchos*, the natives make finer articles of Vacuña wool, which is spun by the women, who merely use a straight piece of wood on which the thread is wound, and which they twist with their fingers. Of this beautiful material they make stockings and gloves of the natural fawn colour, ornamenting the clocks and seams with green silk. A pair of stockings of this description is worth from five to twelve dollars. They also weave fine *ponchos*, in lively colours, with very pretty patterns, which are worth as much as 700 dollars. *Ponchos* and bed-quilts of cotton are likewise made by the Indians, but they are very dear.

There are three species of the Llama or Peruvian sheep: the wild *guanaco*, which is useless excepting

for food ; the *Vacuña,* which supplies the fine wool ;
and the *Llama,* used merely as a beast of burthen.
The Vacuña is wild, and inhabits the *quebradas* of the
mountains : the chase of it affords the Indians great
amusement, and it is caught in the following manner : The Indians form a *corral,* or enclosure, in a
valley frequented by these animals, of upright stakes,
with horizontal strings, to which are attached pieces
of worsted of different bright colours, and this enclosure is left open on one side.   They then take a wide
circuit, and drive the affrighted animals along the
quebrada till they enter the *corral,* advancing gradually upon their timid prey : the Vacuñas, seeing
the pieces of coloured worsted blown about by the
wind, stand together in a flock, alarmed at the unusual sight, and allow the Indians to kill them at
their leisure.

Stewart:
View of the Island of Jamaica

John Stewart, *A View of the Past and Present State of the Island of Jamaica; with Remarks on the Moral and Physical Condition of the Slaves, and on the Abolition of Slavery in the Colonies* (Edinburgh: Oliver & Boyd, 1823), pp. 266–79.

In 1808 the British government finally abolished the Atlantic slave trade, after decades of agitation by Nonconformist and Anglican Evangelicals like Granville Sharpe, Thomas Clarkson and William Wilberforce. Yet the planters' lobby, jealous of declining profits in the face of competition from the slave economies of Cuba and the US, held out against full emancipation, despite growing public opposition in Britain. The planters feared mass rebellions by slaves on the pattern of the bloody rebellion in French Saint-Domingue (Haiti) in 1791; they believed (with some justification) that the growing demand for freedom amongst the slaves was being fomented by Methodist and Baptist missionaries, who had been actively and successfully proselytising them since about 1814. In the interests of effecting a compromise between public opinion and the planters' interests, the British government, in the years following the end of the Napoleonic Wars, urged the various legislative assemblies of the West Indian islands to implement reforms to ameliorate the condition of the 750,000 slaves labouring in British colonies (half of these lived in Stewart's Jamaica). High on the agenda were Anglican religious instruction to counter the influence of Baptist and Methodist missionaries; an end to Sunday labour; legalisation of the marriage of slaves; the abolition of flogging; and limitations on the planters' powers of punishment. While implementation was relatively straightforward in the Crown Colonies of Trinidad, British Guyana and St Lucia, it was resisted by the assemblies of older colonies like Jamaica, leading to a heated polemic between the planters and public opinion at home.

This ideological pressure is evident in Stewart's comments in his preface, where he pleads for his book's impartiality in 'steer[ing] clear of all prejudices and party opinions' (p. vii). Given that the author was (by his own admission) a long-term resident in Jamaica, connected to the planting interest, his avowed impartiality is open to question. The fact that he was also a dedicated Anglican (or more correctly an Episcopalian, given that he was Scottish) helps to explain the axe which he has to grind against the activities of the Nonconformist missionaries. Nevertheless, Stewart's informative book followed

Humboldt's *Political Essay on New Spain* in seeking to present the public with a 'historical, topographical and statistical' overview of Jamaica and its past and future prospects, which transcended mere polemic. Stewart's own position bears little resemblance to the extreme views of an earlier pro-slavery work like Edward Long's *History of Jamaica* (1774), which justified slavery on the grounds that blacks were a separate species from whites, whose destiny was to labour for their white masters. Like Henry Nelson Coleridge, Stewart accepted the paternalistic principle of amelioration leading to eventual emancipation. Slaves would be prepared for liberty by religious instruction, as well as by an 'apprenticeship' system, which obliged them to contribute financially towards their manumission, whilst at the same time implanting habits of industry and sobriety. The excerpt below describes the manners and cultures of the Jamaican slaves, focusing on music and dance, festival and funeral rituals, and the practice of *obeah* or witchcraft, which had greatly interested Wordsworth and Coleridge twenty years earlier. While he admired the energy and cultural inventiveness of the slaves in their rare moments of leisure from the toils of the cane fields, the moralist and political economist in Stewart regretted the 'lassitude and languor' which followed the festivities, incapacitating the slaves 'for much exertion or labour' in the following working days (below, p. 342).

With hindsight, the process of amelioration advocated by Stewart here seems to have been too little, too late. In the year in which his book was published, a violent slave rebellion tore apart British Guyana, and in Jamaica there were sporadic uprisings throughout the 1820s and a major rebellion in 1831, which was savagely repressed. In Britain the heated ideological climate in which emancipation was debated in the decade after 1823 was fuelled by the related issues of Catholic emancipation and parliamentary reform. With the election of a new Whig government, however, all three causes were rapidly carried through Parliament. Britain's colonial slaves were freed by the Emancipation Act of 1833, although the slaves of Jamaica, Trinidad, Tobago and British Guyana bitterly resented the apprenticeship system that preceded final liberation in these colonies.

CHAP. XVI.

HOUSES, PROVISION-GROUNDS, FOOD, AND CLOTHING OF
THE SLAVES—THEIR AMUSEMENTS—THEIR FESTI-
VITY AND DISSIPATION—THEIR FUNERALS—THEIR
SUPERSTITIONS.

THE houses of the slaves are in general comfortable. They are built of hard-wood posts, either
boarded or wattled and plastered, and the roof
formed of shingles (wood split and dressed into
the shape of slates, and used as a substitute for
them), or thatched with the leaves of the sugar-
cane, or the branches of the mountain cabbage:*
this latter is of so durable a nature that it will
last for thirty or forty years. The size of the
houses is generally from fifteen to twenty feet
long, and from ten to fifteen wide. They contain
a small hall, and one or two bed-rooms, according to the size of the family. The furniture of
this dwelling is a small table, two or three chairs
or stools, a small cupboard, furnished with a few
articles of crockery-ware, some wooden bowls
and calibashes, a water-jar, a wooden mortar for

---

* A species of the palm.

pounding Indian corn, &c. and various other articles. The beds are seldom more than wooden frames spread with a mat and blanket.

Adjoining to the house is usually a small spot of ground, laid out into a sort of garden, and shaded by various fruit-trees. Here the family deposite their dead, to whose memory they invariably, if they can afford it, erect a rude tomb. Each slave has, besides this spot, a piece of ground (about half an acre) allotted to him as a provision-ground. This is the principal means of his support; and so productive is the soil, where it is good and the seasons regular, that this spot will not only furnish him with sufficient food for his own consumption, but an overplus to carry to market. By means of this ground, and of the hogs and poultry which he may raise (most of which he sells), an industrious negro may not only support himself comfortably, but save something. If he has a family, an additional proportion of ground is allowed him, and all his children from five years upwards assist him in his labours in some way or other. On the sugar plantations the slaves are not allowed to keep horses, cows, sheep, or goats,* and they

---

* On the pens, and coffee and other settlements, they are usually allowed to keep a few goats, but neither horses nor cattle.

are obliged to prevent their hogs from wandering over the estate.

The common food of the slaves is salt meat (commonly pork), or salted fish, boiled along with their yams, cocos, or plantains, mixed up with pulse and other vegetables, and highly seasoned with the native pepper (*capsum Indicus*). Pimento they never use in their food. They receive from their masters seven or eight herrings per week, a food which most of them, who can afford better, despise ; and they accordingly sell them in the markets, and purchase salted pork, of which they are exceedingly fond. They also get about eight pounds of salted cod-fish once or twice a-year : this food is more a favourite with them than the herrings, for no reason that can be imagined, but because the former is a greater rarity than the latter. They cannot afford to indulge themselves with a fowl or a duck, except upon particular occasions.*

The common dress of the male slaves is an osnaburgh or check frock, and a pair of osnaburgh or sheeting trowsers, with a coarse hat. That of the women is an osnaburgh or coarse linen shift, a petticoat made of various stuff, according to their taste and circumstances, and a

---

* Some of the Africans eat the cane-field rat, which they regard as a great luxury.

handkerchief tied round their heads.   Both men and women are also provided with great-coats (or *croocas*, as they call them) of blue woollen stuff.   Neither sex wear shoes in common, these being reserved for particular occasions, such as dances, &c. when all who can afford it appear in very gay apparel—the men in broad-cloth coats, fancy waistcoats, and nankeen or jean trowsers, and the women in white or fancy muslin gowns, beaver or silk hats, and a variety of expensive jewellery.   But it is only a small proportion who can afford to dress thus finely.   The annual allowance of clothing which they receive from their owners is as much osnaburgh as will make two frocks, and as much woollen stuff as will make a great-coat; with a hat, handkerchief, knife, and needles and thread to make up their clothes.   This specific quantity an owner is obliged by law to give to his slaves.   But all of them who can afford to buy a finer dress, seldom appear, excepting when at work, in the coarse habiliments given them by their masters.

The slaves have little time to devote to amusement, but such occasions as offer they eagerly embrace.   Plays, as they call them, are their principal and favourite one.   This is an assemblage of both sexes, dressed out for the occasion, who form a ring round a male and female dancer, who perform to the music of drums and the songs of the other females of the party, one alternately going over the song, while her companions repeat in chorus. Both the singers and dancers shew the exactest precision as to time and measure. This rude music is usually accompanied by a kind of rattles, being small calibashes filled with the seed of a plant called by the negroes *Indian shot.* Near at hand this music is harsh and clamorous, but at a distance it has not an unpleasant sound. When two dancers have fatigued themselves, another couple enter the ring, and thus the amusement continues. So fond are the negroes of this amusement, that they will continue for nights and days enjoying it, when permitted. But their owners find it prudent and necessary to restrain them from it, excepting at Christmas, when they have three days allowed them. This and harvest-home may be considered as their two annual festivals. Little do they consider, and as little do they care, about the origin and occasion of the former of those festivals; suffice it to say, that *Buckra* gives them their three days—though, by the bye, the law allows only two, in consideration of the injury they may sustain by three successive days of unbounded dissipation, and of the danger, at such a time of unrestrained licentiousness, of riots and disorder.

On these occasions the slaves appear an altered

race of beings. They show themselves off to the greatest advantage, by fine clothes and a profusion of trinkets; they affect a more polished behaviour and mode of speech; they address the whites with greater familiarity; they come into their masters' houses, and drink with them; the distance between them appears to be annihilated for the moment, like. the familiar footing on which the Roman slaves were with their masters at the feast of the Saturnalia. Pleasure throws a temporary oblivion over their cares and their toils; they seem a people without the consciousness of inferiority or suffering.

Many of them, however, but especially the men, give themselves up to excessive intemperance, which, with their nocturnal dances, often produces sickness, and sometimes even death. Such is the violent exercise they undergo in these dancings, such the heedless manner in which they abandon themselves for successive nights and days to this favourite amusement, even in the open air, during the Christmas holidays, that were this unrestrained indulgence permitted for two or three weeks, instead of as many days, it would probably destroy a great number of these thoughtless people. After their riotous festivity, they experience a degree of lassitude and languor which for some days incapacitates them for much exertion or labour.

Plays, or dances, very frequently take place on Saturday nights, when the slaves on the neighbouring plantations assemble together to enjoy this amusement. It is contrary to the law for the slaves to beat their drums after ten o'clock at night; but this law they pay little regard to. Their music is very rude; it consists of the *goombay* or drum, several rattles, and the voices of the female slaves, which, by the bye, is the best part of the music, though altogether it is very rude. The drums of the Africans vary in shape, size, &c. according to the different countries, as does also their vocal music. In a few years it is probable that the rude music here described will be altogether exploded among the creole negroes, who shew a decided preference for European music. Its instruments, its tunes, its dances, are now pretty generally adopted by the young creoles, who indeed sedulously copy their masters and mistresses in every thing. A sort of subscription balls are set on foot, and parties of both sexes assemble and dance country dances to the music of a violin, tambarine, &c. But this improvement of taste is in a great measure confined to those who are, or have been, domestics about the houses of the whites, and have in consequence imbibed a fondness for their amusements, and some skill in the performance. They affect, too, the language, manners, and

344 Travels, Explorations and Empires: Volume 7

344   *Travels, Explorations and Empires: Volume 7*

conversation of the whites: those who have it in their power have at times their convivial parties, when they will endeavour to mimic their masters in their drinking, their songs, and their toasts; and it is laughable to see with what awkward minuteness they aim at such imitations. They have also caught a spirit of gambling from their masters, and often assemble and play at games of hazard with the dice, though there is a law against such species of gambling, and such slaves as are found assembled for this purpose are liable to punishment. At horse-races, betting goes on among the negro servants who are present as regularly as among their masters.

On new-year's-day, it is customary for the creole negro girls of the towns, who conceive themselves superior to those on the plantations, to exhibit themselves in all the pride of gaudy finery, under the denomination of *Blues* and *Reds*—parties in rivalship and opposition to each other. They are generally dressed with much taste, sometimes at the expense of their white and brown mistresses, who take a pride in shewing them off to the greatest advantage. Their gowns are of the finest muslin, with blue or pink satin spencers, trimmed with gold or silver, according to their party; and gold necklaces, ear-rings, and other expensive trinkets, shine to advantage on their jet black skins. The most comely young negresses are selected, and such as have a fine and tutored voice; they parade through the streets, two and two, in the most exact order, with appropriate flags and instrumental music, accompanied by their voices, the songs being for the most part such as they have caught from the whites, and which they previously practise for the occasion. Each party has its *queen*, who eclipses all the rest in the splendour of her dress. Their appearance, upon the whole, is tasteful and elegant, and would somewhat astonish a stranger who had associated with the idea of slavery other images than those of gayety and costly display.

These exhibitions are not so frequent as they used to be. The mistresses of the slaves, who were the patronesses of them, and at whose expense much of the requisite finery was provided, find that they cost more money and trouble than they can well spare. The negresses must, however, have their annual display of fine clothes and suitable ornaments, if they should go in filth and raggedness all the rest of the year.

At their funerals, the African negroes use various ceremonies, among which is the practice of pouring libations, and sacrificing a fowl on the grave of the deceased—a tribute of respect they afterwards occasionally repeat. During the whole of the ceremony, many fantastic motions and

wild gesticulations are practised, accompanied
with a suitable beat of their drums and other
rude instruments, while a melancholy dirge is
sung by a female, the chorus of which is performed by the whole of the other females, with
admirable precision, and full-toned and not un-
melodious voices. When the deceased is interred,
the plaintive notes of sympathy are no longer
heard, the drums resound with a livelier beat,
the song grows more animated, dancing and
apparent merriment commence, and the remainder of the night is usually spent in feasting and
riotous debauchery.

Previous to the interment of the corpse it is
sometimes pretended that it is endowed with the
gift of speech; and the friends and relatives alternately place their ears to the lid of the coffin,
to hear what the deceased has to say. This
generally consists of complaints and upbraidings
for various injuries,—treachery, ingratitude, injustice, slander, and, in particular, the non-pay-
ment of debts due to the deceased. This last
complaint is sometimes shewn by the deceased
in a more *cogent* way than by mere words; for,
on coming opposite the door of the negro debtor,
the coffin makes a full stop, and no persuasion
nor strength can induce the deceased to go forward peaceably to his grave till the money is
paid; so that the unhappy debtor has no alter-

native but to comply with this demand, or have his creditor palmed upon him, as a lodger, for some time. Sometimes, however, the deceased is a little unconscionable, by claiming a fictitious debt. In short, this superstitious practice is often made subservient to fraudulent extortion. A negro, who was to be interred in one of the towns, had, it was pretended by some of his friends, a claim on another negro for a sum of money. The latter denied any such claim; and accordingly, at the funeral of the deceased, the accustomed ceremonies took place opposite to the door of his supposed debtor; and this mummery was continued for hours, till the magistrates thought proper to interfere, and compelled the defunct to forego his claim, and proceed quietly on to his place of rest.

The most dangerous practice, arising from a superstitious credulity, prevailing among the negroes is, what is called *obeah*,* a pretended sort of witchcraft. One negro who desires to be revenged on another, and is afraid to make an open and manly attack on his adversary, has usually recourse to *obeah*. This is considered as a potent and irresistible spell, withering and palsying, by undescribable terrors and unwonted sensations, the unhappy victim. Like the witches'

---

* This practice is less common at present than it used to be.

caldron in Macbeth, it is a combination of many strange and ominous things—earth gathered from a grave, human blood, a piece of wood fashioned in the shape of a coffin, the feathers of the carrion-crow, a snake's or alligator's tooth, pieces of egg-shell, and other nameless ingredients, compose the fatal mixture. The whole of these articles may not be considered as absolutely necessary to complete the charm, but two or three are at least indispensable. It will of course be conceived, that the practice of *obeah* can have little effect, unless a negro is conscious that it is practised upon him, or thinks so; for as the whole evil consists in the terrors of a superstitious imagination, it is of little consequence whether it be really practised or not, if he only imagines that it is. But if the *charm* fails to take hold of the mind of the proscribed person, another and more certain expedient is resorted to—the secretly administering of poison to him. This saves the reputation of the sorcerer, and effects the purpose he had in view.* An *obeah* man or woman (for it is practised by both sexes) is a very wicked and dangerous person on a plantation; and the practice of it is made felony by the law, punishable with death where poison has been administer-

---

* The negroes practising *obeah* are acquainted with some very powerful vegetable poisons, which they use on these occasions.

ed, and with transportation where only the charm is used. But numbers may be swept off by its infatuation before the crime is detected; for, strange as it may appear, so much do the negroes stand in awe of those *obeah* professors, so much do they dread their malice and their power, that, though knowing the havock they have made, and are still making, they are afraid to discover them to the whites; and others, perhaps, are in league with them for sinister purposes of mischief and revenge. A negro under this infatuation can only be cured of his terrors by being made a Christian: refuse him this boon, and he sinks a martyr to imagined evils. The author knew an instance of a negro, who, being reduced by the fatal influence of *obeah* to the lowest state of dejection and debility, from which there were little hopes of his recovery, was surprisingly and rapidly restored to health and cheerfulness by being baptized a Christian. A negro, in short, considers himself as no longer under the influence of this sorcery when he becomes a Christian.

But, though so liable to be perverted into a deadly instrument of malice and revenge, *obeah* —at least a species of it—may be said to have its uses. When placed in the gardens and grounds of the negroes, it becomes an excellent guard or watch, scaring away the predatory runaway and midnight plunderer with more effective terror than gins and spring-guns. It loses its power, however, when put to protect the gardens and plantain-walks of the *Buckras*. When an oath is taken by a negro, according to a certain *obeah* process, it binds by ties the most sacred. This ceremony is usually performed over a grave. The creoles, however, think it equally binding to swear on *Buckra book*—the Bible.

The negroes believe in apparitions, and stand in great dread of them, conceiving that they forebode death or some other great evil to those whom they visit; in short, that the spirits of the dead come upon earth to be revenged on those who did them evil when in life.

Coleridge:
Six Months in the West Indies

Henry Nelson Coleridge, *Six Months in the West Indies in 1825* (London: John Murray, 1826), pp. 169–91.

Henry Nelson Coleridge (1798–1843) was a Fellow of King's College, Cambridge, a frequent contributor to the Tory *Quarterly Review*, and was called to the bar in 1826. He is best known today as the nephew, editor and literary executor of Samuel Taylor Coleridge. In 1829 he married his own cousin, the poet's daughter Sara, translator of Dobrizhoffer's *Account of the Abipones*. In 1825, suffering from 'rheumatism proper, rheumatic gout, gout proper, and an affection of the spinous process' (p. 1), he accompanied his uncle William Hart Coleridge, Anglican bishop of Barbados, on a trip to the West Indies for the sake of his health. Coleridge's account of his tour with the new bishop around his Caribbean diocese on board HMS *Eden*, intervened (like James Stewart's book three years earlier) in a contentious debate about slavery and the political and economic future of these islands, once so valuable to Britain's colonial economy. Although Coleridge's political position is similar to Stewart's in his support for establishment Evangelicalism and a strategy of gradual 'amelioration' preceding the emancipation of slaves, his travel book is strikingly different in tone and style. Whereas Stewart presents a dispassionate 'statistical' account of Jamaica, Coleridge adopts the learned egotism and rather heavy, periphrastic style of the Romantic man of letters. Despite Coleridge's disapproval of Sterne's immorality, the book contains a number of allusions to *A Sentimental Journey*. Disavowing any political bias or motivation for making his six-month tour of the British West Indies, Coleridge sought to steer a middle course between the abolitionist African Association and the 'choleric' planters by dwelling instead on his valetudinarian condition: 'if Yorick had written after me, he would have mentioned the Rheumatic Traveller. This book is rheumatic from beginning to end ... I rarely argue a matter unless my shoulders or knees ache' (p. 9). Coleridge's entertaining egotism and pedantic wit are evident in the following excerpt, in which he describes his visit to the Leeward island of Montserrat, which Britain had regained from France by the Treaty of Versailles. His account of the effect of turtle soup on his digestive system, 'the proparasceve of our manducatory energies, the regretted prophagomenon of Apicius', is worthy of the

learned pyrotechnics of his uncle Samuel Taylor Coleridge or the ironic ped-
antry of Charles Lamb. Balancing the ironic tone, however, is a Romantic
appreciation of the island's tropical beauty, as well as a polemic in favour of
extending the Anglican mission to the slaves in order to combat the deficien-
cies of both Roman Catholicism and Methodism, thereby ensuring 'the
peaceable subordination of the whole class' (below, p. 369). At the same time
Coleridge demonstrates his impatience with the blinkered conservatism of
the planters who 'have no more power to arrest this slow but unceasing
march of intelligence [amongst the slaves] than they could have to stop a
mountain in its fall, or divert a torrent in its downward course' (below,
p. 372). The popularity of Coleridge's book lay mainly in its highly written
'literary' quality, exemplifying the new style of 'entertaining' travel account,
which became common in the 1820s, more concerned with the traveller's literary reflections upon foreign people and places than with objective
description. At the same time, he was scrupulous in recording the social and
political condition of the West Indies at a time of transition, and the book's
success was also in part a consequence of its cautious, paternalistic acceptance
of emancipation, now safely wrested from earlier associations with radicalism
and sansculottism. The very notion of slavery, concluded the Tory Coleridge, 'is now hateful to every Englishman, and justly so' (p. 323). He lived
to see emancipation (together with the transitional 'apprenticeship' system
which his book advocated) become a reality, but died in 1843 of a spinal disease, the early stages of which had prompted him to make his voyage of
convalescence to the West Indies in the first place.

MONTSERRAT.

WE stole slowly under the high ridges of Dominica during the night, and were only just clear
of the northern extremity of the island by the
morning.   Then the breeze freshened at E. by
N., and having crossed the scene of the action
between Rodney and de Grasse in 1782, where
Tom Rowland, the mason in my town, lost his
precious leg by a splinter, we passed gaily by the
Saintes, some rocky islets belonging to the French,
but which were chiefly occupied during the war
by the English for the purpose of refitting, when
it might have been difficult to beat up to English Harbour.   In the Grande Sainte there is a
pottery and a few canes.   Marigalante lay on the
horizon due east behind the Saintes.   At three
p. m. we breasted the southern point of the
great island of Guadaloupe, and, as the wind
came round freer, we ran into the roadstead
before Basseterre, and dashed gallantly by the

Frenchmen within fifty yards of the shore. I believe the folks thought we were going to cut out a merchantman, or run ourselves against the shingles for fun. It seemed a very pretty town, and, I am told, is a most convenient one; there was an agreeable show of trees peeping over the tops of the houses, and the hospital built by the English, and the governor's mansion were conspicuous at the northern end. This hospital is said to have been since destroyed in the hurricane of July 1825, when 230 persons or more perished in various miserable ways. The garrison at Prince Rupert's bay in Dominica suffered at the same time considerably. The country, though apparently very fine, had not quite so finished an air of cultivation as in Martinique, but its features were bolder and more magnificent. Some of the planters' houses were upon a larger scale, and more attention to comfort in the adjoining premises seemed to be displayed than is usual in the English colonies. The wind fell, as it almost always does, under the long lee of the high land, and it was about seven a. m. of the 25th, before we cast anchor in the open road of Plymouth.

I must needs say I have a vehement desire to abuse this island through thick and thin. I declare I cannot to this day think of the ducking I got upon first landing or rather watering at Plymouth without an emotion of anger, which forces me to leave my chair and take three or four turns up and down my room before my pulse sinks to its usual quiet pitch. Though a jetty or pier might be constructed with a trifling expense by simply rolling a few large blocks of the stone, which abounds on the spot, into the water, yet these provoking people would rather that themselves and every human being, who visits or leaves their island, should get drenched, than stir one step towards erecting it. In fact they rarely go from the shore themselves, and they are fools enough to be amused with the misadventures of others. And then like true Creoles, what they are too indolent to do, they conveniently declare is impossible to be done at all. Here's a pretty thing! They call their island the Montpelier of the West Indies, (in verity no great compliment,) and when invalids, rheumatics and others, lured by the name, come for relief to breathe its air, the first thing they have to undergo is a forcible anabaptism in salt water, and then to be converted into drying horses for their clothes under a tropical sun. I am sure it is a subject of particular thanksgiving to me, that I did not for ever lose the use of my shoulders and knees on this occasion. Captain Lawrence had severe rheumatism in his left elbow for a week afterwards. I have been trying to make a beginning to this end of a verse,

—— et inhospita littora Montis
        Serrati——,

but it is miserable to feel how quickly all that Eton craft goes out of the fingers. However I mean to be very savage, and I speak my mind the more freely, because in many other respects I admire Montserrat, and regret that a nuisance should be suffered to exist in the threshold of this lovely little country, which must ruffle the temper of any one who is made of flesh and blood, and moreover hath the rheumatism. I am not vindictive; no! I have not a particle of the thing in my nature...I have a grateful recollection of the turtle at the Court House, though we were kept for our dinner so long that any thing but that exquisite soup would have come too late; the Madeira too was pure and milky, and the beer clean. These things do not pass from my mind as they do from my body; they have a post-existent life with me, and I refer to them frequently for the purposes of contrast, similitude, or the reviving of my affections.

It is indeed commonly but, I apprehend, hastily said, that turtle is eaten in greater perfection in England than in the West Indies. The cookery, I confess, is more studied and elaborate, more science is shewn in the anatomy, and superior elegance in the dishing. Besides, it is a greater rarity, and its visits, few and far between, leave something of an angelic smack upon the palate of a worthy recipient in England. But setting aside this last advantage, or rather justly esteeming plenty a blessing, a man of unprejudiced appetite will have no difficulty in deciding in favor of the consumption of turtle on the spot of its birth. The nature of this fine animal is not understood by European cooks; they distrust the genuine savour, and all but annihilate it by bilious additaments of their own composition. The punch too, though pleasurable per se, is drunk so largely as to wash out all remembrance, all rumination of the past, and I have seen some persons so grossly ignorant as to drink once or even twice before they have finished their soup! This should not be. A single lime is sufficient; squeeze it and cut it in slices afterwards over the various regions of your plate. The soup should be served up in a capacious tin shell, and should always be well lined inside with a thin crust of pastry; the worst consequence may follow upon the neglect of this last particular, for the liquor becomes lukewarm, tenuous and watery, by immediate contact with ware or metal. In England I have always found a crassitude, a pinguedinous gravity in the meat which makes one repent the having eaten it; it enervates the body with a sort of dry drunken-ness,

Atque affligit humi divinæ particulam auræ.

In the West Indies turtle is a generous food certainly, but honest and unsophisticated; it administers in a small space that nourishment which the great exhaustion of the system requires, and there is a freshness and a recency in it, which quickens the palate and invigorates the organs of taste. At a dinner in England, it must be, as they say and do in the city, turtle once and turtle throughout; a man indeed has no heart or appetite for any thing else after so much acid punch and morbid soup as is absorbed there. In the West Indies turtle is a gentle alarum, as from a silver trumpet blown; it is the proparasceve of our manducatory energies, the regretted prophagomenon of Apicius. A glass of Madeira (it should be Sercial, if possible) is the best thing after this soup; the wine flows in a kindly stream of coalescence with what has been eaten before, and harmonizes with what is to follow; lime punch creates a discontinuance, as the lawyers say, and in effect spoils your dinner.

Abbé O'Hannam, a tall Irish Romish priest, gave the health of the Bishop of Jamaica, and talked about our eminent prelate and so on. It was bad taste in Abbé O'Hannam to dine with us at all, but it was gross in the Abbé to give such a toast. The compliment was uncalled for from him, and nobody could think the Abbé sincere in what he said.

The Protestants and Papists are as good friends in Montserrat as they are in Ireland. Indeed the faithful Catholic here has anticipated the fruits of emancipation; he considers it highly absurd to suffer himself to be deprived of great political advantages for the sake of a few oaths, when a priest actually resides in the island; and accordingly, having called God to help him as he utterly disbelieves Transubstantiation, he marches into the House of Assembly, and there gives his vote. Nothing can be easier than this process, and I publish it here for the benefit of all the Irish, English and Scotch Papists, who may not have patience to wait till Parliament open the doors of legislation to them. I could not ascertain the numbers of the adherents of the Romish church in Montserrat. Abbé O'Hannam says there are 4,000; the President told me there were forty. They intermarry, and in most cases the Abbé loses; a thing which the Abbé should look into, for the reverse takes place in England.

The negros here have an Irish accent, which grafted on negro English forms the most diverting jargon I ever heard in my life.

But if you ever visit Montserrat, good reader, go, even if you have only one day, to the Soufrière. I have seen a thousand beautiful things in the West Indies, but I cannot even now think over my morning ramble to this Soufrière without feeling my heart swell with love and sorrow that I shall never see it again. Most of our party had gone off to sleep on board, but the sight of the launch in a canoe over and through the surf sickened me; I had no stomach for a repetition of the morning's ducking, and independently of rheumatism, I knew that

albo ventre lavari

was no joke to any one. So I accepted the hospitality of the learned Dr. Dyett, and after a very edifying and abundantly charitable discourse upon the quality and form of Popery, I snoozed away the night in a barrack room in the Doctor's court yard, oblivious of all sublunary things except the barking of dogs. West India turtle lies light as a feather, and claret is as thin as air; so by the first dawn I essayed to rise, what time shoeless and uncinctured Betsy pushed her black eyes, yellow face and white teeth through the door with " How you do, my massa? La! what white skin! gee! gee! gee!" " Ay, Betsy," said I, " the color would be worth something to you; but just at present go and get me some coffee!" And so fortified, and mounting somebody's horse, (many thanks to the unknown owner!) I paced through the quiet old town, and having joined my companion at the very worthy Mr. Luckcock's, we set out upon our excursion.

At first the road lay along the margin of the

sea, then wound inwards by a gentle acclivity towards the mountains. It was like one of my native Devonshire lanes ; no primroses or violets were there indeed, but the snowy *amaryllis drooped her long and delicate petals like a love-sick girl; the thrice gorgeous hibiscus was un-veiling his crown and feathers of scarlet, and the light limes and darker orange trees, which formed a verdant hedge on either side, were exhaling their perfumed incense to Him who made them so beautiful and so good. A thin grey cloud obscured the sun, whilst an Atlantic breeze blew gently and freshly upon my face and open neck. The air was as cool as on a May morning in England, but so inexpressibly soft, so rare and subtle to the senses that I think the ether which angels breathe cannot be purer stuff than this. O! Temples twain, Middle and Inner. O! Courts, together with all houses, outhouses, easements and commodities thereunto appertaining, even then did I think of you!

After this I nearly broke my neck in a dry gulley which was about as good a bridle path as the steps to the top of St. Paul's. I remember, when

---

* Pancratia Carribbæa.

I was at Eton, a great piece of work was made about an officer's riding up the hundred steps, and the discreet Windsorians planted a huge post at the bottom to prevent any such risk of life for the future; ... why, the hundred steps are no more to be compared to the last two miles before you come to the brink of the Corral, or even to this poor gulley in Montserrat than I to Hercules, a meeting house to a church, Westminster to Eton, or any other equally appropriate dissimile.

The gulley ended in one of those green Savanas which nature has oftimes so mysteriously cleared in the midst of the impenetrable virgin woods of tropical regions. No difference of soil or situation can be the cause; you may lean your back against the frontier tree of a forest which no axe or torch hath ever invaded, and stretch your body on the meadow turf where scarcely a weed can be seen. There is no man to fell these trees or divert their growth; there is no hedge or wall or trench to impede their march; but God said to the Forest as he said to the Sea, " Thus far shalt thou go, and no farther." The view was beautiful; behind me the woody mountain rose into the clouds, before me it descended in a long grassy slope to the edge of the sea; on my left

hand to the south, the broad and irregular eminences of Guadaloupe presented the appearance
of a continent; to the north Redonda shone like
an emerald in the midst of the blue waves, and
beyond it stood the great pyramid of Nevis cut
off from sight at one third from its summit by an
ever resting canopy of clouds. The wind was so
fresh, the air so cool, the morning dew so healthy
and spangling that I might have forgotten, but
for the deep beauty that was around me, that I
was still within the tropics. I seemed to have
left all languor and listlessness below, and really
felt for a season the strength, the spirits and the
elasticity of youthful life in England. At this
spot I and my companion (and he was a very pleasant one) tied our horses to a tree and began to
descend a circuitous and overarched path to the
vale of the Soufrière.

This is a very wild and romantic scene. The
whole of the bottom of the valley is broken into
vast and irregular masses of clay and limestone
which are scattered about in the utmost confusion,
and render it a laborious task to scramble and
leap from one to another. The surface of the
ground is hot every where, and so much so near
the streams of water which ran between the frag-

ments that I could not keep my foot half a minute upon it. The water at its source boils up violently, and very gradually cools as it finds its way in a thousand meanders to the sea. A thick vapour slowly rises upwards till it meets the wind which cuts it off at a straight line and drives it down to the coast. The sides of the mounds of clay are entirely crusted with pure alum, formed by the constant action of the sulphuric acid of the water and the exhalations. In the midst of all this there is a green and luxuriant vegetation of bushes and creepers; some of the flowers were marvellously beautiful, and seemed to me to be peculiar to the spot. The mountains, which rampart round this solitary glen, are of a skiey height; they appear indeed higher than they really are, for their lancet peaks are never seen except dimly and at intervals through the vast and moving masses of clouds, which are first driven from the east against the other side of the sierra, then are pressed upwards, and at last come rolling and tumbling over the summits into the vale below. The wood which clothes every inch of Chance's Mountain is soft, level and uniform, feathering him with a grasslike plumage as an Indian warrior, whilst every branch and every leaf bend devotedly forwards to the setting sun under the unceasing breath of the Trade wind.

The people of Montserrat say they are very poor, and, as their friend, I am fain to believe them; for surely nothing but the direst necessity could reconcile their generous hearts to the present accommodations of their legislature and the unworthy destitution of their respectable President. The Council and Assembly of this island hold their important deliberations in two rooms in which a Devonshire farmer would scruple to hoard his apples; and Mr. Herbert, who has worn a cocked hat in their defence for thirty years, has neither a bed to lie on allowed to him, nor a table to feed on, nor a purse wherewith to purchase a few alleviations of the toils of government. His Majesty's authority and His Majesty's revenue shine together with concentric rays from the windows of His Majesty's Custom House. No salary whatever is allowed to the President, and it is only within a year or so that they have consented to indemnify him for the expense of official postage. Now I really must say that all this is discreditable, or in the vulgar scandalous, or in the vernacular blackguard; it should be reformed altogether. Let a plain Government

House be built or bought in the town, and a few hundreds of their currency stuff added to make the head of their community respectable, and enable him to entertain the guests of the colony with propriety.   There is enough wealth in Montserrat to effect this, and it concerns the reputation of the planters, as gentlemen, to do it.

The town, Plymouth to wit, is small, but many of the houses are singularly well built of a fine grey stone, and have a substantial and comfortable appearance.   The jail is the ruinous remnant of an old fort, a sort of parcus clausus where no man of common humanity would imprison a transgressing donkey.   However they are accustomed to it and know no better, as the old woman said of her eels when she put them i' the paste alive; " she rapped 'em o' the coxcombs with a stick, and cry'd, *Down, wantons, down.*"   This precious devil's hole in the wall should be put into the index expurgatorius of my friend Dr. Dyett.

There are two churches in the island; the first within half a mile of the town is in very good condition, which is not a little owing to the zeal and even manual skill of Mr. Luckcock the rector of the parish of St. Anthony.   The other church in St. Peter's parish is a good deal out of repair, and no service has been performed in it for more than a year. Effectual measures however have been taken for putting the building into decent order, and when that is done, another clergyman will be added to the establishment of the colony.

There are 6,396 slaves in Montserrat, a considerable number of whom are entirely debarred from any mental instruction. This is the case with all those who are unfortunately the property of a noted Papist of great influence, and of other planters who have the pusillanimity to sacrifice their consciences to his contemptible prejudice. The residue are taught the catechism by Mr. Luckcock, who also preaches and expounds portions of Scripture to them with more or less frequency according to the distance of their residence from Plymouth. The Bishop has lately placed a catechist under this worthy minister's direction, and it is earnestly to be hoped by every friend to the true interests of the colony, that means will not always be wanting for still further increasing the number and the influence of those, by whose exertions a religious and moral spirit may be excited in the slaves, and the peaceable subordination of the whole class be insured.

The methodists will pardon the freedom I take

in expressing my suspicions that the evil, which they have done upon the long run both at home and abroad, is but scantly counterpoized by a certain sobriety of exterior which they have inflicted on their sect. One remark seems level to the lowest capacity and the most sordid prejudice. The planters in the West Indies profess to be apprehensive of insurrection; nevertheless they admit sectarians of one denomination or another into their estates; the negros are a very curious and observant race, and after they have learnt that there is a God, the next thing they learn is, that their master does not worship him in the same manner with themselves. They believe their worship is true, and therefore they must think their master's false. While they remain on the brink of civilization, this will have but inconsiderable consequences, but the seeds are laid, a beginning is effected; the individual or his family becomes more knowing in process of time; he perceives the ingredients of distinction more clearly, and gradually and necessarily imbibes that spirit of separation which religious schism is sure to generate. Moreover a completely organized espionage is a fundamental point in the system of the methodists; the secrets of every family are at their command; parent and child are watches on each other, sister is set against sister and brother against brother; each is on his guard against all, and all against each. In this manner these sectarians possess an army of dependants already lodged within every house and fixed in the heart of every plantation. Their dominion over these poor people is as absolute as was ever that of Jesuits over Jesuits; the fear of being turned out of their class* operates like the dread of losing the caste in Hindostan, and the negros know that this formidable power rests entirely with their ministers. That this power has been abused I shall not at present take upon me to assert; that it *may* be abused to the most fearful purposes I am sure. This is no imaginary picture of my drawing; let the gentlemen of Antigua say how this matter stands with them! Do they not sometimes look about them, and

---

* In Anguilla a man told me he was in God Almighty's class, but that if the minister knew that he had been at a dance, he would turn him down into the Devil's class.

Thus (worse than) fools rush in where angels fear to tread.

speculate upon possible contingencies? Do they not repent the encouragement; do they not fear the power of the methodists? They will not deny it.*

* I never come alongside of the methodist spy-system without thinking of poor Tom Smith's stanzas. Tom was always humming them by himself, as Johnson with " Aye! but to die——". They allude to his own experience of a practice not uncommon in the present day.

> I knew a maid who did always command
> All her dear swains to a third gentleman
> Them for to try, if they did keep pace
> With the third gentleman's notions of grace.
>
> Three the third gentleman plucked, and the third,
> As I've been told, was hardly deterred,
> In arguend. about Hume et Calvinum,
> A currend. ad argument. baculinum.
>
> Last came a youth whom the third gentleman
> Chose for the husband; he had a can
> Of rottenness full and Predestinate Hell,
> To make a young maiden live happy and well.
>
> Passion o' me! as John Suckling did say,
> That ever a lady should so throw away
> Such a pair of blue eyes, such lips of delight
> On an underhand, yellow-faced, Puritan wight—
>
> And all for because this silly young maid
> Was led astray-by that artful old blade
> The third gentleman;—Devil him take,
> And duck him and souse in his nethermost lake!

The planters, inasmuch as they are members of the church of England, are bound in conscience to see that their dependants are instructed in the principles of that church; but, putting the obligation of duty out of the question, it is palpable to common sense that it is their present interest to do so.   That sooner or later the slaves in the British colonies will all be fully and properly instructed, cannot be a doubt with any one who quietly observes the signs of the times; a large number of them in different places possess at this moment a measure of skill and knowledge, of which their masters are not always aware, and which the slaves value in proportion to its rarity. The colonists have no more power to arrest this slow but unceasing march of intelligence than they could have to stop a mountain in its fall, or divert a torrent in its downward course.   They would be crushed or drowned in the attempt, and I am not sure that their fate in such a case would be much lamented.   Now, if there is one owner of slaves who believes that sooner or later those slaves, themselves or their descendants, will and must be educated, is it not plainly his interest to bind them to him by every moral tie imaginable, and is it not as obviously dangerous to encourage or permit a mode of education which necessarily tends to alienate them from him? Can there be a bond of connexion more sacred or lasting than identity of religious worship; can there be a source of hostility more sure or prolific than sectarian zeal? At present, the educated planter may despise the poor black methodist slave; but we may be sure, if another system be not adopted, the time will come when the methodist slave will be the methodist freeman, and the power to coerce will precisely cease, when the force and danger of license will more than ever call for it.

That the methodists have done some present good amongst the negros in many of the islands I do not deny; it is partly a shame to England, and partly to the colonial clergy that there was any acknowledged field for their services. But as an effective church establishment has at length been commenced, and will, I most fervently hope, be perfected and maintained, so the time should seem to be past, when a Christian minister could think and say that the souls of the slaves within his parish were not within his cure. That time has been, but it is past, or it is passing while I write. The pretence that the numbers of the clergy were inadequate to such a duty is more than half taken away; the sophism, (for so it appears to me,) that the teacher of a lower or, to speak plainly, of a more vulgar stamp is required for the uncultivated negros has been exposed. I am yet to learn why erudition and good manners are to disqualify a minister of the Gospel from teaching and humanizing a negro. Why will we consent that our Christian religion, a religion which enjoins courtesy and prudence as virtues, should unnecessarily and through wilful neglect on our parts be degraded, if I may so speak, and disfigured by the ignorance and coarseness of men who neither are, nor in any nation or age ever were, intended for the ministry? I am sure that quite as much discretion is necessary in the work of instructing the slave population as in the known labors of attending to the spiritual wants of the free; in fact, much more is necessary; for the course of the missionary is through an undiscovered sea, where his charts serve him not, and his experience is baffled by novelty; where the wisest may fail, but where the wise is more likely to succeed and to succeed effectually than the rash, rude, although pious, men whom the perverse benevolence of thousands at home is yearly sending·out with roving commissions against the peace and tranquillity of foreign communities.

But enough of this matter at present, for the Eden is under weigh and has fired a gun and the Captain's gig is waiting for us a cable's length from the shore. So we will shake hands, pretty island; and now for another launch in a canoe!

N. B. The pure old Montserrat rum, however the market may be, is really a choicer spirit than the Jamaica. Grog from this rum, with a dash of lime or lemon juice, is a pretty tipple indeed—— cosa mayor, as the Dons say.

Mackenzie:
Notes on Haiti

Charles Mackenzie, *Notes on Haiti, Made during a Residence in that Republic*, 2 vols (London: Henry Colburn, 1830), vol. I, pp. 158–81.

Charles Mackenzie was appointed British consul in Haiti in 1826, with the task of reporting 'on the state of society, and the actual condition of the new republic in all its relations'. He was a fellow of both the Royal Society and the Linnean Society, and a close friend of the anthropologist and racial theorist James Cowles Prichard. The French sugar colony of Saint-Domingue had been convulsed in 1791 by the first large-scale slave uprising in the West Indies, the bloody course of which provided a terrible example of the consequences of racial war to European colonists and American insurgents alike. The contemporary commentator Bryan Edwards estimated that in the early months of the uprising alone, 2,000 whites (out of a total white population of 10,000) and 10,000 black slaves died, whilst 180 sugar plantations and 900 coffee and indigo settlements were destroyed. White planters, free mulatto *gens de couleur* and revolted slaves destroyed each other without pity. The Jacobin Assembly in Paris sent an army under General Léger-Félicité Sonthonax to contain the violence, but it was soon drawn into the fighting on the side of the slaves. In 1794 Sonthonax took the unprecedented step of declaring emancipation to all slaves in Saint-Domingue.

In 1793 both Spain and Britain, fearing the consequences for their own colonies of Cuba and Jamaica, sent armies to attack revolutionary Saint-Domingue, but both were beaten off after long and bloody campaigns by the charismatic black republican leader Toussaint L'Ouverture. By 1800 Toussaint, a former slave, had won total dominance over the island and declared a new constitution; the French Directory had even appointed him governor-general in order to save face. But he fell foul of the ambitions of the fast rising Napoleon Bonaparte, who resolved to restore slavery in Saint-Domingue and Guadeloupe. In 1802 Napoleon dispatched to the island a powerful expeditionary army commanded by his brother-in-law General Leclerc, with orders to arrest Toussaint and restore colonial rule. Most of Toussaint's black and mulatto generals deserted him for the French side, and he was captured and shipped to France, where he died in prison. In 1803, however, the tide turned against the French: Leclerc died of fever and his ragged, disease-ridden army surrendered to the British in Jamaica. French withdrawal was the cue for the African-born former slave Jean-Jacques Dessalines to crown himself emperor and declare the independence of Saint-Domingue, which he renamed Haiti (a Taino word meaning 'mountainous'). One of Dessalines's first acts was to order the massacre of all remaining whites. In the passage excerpted here, Mackenzie – not without a note of scepticism – describes seeing the coffins of blacks and mulattos drowned by orders of the French general Rochambeau on the shore of Petite Anse (below, p. 389).

On his death in 1806, Dessalines (whom C. L. R. James, in *The Black Jacobins*, describes as 'a barbarian') was succeeded by another of Toussaint's generals, the former pastry cook Henri Christophe, whose bloody career is described in the following excerpt. Seizing control of the northern part of the island (the south was controlled by his bitter rival, the mulatto Pétion), 'King Henri I' reinstated a form of feudal slavery, which perpetuated the colonial plantation system and sustained the failing economy for a further two decades. Christophe ruled in dictatorial style from his palace at Sans Souci and his nearby mountain citadel until his suicide in 1820, after a popular rebellion. In March 1827 Mackenzie visited the ruins of both Sans Souci and the sinister citadel of La Ferriere (described below, pp. 391–403). Even the relentlessly critical Mackenzie – strangely obsessed by the personality of the Haitian tyrant – admitted that there was a more positive aspect to Christophe's rule: 'he assembled men of talent, even from Europe, established schools, built fortifications, disciplined his army, formed courts for the administration of justice, encouraged commerce and agriculture, and undoubtedly promoted activity and enterprise. But the monarch was sullied with remorseless cruelty' (below, p. 387). The best modern account of Christophe's bloodstained regime is the Cuban novelist Alejo Carpentier's 1949 historical fiction *El reino de este mundo*.

Mackenzie everywhere paints a negative picture of the first independent black republic, 'a very curious experiment in the history of man', which is represented as a bizarre compound of ruin, desolation and misrule. 'Nations as well as individuals', he writes, 'can acquire maturity only by imperceptible degrees; and every step taken, to be effectual, must be in accordance with the peculiar character of the people to be improved' (p. xii). Mackenzie's ameliorist philosophy here partly chimes with the sentiments of James Stewart and Henry Nelson Coleridge, although his report on Haiti presented to the House of Commons in 1829 provided powerful ammunition for the beleaguered anti-emancipation lobby. British planters and their political representatives had dreaded all along the possibility that Jamaica or Barbados might share the bloody fate of Saint-Domingue; the condition of Haiti seemed to offer a warning of the dangers of emancipation and autonomous black rule. This explains why Mackenzie's report and book on Haiti were attacked by the emancipation lobby in Britain for their alleged bias against black people.

The recent death of Henry Christophe, and the existence of many of his chief officers, afforded me an opportunity of making many researches into his personal character, and the history of his reign, which was confirmed by some intelligent foreigners; and as I am not aware of any very faithful record of either, I shall note such matters as may be interesting. I had hoped to have seen Dupuy and Prevost, his principal officers, but the one died before, and the other very shortly after, my arrival;

this loss, however, was in a great measure ob-
viated by my having had access to the personal
associates of both, and to the confidential correspondence between Sans Souci and the Cape
for many years, and from them some curious
materials have been obtained.

Henry Christophe was born, according to an
official account sanctioned by himself, in the
island of Grenada, in the year 1769, and
came at an early age to St. Domingo. He was
not a pure black, but a sambo or griffe, as it is
called. He was the slave of a French gentleman, whose daughter resided there when I was
at the Cape, to whom the former domestic was
kind and attentive in his prosperity. He afterwards became a waiter at an hotel, then priva-
teer's-man, and then returned to an hotel and
gaming-house. It does not appear when he
entered the army; but in 1801 he was general
of brigade and governor of the Cape. He distinguished himself on the arrival of the French
expedition, first in his negotiations with Le
Clerc, and second, by filling his house, richly
furnished, with combustibles, and setting fire to
it, as a signal for the conflagration of the whole
city. Before Toussaint submitted, Christophe
had yielded to French ascendancy, and served
for some time, but afterwards joined the bands

that were roused to revolt by the unsparing atrocities of Rochambeau, whose memory has an unenviable celebrity in every part of Haiti. On the expulsion of the relics of that corps in 1803, Christophe was one of the officers that signed the act of independence ; and although he served under Dessalines, he is reported to have entered into a confederacy which led to the assassination of the Emperor Jacques I. at Pont Rouge.   That, however, is resolutely denied by his partisans.

The death of Dessalines was the signal for intrigue ; and Christophe, having failed in obtaining the wished-for ascendancy over the whole, retired to the Cape in the beginning of 1807, and was proclaimed president and generalissimo of Haiti.   On the 28th of March, 1811, he was elected king, under the title of Henry I.   The act called " La loi constitutionnelle du Conseil d'état, qui établit la royauté à Haiti," completely established the feudal law.

With the succession of public events it is not my intention now to meddle ; but rather to confine myself to such anecdotes as are characteristic of the man.

During his presidency, and the early part of his reign, he was mild, forbearing, and humane ;

but afterwards his nature seemed to have been completely changed, and he indulged in whatever his uncontrólled passions suggested—and they suggested almost every act that can violate the charities of life ; and as he proceeded in his career, he became suspicious and wantonly cruel.

He was destitute of even the elements of education, and scrawled a signature mechanically* without knowing a single letter. He however understood English as well as French, and possessed a rare memory as well as acuteness. Yet he never would speak the former when engaged in discussions with the British, by which means he had leisure to consider the topic which his interpreter was translating, and had at the same time an opportunity of determining the fidelity of that officer. A ludicrous story is told of an American captain, who had been brought before him for some violation of law, and who, indignant at the rating he received, and ignorant of his Majesty's accomplishments, muttered to himself a wish that he had the sable king at Charleston. Henry quietly asked him, " How much do you think I should fetch ? " The offender was dismissed,

* See note (A) in Appendix.

nor do I believe that any further notice was taken of his irreverent remark.

All his acts were not equally marked by the kingly virtue of mercy, his want of which began to be felt after he assumed the monarchy; for although he had all the semblance of a constitution, he was practically a thorough despot, dictating to the puppets, who appeared to those at a distance to act independently. On his return from his last unsuccessful attempt on Port-au-Prince in 1812, some busy meddler told him, that the women of colour had gone to the cathedral to implore Heaven to prevent his return. This was sufficient; bands of sanguinary ruffians proceeded from house to house of those destined for slaughter,* in the dead of the night, and massacred, without remorse, an immense number of these hapless beings. Indeed it is reported that, on an order for the indiscriminate murder of all the people of colour, even the sanctities of domestic life were violated; and I have sat at the same table with a black general, who I believe to have put to death, with his own hands, his coloured wife and children, in order to satiate

---

* There can be no doubt of this, from the testimony of eye-witnesses now at Cape Haitian !

his master's thirst for blood.   But even that did not secure him from outrage, for in a fit of passion, he did him the favour to knock out one of his eyes.

He also assassinated some German officers, who had been allured by his promises to erect fortifications, under some vague pretence of treason; but the real motive was to prevent the exposure of his defences.*

Whatever may have been the motives of his early career, those of his latter life, if we can judge from his conduct, were to obtain uncontrolled power, and the most perfect indulgence of all his inclinations, however improper and licentious.   I was told by a person who witnessed the transaction, that having detected one of his servants at Sans Souci stealing a very small quantity of salt fish, he ordered him to be laid down in his presence, in the kitchen, and the man was literally scourged to death, and all entreaty sternly rejected.   His majesty then went to breakfast with as much composure as if he had been performing a very ordinary act.

I had in my possession a copy of the sentence of a court on a man who had been

* See Appendix (B.)

convicted of robbery, with the mandate of
the king to carry it into effect within twenty-
four hours. This gentle punishment was to
scourge the convict to death with rods.

An English resident, named Davidson, fell
under his suspicion as a spy : he was arrested,
confined, and was even tortured. At the instance of all the foreigners he was released, but
compelled to quit the country at considerable
loss. A part of the correspondence between
Christophe and Dupuy, which will also be
found in a note,† will give the best history of
a transaction which has rarely been equalled
in the annals of cruelty and duplicity.

His indulgences are described to have been
of the most abandoned description. He addicted himself to brandy, which added fuel
to his naturally ungovernable passions; and
though, to gratify his European friends, he
insisted on marriage, and set the example in
his own person, yet he habitually broke its
ties ; and the palace acquired a title to a very
degrading designation. It is recorded that
the ladies attended there in regular rotation
to abide the will of their despotic chief; and
not one solitary Lucretia has been immortal-
ized.

† See Note (D.)

Among his other deeds, he was devoted to a female of colour, the wife of one of his officers, who, even when I saw her, justified her pretensions to beauty and grace. In order to have undisturbed possession of the lady, he voted the husband mad, and consigned him for a long time to a mad-house. Sated, however, with the charms he had so ardently coveted, he discovered that their possessor was an improper character, and, above all, that she had " une mauvaise langue." He then ordered her to go in procession to the " Maison des Fous, with drums and trumpets sounding," to take out her husband, and to restore him to his connubial rights;* and though these violations of decency were public, yet no one dared to report them in Europe, such being the vigilance of his police, and such his dreaded severity.

His archbishops (two) were privately taken off; and so was Medina, the French agent. In short, the dagger and the cord were unsparingly used, and occasionally the poisoned chalice took off an unsuspecting victim, whom it would have been imprudent to have sacri-

* See Note (E.)

ficed more openly. But though I consider it more than probable that such statements are correct, yet as they may have been exaggerated, I do not relate them with the same confidence that I have felt in such details as are supported by documents.

In the midst of all this brutality, Christophe was intent on exalting the condition of his kingdom; although his personal gratifications were probably the mainsprings of his action. He was the principal dealer in the country; and some English merchants, who had had extensive transactions with him, have described him to me as singularly well informed on all matters connected with this branch of his business. To promote the civilization of his subjects, he assembled men of talent, even from Europe, established schools, built fortifications, disciplined his army, formed courts for the administration of justice, encouraged commerce and agriculture, and undoubtedly promoted activity and enterprise. But the monarch was sullied with remorseless cruelty. As an ignorant untaught man, he may be considered one of those phenomena that occasionally excite attention, but leave scarcely any beneficial trace behind. He seems to have possessed a rare degree of native acuteness, activity, intrepidity, and the art of commanding the respect of those around him. These qualities, however, united with his absolute ignorance, were disadvantageous, as, while they made him thoroughly master of one view of a subject, he was blind to every other; and thus knowing nothing of the almost imperceptible degrees by which alone civilization can be rendered permanent, he attempted to carry his object by storm, and succeeded, until bodily infirmity convinced his barbarians that he was mortal. With all his strength of mind, he could not resist the temptation of encouraging a belief that he was protected by a tutelary demon, who would have instantly avenged any insult offered to him. It is also said that he had great faith in *Obeah*. With all his atrocities he was an affectionate father, and endeavoured to place his children above himself in mental culture.

Towards the close of his reign his cruelty became dreadful. He buffeted his generals—beat the governor of the Cape, Richard, with a huge stick whenever he displeased him—degraded generals to the rank of private soldiers—

sent his ministers to labour on the fortifications ; * and, above all, kept his soldiers in
arrear of their pay from extraordinary avarice.
A fit of apoplexy gave confidence to the dissatisfied, and revolt broke out, and terminated,
as is well known, in the destruction of the monarchy.

On the shore of Petite Anse, immediately
below high-water mark, the remains of coffins
are exposed to the view of the passenger. On
inquiry, I was told that they contained the
bodies of the Haitians who underwent the
" Noyade" under Le Clerc and Rochambeau ;
that there was a vessel, with an open bottom,
into which were consigned the unfortunate
wretches who were doomed to death, that
sailed every night with the land breeze, and
returned the following day with the sea breeze,
having disposed of her cargo ; that, with the
tide, the bodies that escaped the voracity of
the sharks were cast on shore ; and it was a
part of the duty of the Haitian soldiers to
collect and inter the bodies of their friends.
The statement may be true, but I suspect that
in such a climate twenty-four years would not

* See Appendix (F.)

leave even the miserable vestiges of coffins that were visible. I rather suspect that some old burying-ground has been exposed.

The President Boyer narrowly escaped this fate, through the intercession of the French general Boyé, who is, I have understood, now in Egypt; and similar tales are rumoured in every part of Haiti, with circumstances of aggravation, that it is unnecessary, without full evidence, to repeat. I am, however, inclined to give credit to the atrocity, though I doubt its connexion of the fact on which the statement I received was founded. The French have left there, as well as in Germany, Spain, and Portugal, fearful records; yet whenever they again appear, a veil of oblivion is readily thrown over the past.

30th March.—As a matter not to be omitted, I formed a party to visit the ruins of Sans Souci, or Millot, the former residence of Christophe, in the time of his greatest splendour, and the " Citadelle Henri," or " La Ferriere," which is only three leagues from the palace; and, as a permission from the authorities at the Cape is necessary for so doing, I applied to the commandant General Leo, in the absence of General Magny, and he very readily granted it, directing, at the same time, one of his aides-de-camp, Captain Emile, to accompany us.

Sans Souci is on the southern confines of the plain of the north, and the district of Limonade, which gave the title of duke to Christophe's foreign secretary General Prevost. We travelled over a tolerably good road, through the ruins of sugar plantations, of one of which the plate gives a very accurate representation.

We stopped at the village of Millot, at a small house, where strangers are able to procure refreshment, and having breakfasted, we paid our respects to Colonel Belair, the commandant, a black officer, who had been on guard at the palace at the time of Christophe's suicide. He also accompanied us to visit the remains of a place in which, I believe, for a time, more unlimited despotism had been exercised than has ever prevailed in any country aspiring to Christianity and civilization. It is a large clumsy building on the side of a mountain, resembling a huge cotton factory. The accompanying view is tolerably correct. We ascended through the gateway up a spacious flight of steps, which are pretty well expressed in the engraving, and then passed through a series of ample apartments, all now dismantled, but the uses of which were well remembered by our conductor. Some were destined for the reception of treasure, some were private, others public apartments ; others were occupied by the military and civil functionaries. The floors, which had been of mahogany, had all been torn up. I visited with particular interest the bed-chamber of Christophe, in which he had terminated his life ; and as I heard most of the details at the time of this visit, I shall give them in this place, although some particulars may appear that have been gleaned at other periods.

When the royal army, which had been sent under the Prince de Limbé to repress the insurrection at St. Mark's, had declared in favour of the revolution, some dissatisfied chiefs, among whom were the Governor of the capital and Generals Nord and Profete, excited the garrison to revolt against Henry, who at that time was labouring under a partial paralysis. On the news reaching Sans Souci, he, with accustomed energy, by the use of stimulants, enabled himself to mount his horse, for the purpose of placing himself at the head of his household troops, who still appeared to remain faithful. But disease had made too extensive inroads to be resisted, and he was compelled to abandon his intentions. This was a complete death-blow to his power. His presence alone would have been a host. Resistance, however, was necessary, and he confided the command to his friend and relation, Prince Joachim, retaining only the few guards required for duty at the palace.

The little army consisted of the élite of Haiti, but had been a little mutinous, in consequence of their pay having fallen into arrear, owing to a foolish niggardliness that latterly influenced their chief. In order to restore a proper tone of feeling, the arrears were paid and a donation given, and they commenced their work with probably the same integrity of purpose that prompted Ney to pledge himself to bring his former master in a cage of iron. On arriving at a well-known place called "Haut du Cap," they found the insurgents in position. A parley having failed, Joachim ordered his troops to fire; but, instead of doing so, they joined the ranks of their opponents, and commenced a fire on their late general, and some few individuals who retained their fidelity. Flight was their only resource, and I have the details from one of Christophe's secretaries, who shared in the disgraces of the day, and could sing of his "parmula non bene relicta." He was the first to reach Sans Souci, and to communicate them. He found Christophe, who had been calmly discussing with his medical adviser (the late Dr. Stewart, a Scotch physician, who had been long his confidential attendant) the most vulnerable parts of the human frame. The disastrous intelligence was privately given to him, and he then communicated it to his family, whom he desired to leave him alone, that he might meditate on the best course to be adopted in the emergency. So perfectly calm did he appear that no apprehension was excited of his purpose. One of his attendants, on hearing him lock his bed-chamber door, looked through the key-hole to ascertain what was going on, and he saw the king apparently adjusting himself in an arm-chair, and immediately discharging one pistol through his head and another through his heart, he fell back dead before any alarm could be given. This happened about ten o'clock, on the night of the 20th of October, 1820, and terminated the life of a remarkable man, whose career exhibits extraordinary changes, singularly opposed traits of character, and proves how much may be effected by uncultivated talent, while it marks the insecurity of trusting a barbarian mind with excessive power.

The rapid approach of the insurgent troops

rendered it necessary to remove his body, lest it should be exposed to the brutal insults of a ruffian soldiery ; and the performance of this act was the last proof that could be afforded of the devotion of Dupuy and Prevost, who personally assisted in conveying his remains to the Citadelle Henri, where it was hastily interred.

The family of the deceased king, consisting of his widow, two daughters, and his son, proceeded to the Cape, and placed themselves under the protection of some of the revolutionary leaders. They were all treated, at first, with respect, and the females were placed in safety. The Prince Royal, and his brother the Duke de Mole, a natural son of Henry, and Prince Joachim, were eventually lodged in a prison, where, in the dead of night, they were basely murdered by the governor of the Cape, Richard Duke of Marmalade, (who was afterwards shot for treason at Port-au-Prince,) at the moment that General Nord was interceding for the youthful prince.

The view from the palace towards the sea is exceedingly fine, stretching over the plain of the north to the city of the Cape. Behind there is a terraced garden, filled with fruit-trees of different kinds, and admirably supplied with water, in which the females of Christophe's family are said to have spent much time.

In the court there is a fine star apple-tree, with seats around its trunk, under which, in good weather, Christophe held his levees; and in the coach-houses we found the royal carriages wholly unfit for use. Indeed his death seems to have been the signal for destruction, for even the guard-houses, and the houses in the village for his nobility, are quite dismantled. The only building that has the semblance of being kept up is the church, the roof of which is a cupola. Abbé Besson officiates there, and presides over a college that had been just set on foot, for the formation of *a national clergy.* How this is to be done without the concurrence of the pope, I do not know, unless the suggestion of a very influential man in Haiti to me be adopted, of *" framing a religion suitable to the character of the people."* In such a case, the president of the new university may be no bad Mahomet: for it is confidently asserted that he is a lieutenant in the French navy, and that his priesthood is quite imaginary.

After this visit we ascended, by a rugged and steep road, about one league and a half, to a small coffee plantation occupied by Mr. Laroche, a partner in an English house at the Cape. There we breakfasted, and rested during the heat of the day; and in the afternoon commenced our journey to La Ferriere, or the Citadel. We ascended nearly a league and a half over a narrow paved road, at times overhanging considerable precipices, and at last arrived at this monument of barbaric power. It is situated at the extremity of a mountain range of considerable elevation, which runs nearly north and south, and is a huge ungainly pile, rivalling, in my imagination, the tower of Babel, both in point of utility and extent. As far as I could see, it has three tiers of guns on every side, and there is infinite accommodation for a large garrison, and it is said for three years' provisions, with a profusion of water. The walls are prodigiously thick; but on one side the use of the plummet must have been sadly neglected, as they literally bulge out. Within the walls there is a palace, and complete plans of security for the royal household, as well as for the reception of treasure. We also saw the marble tomb of Prince Noel, the queen's brother, who was killed by the lightning that destroyed a portion of the fortress, and scattered about some of the hoarded dollars. But I cannot pretend to give anything like a description of the buildings ; for there was evidently a vast suspicion on the part of Belair and the other black officers, trained in the school of Christophe, who never admitted any foreigners within the sacred precincts. He laid hold of my hand under the pretext of guiding, but it was evident that his object was to prevent any accurate examination ; and from being hurried from point to point, my observations became confused. Several circumstances occurred which confirmed my belief. In order to ascertain the height, I had with me one of Carey's very excellent portable barometers, which I requested permission to use, having fully explained the object, which could be in no way injurious to any one ; but it was refused, and the aide-de-camp with us, although he felt the folly, was obliged to acquiesce. I had a similar refusal when I wished to take the bearings of the Cape with an azimuth compass ; and I have little doubt that some magical influence was ascribed by the old barbarians to the instruments.

Notwithstanding all this folly, I was strongly affected by the deep feeling displayed by these old men, whenever their former chief or his institutions were the subject of conversation. They never mentioned his name, but emphati-

cally called him " l'homme," or " le roi." I
shall not soon forget the manner in which
my conductor grasped my hand, when we had
reached the chamber in which the remains of
Christophe repose, nor the manner in which
he pointed out the spot where his uncoffined
remains have their last resting-place. Among
other anecdotes that are treasured respecting
him, one of them mentioned that after the interment it was discovered that his right hand
was extended above the surface, as if in de-
fiance of his enemies.

Over the grave some planks are placed
across the transverse beams, which have never
been boarded, under which two of our party
rather indiscreetly went, and were pursued
with extraordinary alacrity by one of the
officers and two of his men. I apprehend
that some violation of the grave was feared,
for some angry Creole discussion took place,
and at last the ire was assuaged.

In return for the privation of all opportunity
of accurate observation, many wondrous tales
were recounted ; such as that the king wished
to try the range of a gun, and seeing a fisher-
man carrying a basket at the " Haut du Cap,"
at least nine miles off in a straight line, he
fired at and cut the man in two. On another

occasion, to show that the guns commanded a certain part of the road, he ordered a shot to be fired at a horseman just at the angle, which was done, and both man and horse were killed. Such feats seemed to be recounted with satisfaction, as evidence of the power of the sovereign. I was also shown a place in which a refractory officer, " Count d'Ennery," had been tortured to death, by being fixed in a situation in which water was incessantly dripping on his head.

This huge pile is said to contain three hundred pieces of artillery, and the construction of it (which occupied many years) must have cost almost inconceivable labour. The materials for building, and the artillery, were all dragged by human hands; for which, in addition to the troops employed, there were regular levies of the peasantry. In looking back at the precipices to be surmounted, I can easily believe that it cost the labour of an entire regiment a whole day to drag up a single thirty-two pounder. Neither age nor sex was exempt from this duty, and the royal officers were unsparing in their exaction of labour. I saw a young woman at Gonaives, whose back was deeply whealed by a cow-skin applied to it *by the general in command,* when employed in carrying stones on her head. The mortality was very great, and it is said that the severity of this service was one of the prin-cipal causes of the revolution. No doubt other cruelties and oppressions had their share.

I cannot suppose that the citadel was ever intended to be any thing else than a strong-hold, into which, in case of rebellion or invasion the chief might have retired; and I believe that such would have been the case, had he been in the enjoyment of his original vigour both of mind and body. All his disposable money was there hoarded, and it is said that at one time no less than thirty millions of dollars were collected. At the revolution it is calculated that about six millions found their way into the republican treasury. There are various surmises as to the remainder.

At a short distance from the citadel stands a small palace called " Le Ramier," also built by Christophe, to which he occasionally re-tired. We did not visit it.

The mist becoming very dense, and the cold severe, we descended; and, as is usual in Haiti, a few dollars were given to the colonel for the men, and he very quietly divided them between the officers and men.

An instance occurred of the " jactance " of

these people, when Captain Elliot of the Harlequin, who had accompanied me, unconscious of error, looked at some forbidden object. He was warned, and when, to assure them that he had no sinister design, he said, " n'ayez pas peur," the old gentlemen clapped their hands upon their swords, and uttered inconceivable nonsense, which was not terminated for some minutes. The division of the money had a most soothing influence, and restored the most perfect harmony; so that at the castle gate we shook hands with infinite cordiality.

On the way back to Mr. Laroche's, where we were to spend the night, I observed some clearing for coffee, which here as well in the other parts that I had seen, is the favourite; but, generally speaking, the old coffee-trees in bearing were over-run with weeds. In short it seemed that, if they produced coffee, it was gathered ; if they were unfruitful, no effort was made to render them otherwise.

FURTHER READING

PRIMARY SOURCES

Joseph Andrews, *Journey from Buenos Aires through the Province of Cordova, Tucuman, and Salta to Potosi* (1827).

Charles Brand, *Journal of a Voyage to Peru* (1828).

Charles Cochrane, *Journal of a Residence and Travels in Colombia during the Years 1823–4* (1825).

Thomas Cochrane, *Narrative of Services in the Liberation of Chili, Peru, and Brazil* (1859).

Charles-Marie de la Condamine, *Brief Narrative of Travels through the Interior of South America* (1745).

Charles Darwin, *Charles Darwin's Voyage of the Beagle*, edited and annotated by Janet Browne and Michael Neve (Harmondsworth, 1989).

James Hackitt, *Narrative of the Expedition which Sailed from England in 1817, to Join the South American Patriots* (1818).

John Hamilton, *Travels through the Interior Provinces of Colombia* (1827).

Gustavus Hippisley, *Narrative of the Expedition to the River Orinoco and Apure in South America* (1819).

Alexander von Humboldt, *A Political Essay on New Spain* (1809).

Matthew Gregory Lewis, *Journal of a West Indian Proprietor, Kept during a Residence in Jamaica* (1834).

George Lyons, *Journal of a Residence and Tour in the Republic of Mexico in 1826* (1828).

John Miers, *Travels in Chile and La Plata* (1826).

Robert Southey, *History of Brazil* (London, 1810–19).

——, *New Letters of Southey*, ed. Kenneth Curry, 2 vols (New York and London, 1965).

——, *A Tale of Paraguay* (London, 1825).

John Stedman, *Narrative of a Five-Years Expedition against the Revolted Negroes of Surinam* (1796), ed. R. A. J. van Lier (Barre, 1971).

Antonio de Ulloa, *Noticias americanas* (1772).

Henry Ward, *Mexico in 1827* (1828).

SECONDARY SOURCES

José Alberich, 'English Attitudes towards the Hispanic World in the Time of Bello as Reflected by the *Edinburgh* and *Quarterly* Reviews', in Lynch, ed., *Andrés Bello*, pp. 67–81.

Stephen Bann, *The Clothing of Clio: A Study of the Representation of History in Nineteenth-Century Britain and France* (Cambridge, 1984).

David Brading, *The First America: The Spanish Monarchy, Creole Patriots, and the Liberal State, 1492–1867* (Cambridge, 1991).

Mark Burkholder and Lyman Johnson, *Colonial Latin America*, third edition (New York and London, 1998).

Alejo Carpentier, *The Kingdom of this World* (1949), trans. Harriet de Onís (London, 1967).

Ricardo Cicerchia, *Journey, Rediscovery and Narrative: British Travel Accounts of Argentina 1800–1850* (London, 1998).

Antonello Gerbi, *The Dispute of the New World*, trans. Jeremy Moyle (Pittsburgh, 1973).

C. L. R. James, *The Black Jacobins: Toussaint L'Ouverture and the San Domingo Revolution* (London, 1938).

John Lynch, *The Spanish American Revolutions 1808–26*, second edition (New York and London, 1986).

———, 'Great Britain and Spanish American Independence 1810–30', in Lynch, ed., *Andrés Bello*, p. 22.

John Lynch, ed., *Andrés Bello: The London Years* (London, 1982).

R. A. MacNeil and M. D. Dean, *Europeans in Latin America: Humboldt to Hudson* (Oxford, 1980.

J. H. Parry and P. M. Sherlock, *A Short History of the West Indies* (London and New York, 1965).

Mary Louise Pratt, *Imperial Eyes: Studies in Travel Writing and Transculturation* (London and New York, 1992).

Michael Taussig, *Shamanism, Colonialism and the Wild Man* (Chicago and London, 1987).

Hugh Torrens, 'Under Royal Patronage: The Early Work of John Mawe in Geology and the Background to his Travels in Brazil in 1807–10', in M. Lopes and S. Figueiroa, eds, *O conhecimento geologico na America Latina: questoes de historia e teoria* (Campinas, Brazil, 1990), pp. 103–13.

NOTES

I am indebted to Professor James Diggle, Dr Christopher Pountain and Dr Evelyn Arizpe for their assistance with translation and attribution.

ULLOA AND JUAN: VOYAGE TO SOUTH AMERICA

p. 3, l. 2: *Carthagena*] Cartagena de Indias, important port town on the Caribbean coast of the viceroyalty of New Granada (modern Colombia).

p. 9, l. 2: *Fr. Benito Feijoo*] Spanish savant, author of *Téatro critico universal* (1730).

p. 12, l. 27: *beaterio*] a magdalen hospital or refuge for 'fallen women'.

DOBRIZHOFFER: ACCOUNT OF THE ABIPONES

p. 47, l. 12: *Naturam expelles furcâ, tamen usque recurret*] 'Even if you expel nature with a pitchfork, she nevertheless returns' (Horace).

HUMBOLDT AND BONPLAND: PERSONAL NARRATIVE

p. 53, l. 3: *Cross of the south*] The constellation known as the Southern Cross, first seen by Humboldt and Bonpland during their Atlantic crossing to Venezuela on board the corvette *Pizarro* in the summer of 1799.

p. 54, ll. 5–10: *Io mi volsi ... di mirar quelle!*] Dante, *Purgatorio*, canto I, ll. 22–7:

> Right-hand I turned, and, setting me to spy
> That alien pole, beheld four stars, the same
> The first men saw, and since, no living eye;
>
> Meseemed the heavens exulted in their flame –
> O widowed world beneath the northern Plough
> For ever famished of the sight of thee!

p. 55, l. 9: *that affecting scene*] J. H. Bernardin de Saint-Pierre, *Paul et Virginie* (1788), a sentimental novel set in Mauritius, translated into English by Helen Maria Williams in 1795.

p. 56, l. 4: *Cumana*] port on the Caribbean coast of Venezuela.

p. 56, l. 17: *Dollond's telescope*] a three-foot achromatic telescope made by Dolland of London.

p. 56, l. 18: *eudiometrical tube*] an instrument used to measure the amount of oxygen in the atmosphere.

p. 56, l. 19: *galvanism*] animal electricity, named after the Bolognese natural philosopher Luigi Galvani (1737–98).

p. 57, l. 21: *Haller, Cavendish, and Lavoisier*] Albrecht von Haller; Henry Cavendish (1731–1810), chemist; A. H. Lavoisier (1743–94), celebrated French chemist.

p. 58, l. 25: *In this village*] Arenas, near Cumana in Venezuela.

p. 60, ll. 13–16: *Among the signs ... breasts of men*] The 'lactiferous' nature of American males was educed by critics like De Pauw and Buffon to illustrate the debilitated and effeminate tendencies of the inhabitants of the New World (see Gerbi, *Debate of the New World*).

p. 67, l. 7: *Mr. Cuvier*] Georges, baron de Cuvier (1769–1832), comparative anatomist and founder of modern palaeontology.

p. 67, ll. 13–14: *Observations on Zoology and Comparative Anatomy*] *Recueil d'observations de zoologie et d'anatomie comparée*, 2 vols (Paris, 1805–33), which formed vols XXV– XXVI of *Voyage aux régions équinoxiales du Nouveau Continent*.

p. 69, l. 15: *copal*] A fragrant resin derived from the copal tree.

p. 73, l. 23: *Calabozo*] town in the province of Guarico, Venezuela.

p. 75, l. 18: *gymnoti*] electric eels. Another version of this section appears in Humboldt's essay 'Steppes and Deserts', in *Aspects of Nature, in Different Lands and Different Climates; with Scientific Elucidations*, trans. Mrs Sabine, 2 vols (London, 1849), vol. I, pp. 22–4.

p. 83, l. 9: *Having passed the Diamante*] Humboldt and Bonpland were travelling by canoe down the Orinoco river to San Carlos del Rio Negro.

p. 86, l. 16: *Rio Apure*] a tributary of the Orinoco.

p. 87, l. 3: *I believe this agitation is*] Humboldt reworked this passage in his essay 'The Nocturnal Life of Animals in the Primeval Forest', in *Aspects of Nature*, vol. I, pp. 259–82.

p. 95, l. 4: *these stupendous scenes*] the cataracts of the Orinoco at Maypures.

p. 98, l. 4: *the mission*] the mission of San Balthasar, in Venezuelan Amazonia.

p. 99, l. 5: *Missionary of San Fernando*] San Fernando de Atabapo, on the confluence of the Orinoco, Guaviare and Atabapo rivers.

p. 104, l. 1: *The morning was cool*] Humboldt and his party had finally reached the Rio Negro, a tributary of the Amazon, and had determined the exact location of the Casiquiare Canal, which joins the Orinoco and Amazon river systems.

p. 112, l. 25: *Blumenbach*] J. F. Blumenbach (1752–1840), Humboldt's professor of natural history at Gottingen, author of *De generis humani varietate nativa*. Blumenbach collected skulls from diverse human groups in an attempt to ground his theory of racial types on cranial conformation.

p. 114, ll. 3–4: *The independence of the colonies*] The third French volume of Humboldt's book was published in 1825 (the English vol. VI, from which this passage is excerpted, was published the following year). By this time the Latin American wars of independence were nearly concluded.

p. 115, ll. 14–16: *This struggle ... drawing gradually to an end*] i.e. in 1810.

p. 116, l. 1: *Havannah*] Havana, capital of Cuba, which remained under Spanish dominion until the end of the nineteenth century. Humboldt visited Cuba in 1800–1 and again in 1804 on his return journey.

WATERTON: WANDERINGS IN SOUTH AMERICA

p. 133, l. 7 *Mungo Park's*] Mungo Park, Scottish traveller and author of the best-selling *Travels in the Interior Districts of Africa* (1799).

p. 136, ll. 16–17: *the wild man of the woods*] see Humboldt's account, above, p. 91.

p. 136, l. 21: *'erubuit domino, cultior esse suo'*] 'He was ashamed to be more cultivated than his master' (Ovid, slightly rephrased).

p. 138, l. 12: *wourali poison*] more commonly known as curare, a bitter resin from plants of the genus *Strychnos*, which paralyses the motor nerves. It is used by Indians to poison arrows.

p. 142, l. 14: *maams, maroudis, and waracabas*] Note Waterton's frequent use of indigenous, rather than Linnaean, names for flora and fauna.

p. 145, ll. 23–7: *'The cloud-capt towers ... Leave not a wreck behind'*] Shakespeare, *The Tempest*, IV. i. 152–6. (misquoted).

p. 156, ll. 28–9: *'And matted woods ... clusters cling'*] Oliver Goldsmith, *The Deserted Village*, ll. 351–2.

p. 159, ll. 5–7: *faedissima ventris proluvies ... properamus ad unam*] 'the very foul effluvium'; 'sooner or later, we hasten to the same seat' (Horace). Note Waterton's learned pun.

p. 161, ll. 21–2: *'Whose care was ... her friend'*] John Gay, *Fables* (1727), fable 50, 'The Hare and Many Friends', ll. 11–12 (misquoted).

HALL: EXTRACTS FROM A JOURNAL

p. 166, ll. 17–18: *In Chili ... national independence had been for several years established*] At the battle of Maipo (5 April 1818) the Spanish army was defeated and O'Higgins was established as supreme director.

p. 167, l. 5: *San Martin's cannon*] José de San Martín led the Chilean expedition to liberate Peru in August 1820, but at the time of Hall's visit Lima still remained in royalist hands.

p. 171, ll. 19–20: *Lord Cochrane*] Admiral Thomas Cochrane assumed command of the Chilean navy in November 1818.

p. 175, ll. 17–18: *the Viceroy ... they forthwith deposed him*] The ineffectual Joaquín de la Pezuela was deposed as Spanish viceroy of Peru on 29 January 1821 by a miltary *golpe*, which appointed General José de La Serna as his successor.

p. 193, ll. 18–19: *Iturbidé*] Agustín de Iturbide, who crowned himself emperor of independent Mexico in May 1822.

p. 194, ll. 11–12: *the device which Iturbidé fell upon*] Iturbide's Plan de Iguala of 24 February 1821 called upon Spaniards to recognise Mexico as their patria, to be ruled by a constitutional monarchy.

p. 196, ll. 5–6: *'superior ilustracion' ... 'ignorancia barbara'*] 'superior enlightenment'; 'barbaric ignorance'.

GRAHAM: JOURNAL OF A VOYAGE TO BRAZIL

p. 201, l. 1: *Pernambuco*] Now called Recife, situated near the most easterly point of the Brazilian coast.

p. 202, l. 18: *His Majesty's brig Alacricity*] the Grahams' ship, a 42-gun frigate.

p. 203, ll. 13–14: *Colonel Patronhe*] Colonel Luiz do Rego. As Graham's note explains, Pernambuco was still in royalist hands during her first visit.

p. 207, l. 3: *Egina Marbles*] Graham's 'ethnographic picturesque' often compares non-European peoples to Greek sculpture, whilst organising them in an artistic 'grouping'. Although this was a convention of contemporary travel writing, it also reflects her own training as a picturesque painter and art critic.

p. 211, l. 8: *Sir John Lancaster*] He raided Recife in 1595, the last official attack made by England on the Brazilian coast.

p. 212, ll. 3–4: *a Claude or a Poussin*] Claude Lorrain (1600–82) and Nicolas Poussin (1594–1665), renowned French artists.

p. 212, ll. 13–14: *Salvator Rosa*] Salvator Rosa (1615–73), Neapolitan painter, an important influence on the picturesque style.

p. 214, ll. 3–6: *Camoens ... e salvamiente*] Luís de Camões (1524–80), Portuguese poet. The lines are from his epic poem *Os Lusíadas* (1572), canto IV, stanza i (slightly misquoted):

> After the stormy tempest,
> Dark night and whistling wind,
> The morning brought a calm brightness
> Hope of harbour and salvation.

p. 214, l. 7: *the revolution in Portugal*] This began in Oporto in 1820, and quickly saw the establishment of juntas in Oporto and Lisbon, demanding the dismissal of General William Carr Beresford, British proconsul of Portugal, and the return of King John VI from Brazil. A constituent Cortes was established the following year, the first representative assembly held in Portugal since 1689, which seriously curtailed the king's power.

p. 216, l. 13: *Mademoiselle Clairon*] Claire Leyris de Latude, called Mlle Clairon, French actress and friend of Voltaire. Graham quotes from *Mémoires de Mlle Clairon* (1822).

p. 225, l. 8: *Don Pedro*] Dom Pedro I, Portuguese prince regent, who declared himself emperor of independent Brazil on 7 September 1822.

p. 226, ll. 16–17: *Botocudo Indians*] an indigenous group inhabiting the region between the Doce and Jequitinhonha rivers in eastern Brazil, which successfully resisted European incursions for 300 years.

p. 226, l. 33: *Southey's Brazil*] Robert Southey, *History of Brazil* (1810–19).

BULLOCK: SIX MONTHS' RESIDENCE IN MEXICO

p. 232, ll. 14–15: *Many of the streets are nearly two miles in length*] Bullock refers to Avenida Churubusco and Avenida Iztapalapa, which follow the course of the original causeways linking the Aztec city of Tenochtitlan to the land. They are major arteries of modern Mexico City.

p. 236, l. 16: *panoramic view*] John and Robert Burford's panorama of Mexico City, based on Bullock's drawings, was exhibited at the Rotunda in Leicester Square in 1825.

p. 239, 14: *equestrian statue of Charles V.*] now standing outside the Antigua Colegio de Minería in Mexico City.

p. 239, l. 21: *Ex-Emperor*] Agustín de Iturbide.

p. 243, l. 6: *Viceroy Galvez*] José de Galvez, architect of Bourbon reform in the Americas and viceroy of New Spain.

p. 252, l. 4: *pulque*] alcoholic drink made from the fermented pulp of the agave cactus.

p. 268, ll. 2–3: *humming birds, beetles, butterflies, and lizards*] Bullock was a naturalist and taxidermist, and Fellow of the Linnean Society.

HEAD: ROUGH NOTES

p. 282, *Olim juventas ... atque pugnae*] 'Once youth and inherited vigour ... ' (Horace, *Odes*).

p. 287, l. 20: *Quien sabe?*] 'Who knows?'

p. 312, l. 18: *Araucana Indians*] Chilean natives immortalised in Alonso de Ercilla y Zúñiga's heroic epic poem *La Araucana* (1569–89).

p. 313, l. 22: *Montaneros*] Guerrilla bands fighting in support of independence, mainly in Rio de la Plata and Peru.

PROCTOR: JOURNEY ACROSS THE CORDILLERAS OF THE ANDES

p. 320, l. 1: *tapias*] mud or adobe walls.

p. 320, ll. 16–17: *General Miller*] William Miller, British mercenary commanding the armies of liberation in Bolivia.

p. 321, l. 13: *godo*] supporter of the Spanish cause.

p. 329, l. 23: *Montonero*] i.e. montanero; see above, note to p. 313, l. 22.

p.331, l. 4: *Riva Aguero*] José de la Riva Agüero, Peruvian aristocrat, declared president in the military coup of February 1823. He betrayed the independence cause in October 1823 by treating with the royalists rather than submit to Bolívar.

p. 333, l. 18: *Vacuña*] species of llama renowned for its fine wool.

STEWART: VIEW OF THE ISLAND OF JAMAICA

p. 341, l. 23: *Buckra*] name given by slaves to their European masters.

COLERIDGE: SIX MONTHS IN THE WEST INDIES

p. 355, l. 20: *Montpelier*] French spa town renowned for its therapeutic waters.

p. 356, ll. 7–8: *et inhospitia littora Montis Serrati*] 'the inhospitable shore of Montserrat'.

p. 358, l. 9: *a crassitude, a pinguedinous gravity*] 'thickness'; 'oily heaviness'.

p. 358, l. 13: *Atque affligit humi divinae particulam aurae*] 'casts on the ground a particle of divine breath' (Horace, writing of a diner who collapses on the ground after a heavy meal).

p. 359, ll. 1–3: *the proparasceve of our manducatory energies, the regretted prophagomenon of Apicius*] 'a fore-preparation for our power of chewing' (i.e. a first course). Apicius was a proverbial Roman glutton.

p. 359, l. 26: *Transubstantiation*] The Anglican doctrine of the Eucharist, as opposed to Catholic consubstantiation, the doctrine of the Real Presence.

p. 360, l. 6: *Parliament open the doors*] Coleridge refers to the demand for Catholic emancipation in Britain.

p. 361, l. 3: *albo ventre lavari*] 'to wash with an unsettled stomach' (Persius).

p. 365, l. 12: *parcus clausus*] 'enclosure'.

p. 365, l. 26: *index expurgatorius*] the papal index of banned books.

p. 375, l. 12: *cosa mayor*] 'a better thing' (Spanish).

MACKENZIE: NOTES ON HAITI

p. 379, l. 1: *Henri Christophe*] Emperor of Haiti, who committed suicide in 1820.

p. 380, l. 4: *Sans Souci*] Henri's palace in northern Haiti, named after the palace of Frederick the Great.

p. 380, ll. 22–3: *Le Clerc*] General Charles-Victor-Emmanuel Leclerc (1772–1802), Napoleon's brother-in-law, commander of the army sent to crush the Haitian revolution in 1802.

p. 380, l. 26: *Toussaint*] Toussaint L'Ouverture (*c.* 1744–1803), leader of the Haitian revolution.

p. 381, l. 7: *Dessalines*] Jean-Jacques Dessalines (*c.* 1758–1806), African-born general of Toussaint's army, declared Emperor of Haiti in 1804. He ordered racial genocide against whites and mulattos, in emulation of French policy against blacks.

p. 383, l. 12: *women of colour*] translates the French phrase *gens de couleur*. Mulattos formed a distinctive social group in Saint-Domingue; many were massacred by Dessalines in 1800, on Toussaint's orders.

p. 388, l. 19: *Obeah*] magic or witchcraft originating in Africa, often used to cast spells.

p. 389, l. 13: *Rochambeau*] Jean-Baptiste-Donatien de Vimeur, comte de Rochambeau (1725–1807), marshal of France who initiated systematic racial genocide against blacks in Haiti.

p. 394, l. 26: *'parmula non bene relicta'*] 'his shield ingloriously abandoned' (Horace).

p. 399, l. 21: *azimuth compass*] compass used to measure the arc of the celestial or great circle from the zenith to the horizon.